Whistleblowing –

subversion or corporate citizenship?

Edited by
Gerald Vinten

P·C·P
Paul Chapman
Publishing Ltd

Paul Chapman Publishing Ltd
144 Liverpool Road
London
N1 1LA

British Library Cataloguing in Publication Data

Whistleblowing: Subversion or Corporate
Citizenship?
  I. Vinten, Gerald
  658.3

  ISBN 1-85396-238-4

Typeset by Dorwyn Ltd, Rowlands Castle, Hants
Printed and bound by Athenaeum Press Ltd, Gateshead, Tyne & Wear.

A B C D E F G H 9 8 7 6 5 4

15.95

N658·3

Contents

Acknowledgements

Chapter 3 is reprinted by permission of Blackwell Publishers, from *Business Ethics: A European Review 1*. Chapter 6 is reprinted by permission of *The American University Law Review*. Chapter 5 and Chapter 8 are reprinted by permission of MCB University Press Ltd, from *Managerial Auditing Journal*.

Contributors

James F. Brown, jr, is Associate Professor of Accountancy at the University of Nebraska.

Michael Cover, head of DAC's intellectual property group, is a graduate of the University of Southampton, and has been a partner of Davies Arnold Cooper since 1989. Before joining DAC, he was in-house counsel at Allied-Lyons plc, and a director of that group's patent holding-company. He is experienced in all aspects of intellectual property and has a substantial practice in the information technology area. He is the Chairman of the Dictionary Listings Committee of the International Trademark Association.

Bruce D. Fong is Senior Trial Attorney, Office of Special Counsel, JD 1980, Boalt Hall School of Law, University of California, Berkeley.

Dr Simon Holdaway is a Reader in Sociology in the Department of Sociological Studies at Sheffield University. A former police officer, he has published widely on many aspects of policing. His books include *Inside the British Police: A Force at Work* and *Recruiting a Multiracial Police*.

Carolyn Hooker is a regional manager for the Open Business School of The Open University. She has experience in management teaching and research and for many years specialized in the management of charities. Before joining The Open University she worked for Henley Management College.

Gordon Humphreys has a masters degree from the University of Wales, Cardiff, as well as a *licence en droit économique* from the University of Liège. He is a barrister who undertook pupillage in London, and then worked for a major Belgian law firm. He has written a number of reports and articles in both English and French of EU, maritime and international private law topics and also on the environment. He is also about to become a member of the Brussels Bar. He is based in DAC's Brussels office.

Dr Alan Lovell is Head of the Accounting Education Research Centre at Nottingham Business School, Nottingham University.

Christopher Mabey is Head of the Centre for Human Resource and Change Management at the Open Business School, where he writes, teaches, researches and consults in the area of individual and organizational development. Before joining The Open University he worked as an internal change consultant for Rank Xerox and British Telecom.

Robin Robison was educated at Loretto School, Edinburgh, and at the University of Kent, graduating in 1984 with a BA Hons in English and History. Since then, he has worked in the civil service, and for the last three years, for the Religious Society of Friends' (Quakers) Truth and Integrity in Public Affairs Committee. He is married and lives in Brighton.

Gerald Vinten is Whitbread Professor of Business Policy at the University of Luton, and director of research in the faculty of business. He holds postgraduate qualifications from Balliol College, Oxford and City, Leeds, South Bank and London Universities. In addition he was World Council of Churches scholar at Union Theological Seminary in Virginia. He was director of the M.Sc degree in Internal Audit and Management at the City University Business School, London, and and is now senior visiting fellow there, and has taught business ethics on that degree as well as on two M.B.A. degrees, one being at an American University. Professor Vinten is uniquely qualified in business ethics having obtained his first degree in theology and philosophy before going on to qualify as an accountant and to work in the hotel and printing industries, as well as in central and local government, and the National Health Service. He is editor of the *Managerial Auditing Journal*, with volumes 5.2 and 5.3 of 1990 being special editions compiled by him on business ethics, and with 8.4 of 1993 being on corporate governance. The joint editorship of the *Journal of the Royal Society of Health* is another of his responsibilities. He sits on the editorial board of twelve journals, and has been twice named as Outstanding Contributor to a U.S. professional journal. He is a trustee of South Place Ethical Society, and in 1994 was elected deputy president of the Institute of Internal Auditors, UK.

He was a part-time assessor in business and management for the Higher Education Funding Councils of England and Wales for 1993–1994, and remains a part-time Inspector with the Further Education Funding Council.

Marlene Winfield is a policy analyst and author of *Minding Your Own Business: Self-Regulation and Whistleblowing in British Companies*. She is a director of Ethical Investment Research Service (EIRIS), a trustee of Public Concern at Work, an honorary lecturer at the European Centre for Professional Ethics, and is on the Committee of Reference of Friends Provident's Stewardship ethical investment funds.

Michael K. Shaub is Assistant Professor of Accountancy at the University of Nebraska.

Part I

GENERAL ISSUES

1

Whistleblowing – fact and fiction
An introductory discussion

Gerald Vinten

THE SCOPE OF THE BOOK

Whistleblowing – informing on illegal and unethical practices in the work-place – is becoming increasingly common as staff speak out about their ethical concerns at work. It can have tragic consequences for the individual, as well as threatening the survival of the organization that is being com-plained about. It is therefore an issue that will interest managers, students of business and management, workers and others. This book aims to provide a balanced approach to a topic which generates much emotion, concern and debate, through critical contributions from academics, lawyers and from the whistleblowers themselves. A continuum from valid to invalid is suggested, both for whistleblowers and for the employer response. We recommend a possible code of practice and agreed procedures, including arbitration, as a means of taking the sting out of an activity which generally leaves bruises, if not fatalities, on both parties. In the USA, whistleblowing is portrayed as being one's constitutional right or even duty and, under certain circum-stances, whistleblowers in the USA enjoy legal protection: the law is quite developed and permits some differentiation between degrees of validity of whistleblowing, including the extent to which individual conscience should be the determining factor.

The book is divided into three parts. In the first, we explain what whis-tleblowing is, and outline the major issues. We show that whistleblowing could impact on anyone at any time, whether as actor or reactor. As an ethical issue it is so comprehensive as to be ideal to work out ethical anal-ysis. We consider how an organization may use whistleblowers construc-tively, and preventive measures an organization may take. The John Lewis Partnership and the idea of corporate commitment are suggested as ex-amples of such preventive measures.

The second part deals with professional perspectives. It contains import-ant chapters on the legal background both in the USA and the UK, and examines internal auditors and management accountants as well as staff in human resources who often have to deal with the aftermath of whistleblowing. It is rare to be able to read an employer's view, and for the first time the other side of the case of nurse Graham Pink is revealed.

The final part allows the whistleblowers to speak for themselves. These are a civil servant who informed on the secret services, an accountant concerned at false accounting, and a police sergeant who observed ill-treatment of prisoners.

WHISTLEBLOWING – ITS NATURE AND PRACTICE

Whistleblowing is a new name for an ancient practice, which dates from the development of the concept of individualism. In the eighth century before Christ, the Hebrew prophets in the Middle East, such as Hosea and Amos, did not hesitate to criticize rulers and their social injustices, and in so doing risked their lives.

The first time the term 'whistleblowing' is known to have been used was in the 1963 publicity surrounding Otto Otopeka (Petersen and Farrell, 1986, pp. 2–3). Otopeka had given classified documents, concerning security risks in the new administration, to the chief counsel of the Senate Subcommittee on Internal Security. The then Secretary of State, Dean Rusk, dismissed him from his job in the State Department for conduct unbecoming a state department officer.

Alternative terms for whistleblowing may be 'conscientious objector' (Beardshaw, 1981), 'ethical resister' (Glazer and Glazer, 1989), 'mole' or 'informer' (Benson, 1985), 'concerned employee' (Thompson, 1987), 'rats' (quoted in Orr, 1981) or 'licensed spy' (Clitheroe, 1986).

The topic of whistleblowing is gradually achieving prominence. It has been dealt with in a number of official reports: the US Leahy Report (1978), with equivalents in both Canada (Ontario Law Reform Commission, 1986) and Australia (Electoral and Administrative Reform Commission, 1990). All of these recognized the value and public interest to be derived from certain types of whistleblowing, and legislation was introduced following each report. These countries generally have a more open and positive attitude to whistleblowing than that which applies in the UK. They have Freedom of Information Acts, which should reduce the need for whistleblowing. In the UK, the Campaign for Freedom of Information has had an uphill struggle. The 'open government' white paper of July 1993 contained some helpful advances, but it stopped short of delivering real freedom of information such as exists in more progressive countries. One could treat freedom of information and whistleblowing as measures of the democratic maturity as well as the humaneness of a country. If Britain likes to regard itself as the 'mother of democracy', it is clear that it has been overtaken by younger democracies.

Some influential voices suggest that, far from informing on an organization representing disloyalty, it may in certain circumstances be an activity deserving high praise. Inevitably, whistleblowing entails huge risks to the activist, and these risks need to be considered personally and carefully. Sir John Banham, former Director General of the Confederation of British Industry, wrote in support of the Social Audit report on the subject (Winfield, 1990), and a committee established by the Speaker of the House of Commons (Stonefrost, 1990) has suggested the possibility of honouring whistleblowers in the British honours system for their good corporate citizenship.

Definitions tend to be short on the ground. Often a series of examples are provided from which a definition is to be assumed. My own working definition is: 'The unauthorized disclosure of information that an employee reasonably believes is evidence of the contravention of any law, rule or regulation, code of practice, or professional statement, or that involves mismanagement, corruption, abuse of authority, or danger to public or worker health and safety.'

There may be either internal or external whistleblowing. The internal variety is where normal or immediate channels are bypassed, to the chagrin of those who expected to be consulted or involved. The external variety applies when the employee resorts to an outside agency, such as a newspaper or pressure group (e.g. Friends of the Earth or Greenpeace). Reporting cases of racial or sexual discrimination is frequently regarded as whistleblowing and, knowing the consequences, too many victims prefer to suffer in silence. Bullying at work is also not uncommon, and here, too, employees are under daily and constant fear and intimidation and dare not speak out.

CASE STUDIES

What is this activity that often seems to have sweetness and light in its favour, yet drags down hot coal on the heads of those who practise it? Here are some short case studies, followed by discussion of other whistleblowers.

Vivian Ambrose of BCCI

The fate of Bank of Credit and Commerce International counts as the world's greatest banking scandal. The internal audit's role was severely compromised as it was denied access to those significant parts of the bank in which fraud was most prevalent, as well as being denied independence and effective reporting channels. No evidence has so far surfaced that this ever became a matter of comment by the external auditor. Despite this, Mr Vivian Ambrose of the UK regional inspection department decided that matters had gone unchecked for far too long at the bank, and he decided to blow the whistle. He wrote to Tony Benn MP on 14 July 1990, alleging widespread corruption and nepotism and 'apparent incompetence by executives'. Unfortunately the letter was lost in central government bureaucracy when Tony Benn forwarded it to two relevant government departments. A further gloss on this story was the arrest by the Abu Dhabi authorities in early September 1991 not only of chief executive, Zafar Iqbal, and his predecessor, Swaleh Naqvi, but also of more than thirty others including the former head of internal audit and inspection, Selim Siddiqui (Vinten, 1992b).

In a telephone interview with the writer, Mr Ambrose stated that he did not like the culture of BCCI right from the beginning, but the bank's poor reputation in the banking community made it very difficult to find employment elsewhere. One was effectively locked in.

Arthur Suchodolski

From 1972 to 1976, Arthur Suchodolski worked for the Michigan Consolidated Gas Company – the largest gas-distribution company in Michigan – as an internal auditor. When he uncovered evidence of mismanagement and possible fraud in the credit division of the company, his report was ignored by top company officials. He found that audit reports were often dressed up to present a rosy picture to company management. Despite promises to the contrary, Arthur was passed over for promotion and, finding himself increasingly out of sympathy with audit procedures and practices, he requested a transfer to another job within the company. He was asked to start the audit of the credit division without a proper plan. Even so, he immediately located lax procedures and a mass of problems, with fifty major areas all requiring attention. The most significant of these involved the State of Michigan's Aid to Families with Dependent Children Program, from which welfare families received a lump-sum payment by which they were supposed to manage their financial affairs, including their gas bills. After some embarrassing publicity over service disconnections to welfare customers, Michigan Consolidated entered into a 'sweetheart' deal with the Michigan Department of Social Services. The company agreed to inform the department prior to cut-off action; the state reciprocated by agreeing to pay the bills for delinquent accounts out of the state's emergency aid fund. Initially payments were modest. However, as word spread, abuse multiplied, with welfare recipients receiving duplicate payments. Michigan Consolidated sunk into a lethargy in which it took no action to clear up arrears. In fact the sum cheated out of state funds was $19 million. Suchodolski's audit was taken over by his manager, who repackaged it in a way Arthur found unacceptable. Shortly afterwards he was dismissed.

Suchodolski appealed to the company audit committee about both his audit findings and his dismissal, but to no avail. His by-now public revelations were taken seriously by the state, which refused that part of a Michigan Consolidated price increase that appeared to be a result of the fraud. The next 14 years saw several civil court appearances and gradual vindication, with various other episodes coming to light to shed doubt on the corporate integrity of Michigan Consolidated. Both the company president and the board-member chair of the audit committee resigned.

The Institute of Internal Auditors found itself unable to give any professional support to Suchodolski. This was partly due to the problem of achieving a judicious overview of the situation from the outside, but was also no doubt due to the ambivalence and mixed emotions to which whistleblowing gives rise. It is interesting to note that the procedural problem does not obstruct investigation of cases of alleged professional misconduct, and if whistleblowing were to be the cause of the complaint, then the Institute of Internal Auditors would be forced to investigate.

Stephen F. Wells

Stephen Wells was working for a state agency funded by several sources, including a federal agency. The federal agency required a financial and compliance audit governed by the US General Accounting Office's standards which enjoin a legitimized whistleblowing: 'Unless legal restrictions, ethical considerations, or other valid reasons prevent them from doing so, audit organizations should make audit findings available to the public and to other levels of government that have supplied [them with] resources.'

It soon became clear to Wells in his audit that there had been a failure to comply with federal regulations requiring accurate, current and complete disclosure of project costs, federal reporting requirements and federal property-management standards. Highlighting significant internal control weaknesses placed continued support from federal funding in jeopardy. Pressure was applied by top management to substantially modify the audit report. Wells and colleagues identified four major ethical issues:

- Should internal auditors exhibit loyalty to the extent that an incomplete and misleading report be issued so that management can ensure continued funding?
- Should internal auditors jeopardize the independence of the entire auditing function by allowing organizational impairments to limit the extent of disclosure?
- Should internal auditors recognize as pre-eminent their obligation to the general public to disclose all relevant information, whether favourable to their agency or not, regarding public officials' stewardship of public funds?
- Should internal auditors knowingly become involved in what would be improper, if not illegal, activities by failing to disclose information specifically required by the federal agency?

To Wells the way forward was clear: the report was issued, with only minor changes. Subsequently the agency head decided that internal audit was overstaffed, and Wells was given redundancy notice. He promptly started labour grievance procedures. Following months of appeals, an independent arbitrator declared that the agency's actions were improperly motivated, vindictive and without cause. Wells was reinstated one year after his dismissal, and the senior management mentioned adversely in the audit report were no longer with the agency. Wells considered that there should be some specific avenues of direct, professional support and encouragement for internal auditors who uphold professional standards and ethics at the expense of their own personal welfare. He found that such professional support had been minimal.

Christopher Urda

In 1992, Urda was an internal auditor with the US defence company, the Singer Corporation. Aged 35, he helped prove that his company had cheated the Pentagon out of the equivalent of £38.5 million over eight years. As the newspaper reported, 'Honesty really is the best policy as auditor Christopher Urda discovered after Uncle Sam awarded him £3.75 million for shopping crooked bosses ripping off the American government.' The judge made the award 'under legislation known in America as the Whistleblower's Charter, which rewards citizens who report corporate dishonesty'. Urda stated, 'I was just an ordinary guy, but it was the right thing to do.'

GLOBAL WHISTLEBLOWING

Leslie Chapman took the exceptional step of breaking civil service convention, if not the Official Secrets Act, and speaking out about waste and extravagance in the British Civil Service in the 1970s.

Clive Ponting received considerable publicity when he sent secret Ministry of Defence documents to Parliament revealing government cover-up over the sinking of the Argentinian warship, *General Belgrano*, during the skirmish over the Falklands. One has to question an action which was perhaps aimed more at restoring naval and government credibility than reaching a diplomatic solution, and which led to substantial loss of life, including the retaliatory action of sinking *HMS Sheffield*.

The 1983 film, 'Silkwood', deals with the true story of Karen Silkwood and her crusade against her company and its poor safety procedures in plutonium processing in the USA. Silkwood was among several who suffered contamination, and her mysterious death in suspicious circumstances suggested the possible dangers of opposing procedures in such a powerful industry.

In Hong Kong, Elsie Elliot, now Elsie Yu, had long been a thorn in the flesh of the establishment with her constant revelations about fraud and corruption. She led a courageous series of campaigns, at the expense of her health, and became a folk hero, particularly among the majority Chinese population.

Dr Prem Sikka, Reader in Accountancy at the University of East London and an avid commentator on the inadequacies of accountancy, made public in late 1993 his concerns about a perceived lack of democracy in his professional accountancy body, the Chartered Association of Certified Accountants. The Chief Executive of the association then wrote to Prem's Vice-Chancellor, questioning Prem's use of university letterhead. The Vice-Chancellor supported Prem; the Chief Executive and President of the accountancy body issued apologies as well as promises to improve the democratic inadequacies. Austin Mitchell, MP, tabled two early-day motions in the House of Commons on 1 December 1993. Referring to the letter to the Vice-Chancellor, it states:

> The Association did not inform him of such actions and subsequently refused to answer his questions. Such action is, however, the latest example by which the accountancy bodies, major firms and other organisations are seeking to silence critical voices and stifle research which they find threatening. Such actions are contrary to the traditions of a free and democratic society.

A number of cases have arisen in the National Health Service, and it looks as if this is only the tip of the iceberg. Dr Wendy Savage criticized the facilities for women in Tower Hamlets Health Authority; Dr Helen Zeitlin the haematological services in Redditch, particularly as they impacted on elderly patients; biochemist Dr Chris Chapman exposed fraud at the Leeds General Infirmary and charge nurse Graham Pink the nurse staffing levels for geriatric patients on the night shift. All believed they were acting according to their codes of professional conduct and all faced dismissal. All except Graham Pink achieved eventual reinstatement, and he was awarded monetary compensation after his employer withdrew from the industrial tribunal case, for reasons explained in Chapter 9.

In a period of mass education it is perhaps not surprising that some will perceive a fall in standards, and others will be concerned about some of the financial expedients that may be taken. University politics at their worst can be among the most ferocious and duplicitous of any organization, as C. P. Snow reflected in his novels. Tutors in a university hall of residence who dared to criticize the way in which it was managed, and the fact that a freemasons' cell met there without paying the promised hire fee, found themselves the subject of a campaign to be replaced by a more compliant group of tutors. Bogus interviews were set up, contrary to previously agreed procedures, and reasons for non-appointment were contrived. One tutor who refused to leave under such circumstances was subject to intimidation and High Court action, with subsequent arbitration resulting in penalties being awarded against the university. The university then broke its agreement to give impartial consideration to application for a tutorship by withholding the application from proper consideration.

Some universities operate double standards in their promotion systems, in which political and administrative influence could be more significant than academic merit. An individual was promoted to professorship who had no direct experience of the area in which he professed, who had produced no significant publications and who was virtually unknown among the academic-subject peer group. A member of staff who raised concerns and who claimed undue freemasonry involvement was subjected to a court case for spending monies that were allegedly unauthorized. The case was dropped, but a gagging agreement was entered into so that the true story will never be known. This can scarcely be regarded as accountable management.

University College, Swansea's Centre for Philosophy and Health Care, was the scene of another whistleblowing episode when lecturers Anne Maclean, Michael Cohen, Colwyn Williamson and Geoff Hunt expressed their concerns about the standards relating to student assessment – particularly dissertations. Eventually, three of the lecturers were reinstated, who had remained. The 'Swansea Four' were presented with 1993 Freedom of Information Awards at a ceremony in January 1994.

Another academic whistleblower is Dr Bill Mallinson. Mallinson was concerned about the way funds obtained from the ERASMUS Bureau (a European body which distributes funds to universities to promote intra-

European educational co-operation) were used at Bournemouth University. It was being stated that 60 teaching hours had been completed in Rome, whereas it appeared there had been no teaching at all. Mallinson then found himself eased out as course director, discriminated against, disciplined and, in his opinion, pressurized to accept a resignation settlement. On 17 March 1993, the university issued a press statement saying that, as a result of various investigations, £2,343 had been remitted to ERASMUS and had been accepted in full settlement. Dr Mallinson continued to press for a public investigation into what he calls the 'dark secrets' of the university.

A secondary-school case in Harrow, researched by Angela Peek of the University of Luton, involved Harry Whitby. Whitby was unjustly accused by a teenager in a remedial class, and it seemed to suit the headmaster's convenience to discipline and dismiss him despite the evidence being virtually non-existent. As often happens in whistleblowing cases, attempts were made to prove that Whitby was mentally unstable, and the educational medical officers were prepared to go along with this. Professor Anthony Clare, an eminent psychiatrist, found no evidence of personality disorder. A High Court judge found in Harry's favour but, despite this, the education authority continued to play games, and the union was less than helpful – another regrettable characteristic of whistleblowing cases. Ten years later, Whitby is still waiting for justice. Indeed, he would like to return to his old school to give just one lesson to establish his credentials and his dignity.

THE RISKS

The trouble with whistleblowing, either internal or external, is that there is plenty of material to blow through. Gerald Mars (1982) has shown that occupational crime, sometimes referred to as 'part-time crime', is an accepted part of everyday jobs. 'Fiddling' is not exceptional but endemic; it is not marginal but integral to the organization and rewards of work. Whether it is called 'pilfering' or 'the fiddle' (UK), 'skimming' or 'gypping' (US), '*le travail noir*' (France) or '*rabotat nalyevo*' (USSR), Mars argues that it is far from the trivial pursuit it is often made out to be. Covert rewards are so intimately connected with some occupations that it is impossible to understand whole sections of the economy without reference to them. There are, therefore, no problems in finding examples if you want to be a management mole. However, it does appear necessary to be highly selective, if one is not to become a professional full-time whistleblower.

For one thing, the whistleblower's path is not easy, and the bee-sting phenomenon may often apply. One has only one sting to use, and using it may well kill off one's career. In a survey of 87 US whistleblowers from both the civil service and private industry, it was found that all but one experienced retaliation, with those employed longer experiencing more. Harassment came from peers as well as superiors, and most of those in private industry and half of those in the civil service lost their jobs. Of the total, 17 per cent lost their homes, 8 per cent filed for bankruptcy, 15 per cent became divorced and 10 per cent attempted suicide (Soeken and Soeken, 1987). A similar result emerged from a six-year US study of 64 whistleblowers – ethical resisters who felt impelled to speak out because they had witnessed a serious violation of legal or ethical standards. To qualify for inclusion, each resister needed to have persuasive evidence to corroborate observations, and those who appeared to be engaged in personal vendetta or making a deal when charged with improper conduct by a prosecuting attorney, were excluded. Most were in their thirties or forties, and were conservative people devoted to their work and organizations. They had built their careers by conforming to the requirements of bureaucratic life. Most had been successful until they were asked to violate their own standards of appropriate workplace behaviour. Whistleblowing was accompanied by economic and emotional deprivation, and led to career disruption and personal abuse (Glazer and Glazer, 1989).

In another survey, a questionnaire was completed by 161 whistleblowers, 80 per cent of whom were government employees. Severe retaliation and overwhelming personal and professional hardship were reported by many in this group, which was found to be in many ways exceptional and tending to exhibit a distinctive approach to moral issues and decision-making. Committed to certain values, the group was capable of *acting* on this sense of obligation, despite the strong organizational and situational pressures to the contrary (Jos, Tompkins and Hays, 1989). Few studies of this magnitude have been undertaken in the UK, but those that have come to a similar conclusion. One was on mental hospital nurses (Beardshaw, 1981). More individualized biographies also confirm the same point. There could be few more tragic stories than that of Stanley Adams, a former executive with Swiss pharmaceutical manufacturer, Hoffman La Roche, who was imprisoned under Swiss law for exposing in 1973 the company's illegal price-fixing methods to the European Commission. His wife's probable suicide, his financial ruin and lack of useful support from the European Commission were all graphically portrayed in the film 'Song for Europe'.

THE ANTI-WHISTLEBLOWERS

Not all commentators favour whistleblowing. In 1971 the Chair of General Motors, James Roche, expostulated that

> Some of the enemies of business now encourage an employee to be disloyal to the enterprise. They want to create suspicion and disharmony and pry into the proprietary interests of the business. However this is labeled – industrial espionage, whistleblowing or professional responsibility – it is another tactic for spreading disunity and creating conflict.
>
> (Walters, 1975)

General Motors has had more than its fair share of turbulence, as one can divine from reading Sloan's reprinted classic of 1963 on the early years (Sloan, 1986), and from a more explicit source which details sixty years of conflict at General Motors and the serious lack of corporate and social responsibility, with cover-up and deceit the order of the day (Neimark, 1992). As just one example, a joint General Motors–Union of Auto Workers study of 1989 found that workers at the Lordstown, Ohio, complex are dying from cancer at a substantially faster rate than the general population, yet the company's initial claim was that 'records and test data indicate that there is no problem' (*ibid.*, p. 169). It is clear that James Roche may be regarded as having a vested interest rather than someone who is likely to be considering the wider public interest, which the company seems to have a legacy of ignoring.

The most notable anti-whistleblower is Peter Drucker, whose original spring 1981 article in *The Public Interest* has been reprinted (Iannone, 1989). His view is that whistleblowing is simply another word for 'informing'. Using the misleading analogies beloved by him, he indicates that the so-cieties in Western history that encouraged informers were bloody and in-famous tyrannies – Tiberius and Nero in Rome, the Inquisition in the Spain of Philip II, the French Terror and Stalin. Mao is an Eastern example. To Drucker, under whistleblowing mutual trust, interdependencies and ethics are impossible. He roots ethics in an individualism which he attributes to Confucius, and considers that whistleblowing interferes with this. Drucker's view has not gone unchallenged. Milton Friedman is also of this school of thought. One critic has stated:

> But 'informing' is itself a value-laden interpretation, not a neutral description, of whistleblowing. It is by no means self-evident that whistleblowing *is* 'informing', and Drucker offers us no support for his claim. Such support requires as its basis rigorous normative reflection; and it is reflection of this kind that is precisely the province of business ethics.
>
> (Hoffman and Moore, 1982)

There was also an editorial survey in *Business and Society Review* (Orr, 1981), in which a group of leading business people and thinkers were invited to comment on the Drucker article. Although there was a variety of views, Drucker was generally found oversimplistic, and Monte Throdahl, senior Vice-President of Monsanto, said that his company had made a virtue out of whistleblowing, particularly in relation to safety and environmental issues. Alan Westin reckoned that Drucker and those like him who referred to whistleblowers as rats, and whistleblower protection legislation as rat pro-tection, more properly deserve the label of 'totalitarian'. They would, he suggests, elevate silent loyalty to employers who act unlawfully or in clear disregard of public interests, above any moral or social duty.

Whistleblowing sounds like a less exotic response to organizational life if you argue that the study of ethics in business is primarily concerned to help individuals operating in organizations to identify behaviour which will not be detrimental to human welfare and, more positively, to encourage behaviour which will benefit it. It follows that ethics will also help to de-termine which organizational systems make the attainment of ethical behaviour more or less difficult for the individual. It can certainly be argued that evading questions about the ethical implications of one's actions constitutes moral negligence. Sound ethical thinking must be based on as full an understanding of a situation as it is possible to obtain in a given situation, and there is also a need to consider unintended or undesirable consequences of decisions. Any view of life that stops short of a rigid totalitarian attitude must make allowances for the legitimacy of individuals asserting alternative moral standpoints and, occasionally, *in extremis*, blowing the whistle.

The Director of the University of Leeds Centre for Business and Professional Ethics has raised the intriguing question: should we credit whistleblowers with having acted from a sense of duty, if they are known to have grudges against their employers? She considers that this is a *Catch 22* aspect to the whistleblower's predicament. If they do not exhaust internal channels, their deed seems irresponsible; they do harm without being able to show that it was necessary. Yet if they do exhaust all internal channels, they must surely have acquired grouses against their employers – if they did not have them already – since their employers have failed to heed their appeals. Thus she argues that whistleblowers, it may seem, never deserve our respect: they either act irresponsibly or they act maliciously. The rest of her exposition shows that mixed motives are common, and that it is necessary to examine the evidence on each separate occasion (Jackson, 1992).

Another writer has drawn comparisons between civil disobedience and whistleblowing (Elliston, 1982). A text on strategic management (Benson, 1990) includes a chapter on business ethics, and the contributor suggests that thoughtless observers may criticize whistleblowing as 'squealing' (an adult version of the school child's criticism of 'tattling'), whereas in fact any enforcement of law and ethics must rely partly on whistleblowers. Examining specific cases would certainly seem to suggest the public good emanating from whistleblowing. We have the case of the problems with the cargo doors on the DC-10 aircrafts in the 1970s (Beauchamp, 1989, pp. 40–7); or the security guard in the shopping mall who refused to let drunk drivers on to the public highway, and who called police, as the security officers' manual dictated. He was dismissed, and the National Labor Relations Board found against him, since whistleblowers were legally protected only if they engaged in 'concerted activity' together with their fellow workers (*ibid.*, pp. 48–52). This shows whistleblowers' vulnerability under labour law.

The best approach is to institutionalize and internalize whistleblowing. Managers may prefer to find out about problems before the story hits the news, and companies with foresight are now setting up telephone hotlines to the top, and employing intermediaries and encouraging employees to use them. Some companies may use itinerant company lawyers as the channel of communications for whistleblowing. Another approach is to set up consumer advocates with independence and a direct line to the top. Government has various channels to assist, with a requirement for supporting documentation and periodic audit of it. But what protection does there need to be if, under pressure of competition, the intermediaries and advocates become co-opted into the company agenda?

THE EUROPEAN PERSPECTIVE

It is difficult to make a systematic study of whistleblowing since there is no available sampling frame. This is a sensitive subject, and not all wish maximum publicity. Most researchers try to accumulate leads from whatever sources present themselves. Thus the Glazers' six-year travels throughout the USA interviewing whistleblowers, was based on those few mentioned in previous academic studies, on journalistic accounts, those known to the Government Accountability Project (the major whistleblower defence organization, situated in Washington DC) and self-reports from those who learnt of the research (Glazer and Glazer, 1989, p. xiii). Another study refers to the problem of having to rely on the anecdotal evidence of those who choose to sound their concerns, and these researchers, too, had to rely on a networking of contacts to achieve their sample of 213 individuals (Jos, Tompkins and Hays, 1989).

The discovery of widespread fraud in the EEC's wine industries is documented to have been attributable to informers on certain occasions. North Sea oil rigs have provided another example such as the Piper Alpha disaster, with the deaths of 165 workers. It would almost be possible to write a common-core report which would readily apply to every variety of disaster: the findings of previous reports concealed or not actioned; lack of independence or effectiveness of inspectorates; failure to adopt a participative management style; and, worst of all, the 'not required back' stamp for those employees who dare complain of health and safety abuses, particularly those who threaten to or who actually blow the whistle.

Norway has much more humane industrial relations practices, where whistleblowing is internalized and readily actioned. If it is impossible to emulate Norwegian practice in the oversecretive UK then at the very least anonymous telephone hotlines should be introduced, and safety intermediaries appointed so that those who know and will suffer the consequences will have a sure means of communication, and real penalties may be applied to those who choose to ignore them.

Following the murder of the Greenpeace photographer when the French secret service sunk *Rainbow Warrior* in Auckland harbour by explosives, two members of the service went public. They were arrested on espionage charges which were subsequently dropped. In Germany, a civil servant published an article on deficiencies in his department. He applied to the European Convention on Human Rights. In Hungary, a security service member revealed that Members of Parliament and other political figures continued to be monitored, after the 'liberalization' of the country. He was prosecuted and convicted, because he should have gone through the official channels.

In 1986, Mordecai Vanunu revealed to *The Sunday Times* details of nuclear plants in Israel which officially did not exist. He was enticed from England to Italy, since it was considered easier to kidnap him from there. He was abducted to Israel, convicted and given a 25-year prison sentence. Amnesty International has taken up his case.

In Sweden, three members of the Information Bureau, an intelligence agency whose existence was unknown to Parliament, disclosed its existence to journalists, and articles and a book resulted. All three were convicted of espionage. Ian Guillou is now a TV presenter, Peter Bradt wrote *The IB Affair* and Hakon Isakson now works for the Stockholm Education Service, as a result of which he feels unwilling to discuss the affair.

A CODE OF ETHICS FOR WHISTLEBLOWING

There is much value in companies setting up codes of practice for whistle-blowing; this can work to their advantage, as well as protecting whistle-blowers. On the other side of the coin, there is a case for setting up a code for the whistleblowers themselves. Two experts in corporate culture have indicated in their categories of the 'storyteller' and 'spy' that, despite their labels, both are essential to the cohesiveness of an organization (Deal and Kennedy, 1988). Both can be used for the greater good of the organization but, if they are not, it is easy to see how they could engage in a form of external whistleblowing that could damage their organization.

Thus we have Norman Bowie's (1982, p. 143) ideal requirements of justifiable acts of whistleblowing:

(1) that the act of whistleblowing stem from appropriate moral motives of preventing unnecessary harm to others;
(2) that the whistleblower use all available internal procedures for rectifying the problematic behavior before public disclosure, although special circumstances may preclude this;
(3) that the whistleblower have 'evidence that would persuade a reasonable person';
(4) that the whistleblower perceive serious danger that can result from the violation;
(5) that the whistleblower act in accordance with his or her responsibilities for 'avoiding and/or exposing moral violations';
(6) that the whistleblower's action have some reasonable chance of success.

Other writers have suggested practical points for whistleblowers to ponder:

1. How comprehensive is the worker's knowledge of the situation? Is the worker's information accurate and substantial?
2. What, exactly, are the unethical practices involved? Why are these unethical? What public values do these practices harm?
3. How substantial and irreversible are the effects of these practices? Are there any compensating public benefits that justify the practices?
4. What is the employee's obligation to publicize such practices by working within the organization or by going outside? What probable effects will either alternative have on the company's practices? On society? On the firm? On other organizations? On the employee? (Velasquez, 1988, p. 381)

Similarly, Bok (1980) catalogues three levels of moral conflict, which one may regard as in a cascade. First, consider whether whistleblowing is truly in the public interest. Secondly, there is the professional ethic requiring collegial loyalty, with codes of ethics often stressing responsibility to the public over and above duties to colleagues and clients. Thirdly, there is the fear of retaliation. Jenson (1987) refers to ethical tension points (ETPs) in whistleblowing, and distinguishes procedural ETPs (e.g. does the whistle-blower have low tolerance for shortcomings? How often and with what intensity does one blow the whistle?) and the more agonizing substantive ETPs, which are one's obligation to the organization, colleagues, the profession, one's family, oneself, the general public and to strengthening basic values, such as truth, independence, fairness, co-operation and loyalty.

Richard T. De George (1986) has suggested three conditions which may turn whistleblowing from being an act of disloyalty – damaging to an organization – into something morally justifiable:

1. The firm, through its product or policy, will do serious and considerable harm to the public, whether in the person of its product's user, an innocent bystander or the general public.
2. The matter should be reported to the immediate superior and the moral concern made known.
3. If no action results, the employee should exhaust internal procedures and possibilities. This usually involves taking the matter up the managerial ladder and, if necessary and possible, to the board of directors.

Some of the problems of whistleblowing have been outlined by Alan Westin (1981) as follows:

1. Not all whistleblowers are correct in what they allege to be the facts of management's conduct, and determining the accuracy of charges is not always easy.
2. There is the danger that incompetent or inadequately performing employees will whistleblow to avoid facing justified personnel sanctions.
3. Employees can choose some ways of whistleblowing that would be unacceptably disruptive, regardless of the merits of their protest.
4. Some whistleblowers are not protesting unlawful or unsafe behaviour, but social policies by management that the employee considers unwise.
5. The legal definitions of what constitute a safe product, danger to health or improper treatment of employees, are often far from clear or certain.
6. The efficiency and flexibility of personal administration could be threatened by the creation of legal rights to dissent and legalized review systems.
7. There can be risks to the desirable autonomy of the private sector in expanding government authority too deeply into internal business politics.

(Westin, 1981, pp. 134–6)

The Government Accountability Project has produced a useful and realistic survival guide for whistleblowers which suggest that 'A well-planned strategy has a chance of succeeding, but unplanned or self-indulgent dissent is the path to professional suicide'. (Stewart, Devine and Rasor, 1989) The problems of reaching an ethical balance sheet are well rehearsed in the extended case study of the Bay Area Rapid Transit in San Francisco (Anderson *et al.*, 1980). The authors could have presented either the three whistleblowing engineers or the BART organization in various shades of purity or chicanery, but find it unrealistic to do so. They do point out that there was far from overwhelming public support for the idea of BART, and that there was a considerable public relations initiative, as seen by the appointment in 1963 of B. R. Stokes, a former newspaperman and BART's first public relations director, as general manager. Management had to work with a politically fragmented and, therefore, relatively ineffective board, and so moved by default into the power vacuum. Relations with the relatively small number of in-house engineers were far from satisfactory. They could observe all the problems, but had little power to intervene. Whether the matters over which they went public were trivial or material is perhaps less significant than the fact that, in the political rough-and-tumble of organizations, such conflicts are bound to happen.

Apart from considering procedural and substantive ethical codes for individual whistleblowers, it is also vital to find reciprocation of organizations who are prepared to act positively towards ethical whistleblowers. In the US, organizations such as the Government Accountability Project and the Project on Government Procurement have been attempting to protect the rights of legitimate whistleblowers. In the UK there are two organizations. Freedom to Care is mainly concerned with health and social services and education. It is a grassroots organization with minimal funding. It runs occasional support meetings and produces a newsletter, *The Whistle*. Contact may be made through Dr Geoffrey Hunt, University of East London, Romford Road, London E15 4LZ.

The other organization is Public Concern at Work, Lincoln's Inn House, 42 Kingsway, London WC2B 6EN. This was set up with a grant of £250,000 and is for those, with concerns in the workplace, who have not blown the whistle. As a legally based charity it will provide free advice protected by the confidentiality of the lawyer–client relationship. It will seek mediation and conciliation, as well as working with employers to introduce best practice. It will also conduct research and issue position papers, such as on the police, local government fraud and education. The charity has a sequential, growth model of the process whereby the concern is aired internally with initially little impact on either the concerned individual or organization, but gradually gathers momentum until the individual feels impelled to go outside the organization. The charity will operate at the very early stages of concerns being raised. The trouble is that the reality rarely conforms to this idealized picture.

In a recent medical study of whistleblowers in Australia, 29 of the 35 in the study found that victimization had started immediately after their first internal complaint (Lennane, 1993). They were effectively regarded as whistleblowers right from the start. It may be that Public Concern at Work's legal view is different from those who are experts in organizational politics and behaviour. In PCAW's first report of 1994 it found that the health service and local councils were the most common sources of staff complaint about malpractice in the workplace. Corruption, financial malpractice and fraud accounted for a third of the cases raised by the 80 workers who sought advice from the charity in the first months of its existence. These were closely followed by worries about public and consumer safety. Among the examples quoted were a group of teachers who suspected that school governors were using funds for private purposes; a senior district council officer suspended after raising concerns about a councillor's involvement in high-value land deals; and a senior nurse who was told by management not to worry about patient malpractice in a hospital. The charity stresses the importance of seeking advice early on. Of those who had already blown the whistle, 25 had been victimized, and 14 of them were sacked. A concern raised in the wrong way, or with the wrong person, allows the response to be focused on the messenger rather than the message. Any organization that wishes to know about a problem before it is out of control needs to show that it values employees who are prepared to speak up.

The charity has a *Speaking up by Sector* series of publications, which includes auditors in the regulated sector; fraud and corruption in local government; the defence industry; abuse in residential care; product safety across Europe; malpractice in medical research; and individuality in the workplace. The first in the series was on the police, and it was recommended that

- systems be established to encourage the raising of concerns about malpractice;
- loyalty to the police service should be seen to come before loyalty to colleagues; and
- the annual appraisal system should view positively speaking up against malpractice.

Those with concerns or who have blown the whistle, or organizations wishing for assistance in introducing and monitoring a code of conduct, or having an ethical audit conducted, are welcome to contact the editor, Professor Gerald Vinten, at 82 Speed House, Barbican, London EC2Y 8AU.

In many cases these channels may be a last resort. One needs to have procedures at an organizational level. Corporate codes of conduct will often be a formal safeguard, and that of the J.C. Penney Company Inc. goes into considerable detail. On the professional side, the Institute of Chartered Accountants in England and Wales issued *Guidance for Members in Business* (December, 1990), and this certainly recognizes the possibility of whistle-blowing. The establishment of the Chartered Accountants' Advisory Service on Ethics (CAASE) in January 1991 to supplement the existing advisory service for members in business (IMACE), is another significant development. Accountants are now enjoined to blow the whistle on examples of poor professional practice among their peers, as well as to inform relevant regulatory bodies (Vinten, 1992a). This may be contrasted with the statement in 1984 that, except in accountancy firms, when an employer's position is challenged, 'the institutional structure of the various professional associations can provide little or no protection to the individual' (Loeb, 1984, p. 6). The Chartered Association of Certified Accountants has also issued some helpful advice on the subject of whistleblowing, and the Institute of Internal

Auditors and the Society of Health Education and Health Promotion Specialists both have position statements on whistleblowing. Trade unions, organizations and professional bodies concerned with nursing, the construction industry, fraud and health and safety have introduced whistleblowing hotlines. An anonymous annual report is issued by the Royal College of Nursing.

The Stonefrost Committee in 1990 reported on the workings of the honours system, and even suggested that whistleblowers might be included in the honours list (Stonefrost, 1990). 'As to "whistleblowing", we all regarded this as an important part of citizenship. We had no special problems with this issue as an element of citizenship although if there was too much "whistleblowing" its effective value could be drowned by the noise' (Maurice F. Stonefrost, 21 September 1990, personal communication).

Whistleblowers may never have it easy. Career mortality and occupational morbidity should be maintained at the lowest possible level. How well a society or organization treats its valid whistleblowers may be taken as an indication of how genuinely ethical and civilized they are. One can but hope that we will perform better in the twenty-first century than we did in the twentieth century. Society owes an immense debt of gratitude to its whistleblowers. Is it not time to express this, rather than wait to record it in an obituary as our whistleblowing martyrs are forced into early graves?

REFERENCES

Anderson, R. M. *et al.* (1980) *Divided Loyalties. Whistleblowing at BART*, Purdue University Press, West Lafayette, Ind.

Beardshaw, V. (1981) *Conscientious Objectors at Work. Mental Hospital Nurses – A Case Study*, Social Audit, London.

Beauchamp, T. L. (1989) *Case Studies in Business, Society and Ethics*, Prentice Hall, Englewood Cliffs, NJ.

Benson, G. C. (1990) 'Business ethics in management strategy', in B. V. Dean and J. C. Cassidy, (eds) *Strategic Management: Methods and Studies*, North-Holland, Amsterdam, Oxford and New York.

Benson, Lord (1985) *The Auditor and Fraud*, Institute of Chartered Accountants of England and Wales, London.

Bok, S. (1980) 'Whistleblowing and professional responsibilities', in D. Callahan and S. Bok (eds) *Ethics Teaching in Higher Education*, Plenum Press, New York and London.

Bowie, N. (1982) *Business Ethics*, Prentice Hall, Englewood Cliffs, NJ.

Clitheroe, J. (1986) 'Reporting fraud', in *Financial Fraud – What Next?*, Institute of Chartered Accountants of England and Wales, London.

Deal, T. and Kennedy (1988) *Corporate Cultures. The Rites and Rituals of Corporate Life*, Penguin Books, Harmondsworth.

De George, R. T. (1986) *Business Ethics* (2nd edn), Macmillan, New York.

Electoral and Administrative Reform Commission (1990) *Protection of Whistleblowers* (Issue paper 90/I10), Brisbane.

Elliston, F. A. (1982) 'Civil disobedience and whistleblowing', *Journal of Business Ethics*, Vol. 1, pp. 23–8.

Glazer, M. P. and Glazer, P. M. (1989) *The Whistleblowers. Exposing Corruption in Government and Industry*, Basic Books, New York.

Hoffman, W. M. and Moore, J. M. (1982) 'What is business ethics? A reply to Drucker', *Journal of Business Ethics*, Vol. 1, no. 4, pp. 293–300.

Iannone, A. P. (1989) *Contemporary Moral Controversies in Business*, Oxford University Press, Oxford and New York.

Jackson, J. (1992) 'Motive and morality', *Business Ethics. A European Review*, Vol. 1, no. 4, pp. 264–6.

Jenson, J. V. (1987) 'Ethical tension points in whistleblowing', *Journal of Business Ethics*, Vol. 6, pp. 321–8.

Jos, P. H., Tompkins, M. E. and Hays, S. W. (1989) 'In praise of difficult people: a portrait of the committed whistleblower', *Public Administration Review*, November/December, pp. 552–61.

Leahy, P. (1978) *The Whistleblowers: A Report on Federal Employees who Disclose Acts of Governmental Waste, Abuse and Corruption*, State Committee on Government Affairs, Washington, DC, 95th Congress, 2nd Session 10.

Lennane, K. J. (1993) ' "Whistleblowing": a health issue', *British Medical Journal*, 11 September, pp. 667–70.

Loeb, S. E. (1984) 'Codes of ethics and self-regulation for non-public accountants: a public policy perspective', *Journal of Accounting and Public Policy*, Vol. 3, pp. 1–8.

Mars, G. (1982) *Cheats at Work. An Anthropology of Workplace Crime*, Allen & Unwin, London and Boston, Mass.

Neimark, M. K. (1992) *The Hidden Dimensions of Annual Reports. Sixty Years of Social Conflict at General Motors*, Markus Wiener, New York.

Ontario Law Reform Commission (1986) *Political Activity, Public Comment and Disclosure by Crown Employees*, Toronto, Ontario.

Orr, L. H. (1981) 'Is whistleblowing the same as informing?', *Business and Society Review*, Fall, pp. 4–17.

Petersen, J. C. and Farrell, D. (1986) *Whistleblowing. Ethical and Legal Issues in Expressing Dissent*, Kendall/Hunt Publishing, Dubuque, Iowa.

Sloan, A. P. (1986) *My Years with General Motors*, Penguin Books, Harmondsworth.

Soeken, K. and Soeken, D. (1987) *A Survey of Whistleblowers: Their Stressors and Coping Strategies*, Association of Mental Health Specialities, Laurel, Md, March.

Stonefrost, M. F. (1990) *Encouraging Citizenship. Report of the Commission on Citizenship*, HMSO, London.

Stewart, J. Devine, T. and Rasor, D. (1989) *Courage without Martyrdom. A Survival Guide for Whistleblowers*, Government Accountability Project, Washington D.C.

Thompson, C. M. jr (1987) 'The auditor and the informant', *Internal Auditor*, February, pp. 24–8.

Velasquez, M. E. (1988) *Business Ethics. Concepts and Cases* (2nd edn), Prentice Hall, Englewood Cliffs, NJ.

Vinten, G. (1992a) *Whistleblowing Auditors: A Contradiction in Terms, Occasional Research Paper 12*, Chartered Association of Certified Accountants, London.

Vinten, G. (1992b) 'Internal audit after Maxwell and BCCI: public responsibility versus loyalty to the organization', *Managerial Auditing Journal*, Vol. 7, no. 4, pp. 3–5.

Walters, K. D. (1975) Your Employees' Right to Blow the Whistle', *Harvard Business Review*, Vol. 53, p. 27.

Westin, A. F. (1981) *Whistle Blowing Loyalty and Dissent in the Corporation*, McGraw-Hill, New York and London.

Winfield, M. (1990) *Minding Your Own Business. Self-Regulation and Whistleblowing in British Companies*, Social Audit, London.

2

Whistleblowers as corporate safety net

Marlene Winfield

In the autumn of 1991, Colin Jewell, a respected design engineer with twenty years' experience in the oil industry, was unemployed. What's more, he had good reason to believe that no offshore contractor operating in the UK would want to hire him. His crime? He had discovered design faults on North Sea oil rigs.

Between 1990 and 1991 he found faults in the design of two oil platforms while working for two different contractors. In both cases, his attempts to raise his concerns internally with his employers failed. The first time he pointed out the faults to his bosses, he was transferred. Afraid to leave things as they were, he reported his fears to the Department of Energy (DE). Because the DE could not guarantee his anonymity, he felt obliged to resign before the investigation.

The second time, he made his concerns public at an oil-industry workers' conference after using an internal procedure called 'Warnings of Preventable Disaster' to no avail. He was trying to alert the main contractor to what he considered to be serious flaws.

In both cases, his concerns proved justified. What had motivated him to take such risky action?

> A small accident had happened. Very fortunately no one had been killed. If it had happened slightly earlier or later a lot more people would have been injured. I thought it was in the interests of everybody that the fact that it wasn't an accident but a foreseeable and preventable potential disaster should be made public.
>
> (unpublished interview)

Colin Jewell's fate is one that too often befalls those who cannot turn a blind eye to what they consider to be shoddy or improper practices. Well-known whistleblowers include Jim Smith and Charles Robertson (accountants); Clive Ponting and Sarah Tisdall (civil servants); John Stalker, Brian Woolyard and Ron Walker (police officers); and Graham Pink (nurse). Common themes run through their cases. All had been valued employees. They acted in good faith and with justification. For a variety of reasons, their concerns could not be resolved internally and were eventually to be made public. They were not able to resume their previous jobs, and some had to change fields in order to find work. Many would say they are worse off than if they had kept silent.

These UK whistleblowers bear an uncanny resemblance to the profile of the typical US whistleblower drawn by psychologist Donald Soeken. In 1987 he studied 87 Americans who had blown the whistle on abuse, fraud, waste, corruption and safety violations (Soeken and Soeken, 1987). He found whistleblowers were often male, around 40 years old and married with children. They had worked for the company on average for 7 years, and blew the whistle only after trying to raise the matter with someone in the organization. Retaliation followed in all but one case. Most lost their jobs. Some lost their homes (17 per cent), were divorced (15 per cent) and attempted suicide (10 per cent). As a result of their experiences, some reported losing faith in themselves, in others, in government and in the judicial system.

A second American study of 'ethical resisters', i.e. whistleblowers, by Glazer and Glazer (1986, p. A23) gives insight into their motives:

> Virtually all of the ethical resisters we studied had long histories of successful employment . . . they began as firm believers in their organizations, convinced that if they took a grievance to superiors, there would be an appropriate response. This naivety led them into a series of damaging traps. They found that their earlier service and dedication provided them with little protection against charges of undermining organizational morale and effectiveness.

TRAITOR OR SAFETY NET?

Are employees who blow the whistle disloyal 'sneaks' or are they a safety net which, when other forms of regulation fail, protects the workforce or the public from fraud, malpractice and preventable disasters? It is time we made up our minds.

While we dither, the world around us is changing rapidly. As businesses, industries and public sector agencies become ever larger and decentralized, it is increasingly unlikely that those at the top will know what is going on at ground level. What is becoming all too apparent is that, as enterprises grow bigger, each dangerous product, unsafe practice, financial impropriety, pollution incident or bit of disinformation can potentially claim more and more victims. The public policy response of the 1980s was to deregulate, putting the onus on employers to be vigilant, and in some cases (like pollution) increasing the penalties when they failed. But is it working?

So far, the outcome is not encouraging. Regulation – from without or within – has failed to prevent major financial scandals, such as the disappearance of vast sums from the Mirror Group pension fund, illegal share support during the Blue Arrow flotation and the misappropriation of funds by the Bank of Credit and Commerce International. It has failed to compel speedy action on safety recommendations which followed the Clapham rail crash, the capsizing of the *Herald of Free Enterprise*, the explosion on the Piper Alpha oil platform, the fire at King's Cross underground station and the

Manchester air-crash fire. Our ability to regulate arms sales has been called into question. Our safety record at work is not one to be proud of: according to the Department of Trade and Industry, there is an accident in the work-place every 3½ seconds. All in all, we appear to be learning worryingly little from past mistakes.

'NEED TO KNOW'

Our best hope of regulating what goes on inside private and public sector enterprises is through the vigilance of individual employees. But much work remains to be done to make employers recognize and develop this form of self-regulation.

Long-standing attitudes and practices of many private and public sector organizations will have to undergo a sea change. Open communication will have to replace the 'need-to-know' principles which govern the flow of information in many organizations – and not just the security services. Too many employers are only prepared to disclose to their employees exactly what they 'need to know' to do their jobs; and too many bosses 'need to know' only good news. The time-honoured tradition of shooting the mes-senger of bad news will have to be abandoned.

In 1990, Public Interest Research Centre asked 510 private sector com-panies operating in the UK what steps they took to create an 'ethical' corpor-ate culture, what mechanisms existed to hear employees' concerns about malpractice and what they felt about employees who blew the whistle on the company outside. Only 53 companies replied, arguably those who had al-ready given the matter some thought. They ranged from huge multinational banks, hoteliers, chemical and oil companies to small manufacturers and engineering firms. Questionnaires were completed by heads of personnel, chief executives, managing directors, chairpersons and company secretaries. Their answers were sometimes surprising and sometimes not:

- Just over half had codes of ethics; just over half had codes of practice.
- Some 19 had formal employee participation policies, some stressing an ethical perspective in policy- and decision-making.
- One or two obliged employees to sign 'ethical contracts' or stressed ethics in training.
- Nearly two-thirds expected employees to raise concerns informally through an 'open door' to senior managers. Around half expected em-ployees to use the regular grievance procedure or involve the union rep.
- Just over half had some sort of employee and/or management committee that could hear employee concerns.
- Two or three had newsletters where concerns could be raised anony-mously, or someone like a 'stress counsellor' to hear concerns in confi-dence, or formal confidential complaints procedures.
- Few had any structured way of monitoring 'ethical' performance. One or two conducted periodic employee, client or customer surveys to pick up prob-lems; or had periodic 'ethical audits'. Two used exit interviews in this way.

What was apparent from this small sample was that companies with codes
of ethics, formal participation policies, committees which could hear employee concerns and 'open door' policies were less likely than the others to
say they had no need to hear employee concerns. Clearly the more you
know, the more you know you 'need to know'. Or put another way, igno-
rance is bliss, at least up to a point.

A FRAMEWORK FOR SELF-REGULATION

Internal self-regulation can only succeed if employers are prepared to open
themselves to scrutiny by their employees. Together, employer and employees need to define and agree their operating standards, publicize them
widely inside and outside and charge every member of the workforce with
upholding them. But this effort must consist of more than producing glossy
codes and mission statements. Policy documents should describe clearly
company standards and objectives. They should contain unambiguous
guidelines on acceptable and unacceptable behaviour, and give credible
assurances that legitimate efforts to uphold standards will not meet with
reprisals.

There should be specific and well-understood procedures to enable employees to raise their concerns about standards – anonymously if preferred –
at the highest levels, and be given a considered response within a specified
time. If doubts remain, the advice of an independent third party should be
enlisted to sort out misunderstanding and take any action deemed necessary.

Employees who use the procedures in good faith should not be penalized
in ways obvious or subtle. In fact, those whose interventions benefit company performance should be rewarded. Rather than being part of a grievance procedure, responding to employee concerns should be seen as part of
quality enhancement.

The John Lewis Partnership's registrar system and Otis Elevator's 'Dialog'
procedure use employee vigilance in this way. John Lewis employs 32 independent 'registrars' to be on the lookout for what the founder described as the
'bowling of no-balls'. Registrars hear employee concerns and 'maintain and
oil communication between managed and management'. They edit and publish local newsletters where concerns can be aired, anonymously if wished,
and will be answered in print by a principal director or the chairman. Employees not satisfied with the reply have recourse to an ombudsman.

'Dialog' is a two-way confidential communication programme through
which any employee can submit a question and receive a mailed reply
prepared by the person best qualified to answer. The Dialog administrator
receives in strictest confidence queries on a special form available throughout the workplace, detaches the name and address and forwards the rest to
the relevant officer at the highest level. A reply must be received by the
employee within ten working days.

The process of defining, reviewing and upholding standards must be
continually reinforced through training. Relevant training courses – from

induction of new employees to preparation of senior managers and directors – should explain the organization's standards and why and how they are to be upheld. The effectiveness of these quality initiatives should be monitored regularly.

When properly operated, an open system of communication should render whistleblowing virtually unnecessary. Virtually but probably never completely. Perhaps the most surprising result of the research was that nearly three-quarters of responders could think of circumstances in which an employee might be justified in reporting concerns to outside bodies, i.e. blowing the whistle. Reasons included breaking the law, endangering health or safety, and discrimination. But nearly all said the employee should exhaust internal channels (such as they were) first. Only 11 responders thought whistleblowing would never be justified. A few had clearly given the matter a lot of thought and their answers raise some particularly interesting issues.

Industrial relations adviser, employment agency:

> We would not look askance at field staff reporting any matter to any group or body or authority. It would, I feel, be a grave demerit on the company should this need to be done in that we attempted to allow the maximum scope to reconcile all company employee problems internally.

Head of personnel, engineering consultancy:

> It is quite possible for an individual to believe quite wrongly but honestly that a company practice is unethical/immoral and for the company to be unable to persuade him of his mistake. If the individual is encouraged to believe that he has a duty to report his company to an external body, the company could find itself facing considerable expense and trouble defending itself – pressure could grow to stifle such people at an early stage if companies found it happening too often.

Manager for corporate affairs, international bank:

> Any report to an outside body which breached confidentiality would be a matter for disciplinary procedures. If an employee felt strongly that agreed bank policy confirmed by a senior manager was unethical, he or she would presumably wish to resign.

Head of personnel, chemical company:

> The individual will decide, but should go to a professional body rather than, say, the media. The process may be slower but whistleblowers whose motivation appears to be to damage the company forego the chance to influence the company.

(Winfield, 1990)

ACTIVE CITIZEN OR INDUSTRIAL SPY?

Clearly, many employers recognize that it is sometimes necessary for serious concerns that cannot be resolved internally to be reported outside. When concerns are reported outside, the law should afford the whistleblower acting in good faith better protection than it does now. Before that can happen, the law, too, needs to examine its attitude to whistleblowing.

Commercial and employment law seems to bend over backwards to protect the trade secrets and reputation of employers, while scarcely sparing a thought for the reputation of an employee who may have to choose between collusion in wrong-doing and blowing the whistle. Under employment law, the employee owes the employer duties of fidelity and confidentiality. These seek to make it a breach of contract for an employee to reveal pretty much anything the employer chooses to call 'confidential', in some cases this can even apply to evidence of wrong-doing. Even where an unauthorised disclosure is justified in law, it is remarkable that it can still result in dismissal. The employer owes duties to the employee as well, but these are less precise and more difficult to enforce.

No matter how pure the motives, an employee who asks awkward questions or blows the whistle risks losing everything. Even if an industrial tribunal rules that an employer has acted 'unfairly' by sacking or forcing the employee to quit ('constructive dismissal'), compensation usually bears little relationship to what has been lost. And should a tribunal take the uncommon step of ordering reinstatement, it can do very little to make the employer comply. It is quite common for an employee who acted in good faith to wind up jobless, blacklisted and broke.

Moreover, the employer can bring a court action against the employee for breach of confidence and claim damages. If the employee claims that disclosure was 'in the public interest', the court will weigh up the seriousness of the wrong-doing disclosed, how the information was obtained, to whom it was given and whether the employee acted in good faith. Different courts do reach different conclusions, for example, about who is a legitimate recipient of information. The onus is on the employee to prove a public interest defence, and the courts often reject it.

Some laws have provisions which protect employees who disclose certain types of information to certain recipients. For example, employees who report discrimination on grounds of race are supposed to be protected from victimization. However, what constitutes 'victimization' is so ambiguously stated (a good example of the law's ambivalence to whistleblowers) that it cannot afford any reliable protection. Employees with a specific health and safety brief are now protected from victimization for reporting health and safety concerns. Welcome though this is, this protection only covers a narrow band of employees and the legislation is as yet too new to judge how it is working in practice.

IF ALL ELSE FAILS, AT LEAST PROTECT THE WHISTLEBLOWER

It looks as though, for the foreseeable future, we will continue to rely on whistleblowers to act as the safety net when other forms of regulation fail. How can we be fairer to them?

First of all, the contractual duties of employer and employee should be clarified, particularly as they affect the reputation and future prospects of the employee. All regulatory legislation should clarify the responsibility of employer and employee for regulating, and contain unambiguous anti-victimization provisions.

The presumption of secrecy which pervades our laws of confidence should be abandoned in favour of a presumption of openness. The onus should be on the employer to prove that there is a public or other compelling interest in keeping information secret, and not on the employee to prove the need for disclosure. The types of employer information courts and tribunals are willing to protect should be restricted to a few carefully defined categories (e.g. genuine 'trade secrets' and real and present threats to national security).

In addition to anti-victimization clauses in individual laws, there should be laws specifically to protect whistleblowers. In so far as possible, they should protect from retaliation and blacklisting those who act in good faith to report safety, fiscal, environmental or other serious concerns to outside bodies. If protection fails, they should entitle the whistleblower to realistic compensation, both for what has been lost already and what is likely to be lost in future.

SEDUCED AND ABANDONED?

One of the most surprising and disappointing things to emerge from my recent interviews with whistleblowers was the cavalier behaviour of regulatory bodies towards the whistleblower once the whistle had been blown. For example, before responsibility for North Sea oil-rig safety was taken away from the Department of Energy (DE), every oil-rig worker used to have a poster on the back of his door saying, 'Your responsibility does not end when you leave this installation. If you are still dissatisfied with a safety matter when you return to shore, you should then contact the Department of Energy Inspector . . . Your anonymity will be respected.'

The reality was much different. When Colin Jewell tried to carry out his 'responsibility' as laid down by the DE, he was told that his anonymity could not be guaranteed, full stop. He was then left to wrestle with his conscience. No attempt was made by the DE to protect him.

When welder Vaughan Mitchell read the poster and reported unsafe welding practices on his oil rig two months after the Piper Alpha explosion, he was sacked. A subsequent DE inquiry found that there were in fact unsafe practices, which the contractor promised to change. No action was taken against the contractor. When Mitchell asked the DE for the inquiry results to assist in his legal action against his employers, he was told the findings were 'confidential'. Apparently the DE did not feel it had any responsibility towards him.

Similarly, chief tax accountant Charles Robertson lost his job for refusing to approve Guardian Royal Exchange's tax returns until he got to the bottom of what appeared to be irregular transactions. The Inland Revenue official to whom he reported his suspicions had to be subpoenaed before he would appear at Robertson's industrial tribunal hearing. (The tribunal subsequently ruled he had been unfairly dismissed.)

Nowhere is our collective ambivalence more starkly visible than in the off-hand way regulatory bodies treat whistleblowers. This sends confused messages to other would-be whistleblowers, which does not make their decisions any easier. It is time regulators came down firmly on one side or the other.

Nor are professional associations (for doctors, nurses, architects, engineers, accountants, lawyers, teachers, etc.) a model of good practice when it comes to supporting whistleblowers. Qualified nurses and accountants, for example, are bound by strict codes of conduct which set firm priorities. But what happens when they are asked to contravene their codes of conduct, say, by turning a blind eye to deteriorating conditions in a hospital ward or signing-off on accounts over which doubts remain?

It must be becoming increasingly apparent to many professionals that, should they choose to uphold their professional codes and get the sack, the august bodies which bind them to those codes will rarely raise their voices above a whisper to defend them. (The Institute of Chartered Accountants in England and Wales deserves mention for at least recognizing the problem and making some effort to help whistleblowers. It operates a hotline and offers initial advice to its members and a few hours of free legal assistance. While this is not quite 'going to the wall' with the whistleblower, it is more than most other professional bodies are prepared to do.)

And how often do we hear a trades union mount a strong defence for a lone whistleblower on a building site, in a police force, on a railway gang, on a food production line, etc.?

The first thing a potential whistleblower must understand is that, *he or she will most likely be acting alone.*

THE REALITY OF WHISTLEBLOWING

Below is a checklist for anyone thinking of blowing the whistle. Based on consultations with whistleblowers and on information from those who have tried to help them, it is a chilling chronicle of the risks whistleblowers run in today's UK. It makes clear that whistleblowing should not be embarked upon by an employee – or provoked by an employer – without giving a great deal of thought to the alternatives.

WHISTLEBLOWERS' CHECKLIST

Examine the facts of the case

1. Ask yourself if the practice is clearly illegal or potentially dangerous or if it is simply questionable business policy. Is the public interest really at stake?
2. Be realistic about the potential human damage caused by blowing the whistle – damage to the company, its shareholders, its clients, your colleagues. Be realistic about what you are likely to achieve.
3. Be optimistic but also be prepared to lose, to be rejected by colleagues and friends and probably to see your family suffer. Consult with your family.

4. Identify the issues carefully and prioritize them. Analyse the grievance; identify who will suffer if the problem goes unchanged and how much suffering will occur. Be able to speak knowledgeably about the costs of inaction.
5. Know and be able to refer to the ethical standards of your professional association or trade union if you belong to one. Identify the laws and regulations which relate to the abuse. Identify organizational policies and documents which support correcting the abuse. Document everything thoroughly and double check your information.

Exhaust internal channels first

1. Take your complaint in writing, with appropriate supporting documents, to the authorities of your company or agency. Ask them to correct the abuse and give them fair warning that you may go outside if this is not done.
2. Exhaust all internal channels, making sure that your efforts to do so are well documented. This is by far the method of choice for resolving the problem – if there are channels through which you will be given a fair hearing. Give the organization time to remedy the situation.

Protect yourself

1. Try to enlist others in the organization to join you.
2. If possible, approach someone higher up in the organization as a sounding-board and to keep you informed of what is happening.
3. Stay on your best behaviour with superiors and peers. Work hard and do your job thoroughly. Bear in mind that all of your past performance may be reviewed if you blow the whistle; and that those you expose may retaliate or try to discredit you.
4. Know your legal rights and contact a good employment lawyer or someone who can advise you on your legal position. Know whether or not you are breaking any laws or terms of contracts, particularly those to do with confidentiality.
5. Look for another job.

Go outside only as a last resort

1. If all internal channels fail, you have several options: resign and speak out; stay and try to expose the abuse anonymously; stay and go public; stay and say nothing more. In any case, the benefits must be weighed against the likely risks.
2. You may choose to take your complaint to a statutory agency, like a regulatory body, or expose it through the media, or go to a pressure group or a Member of Parliament. In any future legal action the courts will consider whether the recipient of the complaint was appropriate.
3. Be aware of the difficulties of blowing the whistle anonymously and, if you do, be prepared for your identity to be discovered. Remember that some third parties may not feel able to act on anonymous information.

4. Keep a log or diary of everything that happens, particularly at work, from the time you decide to take action.

The checklist raises questions that have too long gone unanswered: At the end of this painful process, can anyone – the individual, the company, the community – emerge a winner? Can we expect whistleblowers to go on paying such a high price for acting as the safety net for self-regulation?

MINIMIZING THE RISKS

Employees who discover apparent wrong-doing have several options: they can turn a blind eye and continue as normal, raise the matter internally and hope for the best, blow the whistle outside while trying to remain anonymous, blow the whistle and take the full force of employer disapproval, resign and remain silent, or resign and blow the whistle.

As we have seen, to blow the whistle effectively requires a great deal of care, attention to detail and patience. Yet worried employees do not always make good judgements in the heat of the moment about how to proceed. They may not know how to raise issues in an appropriate way, or may act rashly under pressure, weakening their case and increasing their own vulnerability. Their initial attempts to put things right may founder and they may feel that any further effort will be ignored or worse. In all cases, they would benefit from independent and expert advice *at a very early stage*.

In 1993 Public Concern at Work was set up with funding from the Joseph Rowntree Charitable Trust to provide such advice. It is a specialist legal advice centre whose aim is to promote better communication about these issues between employees and employers. The centre's first priority is to help concerned employees identify the best options and correct procedures for raising their concerns with their employers, based on an understanding of the implications of various courses of action, and knowledge of their rights and duties under law.

Apart from advising on how concerns are raised with employers, Public Concern at Work may be able to assist in a number of ways – contacting the employer on the employee's behalf, providing observers to attend meetings, giving expert second opinions, and where asked organizing mediation services.

It is expected that the majority of employee concerns will be resolved co-operatively in this way. However, when that is not possible, some employees might wish to take matters further. In such cases, Public Concern at Work can advise on other courses of action. Priorities are to maximize chances of correcting the fault while best protecting the employee and avoiding unnecessary damage to the employer. Needless to say, the centre gives a very high priority to minimizing any risk to the public.

Public Concern at Work also seeks to promote greater accountability in the workplace. It is doing this by devising training courses and training materials for employers, and employers' and employees' bodies; by producing reports and briefings; by recognizing and encouraging good practice;

and by making information about good practice widely available to managers, management trainers, students, academics, etc.

Public Concern at Work is located in Lincoln's Inn House, 42 Kingsway, London WC2B 6EN, telephone number 071 404–6609.

CONCLUSION

Employees who blow the whistle are often forced to do so because their concerns are not given a fair hearing by their employers. This can result in damage to both the whistleblower and the organization. Yet, if faults go undetected, they can result in even greater damage to the workforce, the public at large or of course to the employer. It is in everyone's interest that public and private sector enterprises are regulated effectively. The most feasible way to do this is from within, by making every employee responsible for maintaining the highest standards and reporting when those standards are not being met. This requires workplaces to have clearly defined standards and specific procedures for reporting lapses.

British companies are beginning to explore self-regulation through employee vigilance. Until such time as all employers embrace this approach, employees will need independent and expert advice on how to raise their concerns with employers in ways which maximize the chances of a constructive outcome and minimize personal risk.

Even the best internal regulation systems will sometimes fail and employees will feel compelled to blow the whistle outside. The rights and duties in law of the whistleblowing employee must be clarified. Any employee who acts in good faith to report malpractice should be protected from retaliation and blacklisting, and should be able to obtain compensation for present and future loss. The duties owed to the employee by the employer must similarly be clarified. Regulatory bodies, professional associations and trades unions should do more to support whistleblowers.

At present, because of our collective ambivalence, whistleblowers pay too high a price for acting as a safety net when other forms of regulation fail.

IS WHISTLEBLOWING ITS OWN REWARD?

The last word should go to whistleblowers who have found themselves trapped in the safety net. Colin Jewell, oil-rig designer:

> It hurts to suffer what I did when you see other people who do nothing and profit from that. Afterwards you think 'Should I have bothered?'. I spoke to the Health and Safety Executive [recently made responsible for North Sea installations], who said, 'You have a legal responsibility to do this'. But there is no help or protection when you do such things.
>
> (unpublished interview)

Charles Robertson, former tax accountant:

> When I was dismissed the bottom fell out of my world really. I remember it was a lovely weekend, I sat on a lounger in the garden feeling that I had thrown my

career away. And I had . . . It's no good talking about active citizens. You can't have active citizens until you provide the back up for them. Active citizens are left to drown really.

(Winfield, 1990)

Dennis Mitchell, intelligence officer at GCHQ for 32 years, who took early retirement after failing to resolve internally his serious concerns about his own work and the accountability of the security services, generally, and who is still prevented from speaking about his work by an injunction as well as the Official Secrets Act:

Since leaving GCHQ I have created an organisation with the help of others which is an educational charity and has forged links with other cultures. And I work as an unpaid shopkeeper in order to support the charity. My wife and I can live on the pension I get. I have this terrible choice. Do I drop the work I am doing for what I am trying to achieve at GCHQ, which is going to mean going to prison.

(Winfield, 1990)

Maureen Plantagenet, former pharmaceutical sales rep, who quit her job after being asked to pay doctors to prescribe her company's products, and who later made a television programme about her experiences:

I don't think people know what you go through beforehand, but I can understand why there are so few whistleblowers. It's much easier for people to just get out . . . It's very likely that because employment law has become so harsh and because unions are weak that there are a lot of people who do not know what to do.

(Winfield, 1990)

Vaughan Mitchell, oil-rig welder:

They [contractors] are in the business of making money and so they will have an inclination to save money, bend rules, save time, whatever. But we're in the business of staying alive. Out here the working guy knows that there are risks involved, but it's when it gets to the stage that they are unacceptable risks that you have to say 'enough is enough'. Sometimes you feel really down and you think, 'God is it really worth going through all this?' Then something happens and you realise it'll be worth it simply because they won't be able to do to other people what they did to you.

(Winfield, 1990)

REFERENCES

Soeken, Karen L. and Soeken, Donald R. (1987) *A Survey of Whistleblowers; Their Stressors and Coping Strategies*, Association of Mental Health Specialities, Laurel, Md.

Glazer, M. P. and Glazer, P. M. (1986) The Whistle-blower's Plight, *New York Times*, August 13, p. A23.

Winfield, M. (1990) *Minding Your Own Business: Self-regulation and Whistleblowing in British Companies*, Social Audit, London.

3

The Registrar in The John Lewis Partnership, plc: corporate conscience*

Pauline Graham

Under UK company law, every public limited company has to employ a registrar. The main duty of this functionary is to maintain the records of the company's shareholders. He or she or the outside company, if the work is contracted out as is often the case, keeps the Register of Members, updates it, provides information on it to outsiders as required by law, and so on – all in accordance with sections 352 and 353 of the Companies Act 1985.

The John Lewis Partnership (abbreviated to the Partnership), being a public limited company, has one of this kind of registrar. But, in addition, it has many other registrars – of a very different kind.

The registrars in the Partnership are unique to it. To start with, they are women. Thus its founder had decreed, excepting for their chief who could be either a man or a woman. (Nowadays, the advertisements for the post are non-gender specific; male applicants are given serious consideration but, so far, women have turned out to be the more suitable applicants and have been chosen. Currently, the Chief Registrar is a man.)

The Partnership registrar has no counterpart, to my knowledge, in any other company in the UK. She certainly came as a surprise to me when I joined the Partnership. As the general manager of the branch in charge of all its activities, I had to learn to take full account of the views and suggestions of this registrar, a manager with her own little set-up in the place, with an unusual mixture of functions, who reported directly to the centre, a colleague of equal status who advised but could not direct.

The role of the Partnership registrar is not well known, if at all, outside the organization. Current thinking is that the large-scale organization needs a corporate ombudsman to oversee the upkeep of its ethical standards. There is much discussion about the exact activities of such an official and whether the holder should be an employee of the company or an outsider.

* This article is reprinted from *Business Ethics: A European Review* 1 (1992), pp. 185–91, where it appeared under the title 'The Registrar in the John Lewis Partnership, plc: her role and responsibilities'.

It may be useful, in this connection, to look in some detail at the *raison d'être* of the registrar in the Partnership, her function and her value to the organization. In another direction, the overview may encourage other companies to be innovative, tailoring their own creation specifically to their ethos and form of organization.

As the registrar's job is integral to the Partnership philosophy and its organizational mode, it is necessary to know something about these to understand her place in the scheme of things.

THE JOHN LEWIS PARTNERSHIP

Its philosophy: partnership

In the UK the Partnership is recognized as the premier group of department stores in the country. Its promise to its customers of being 'Never Knowingly Undersold' is meticulously upheld. Only the other day, a friend who had bought a freezer from a Partnership store found it being sold more cheaply at one of its competitors. The Partnership immediately refunded her the price difference. The slogan has passed into the language and has been copied by others as a marketing device. In addition to the chain of department stores, the Partnership also owns Waitrose, the equally highly respected chain of food supermarkets. This much is public knowledge about the Partnership.

What is not generally known is that the Partnership is run on co-operative principles. *The Gazette*, its journal, proclaims it every week on the back page:

> The business belongs to those who work in it. All, except those engaged temporarily, are Partners from the day they join and all the ordinary share capital is held by a trustee on their behalf. Under irrevocable trusts, Partners get all the profits, after provision for prudent reserves and for interest on loans and fixed dividends on shares held outside. A large part of the distribution is made direct in the form of Partnership Bonus, shared among Partners at the end of the trading year as a percentage of their pay.

The founder of this Partnership was John Spedan Lewis (1885–1963). As a young man entering his father's drapery business in Oxford Street, London, in the early 1900s, he was struck by the fact that 'the profit, even after £10,000 had been set aside as interest at 5 per cent on capital, was equal to the whole of the pay of the staff, of whom there were about 300'. Years later, in 1957, in a BBC broadcast, he said:

> It was soon clear to me that my father's success had been due to his trying constantly to give very good value to people who wished to exchange their money for his merchandise; but it also became clear to me that the business would have grown further and that my life would have been happier if he had done the same for those who wished to exchange their work for his money.

From this twin realization – that the business would have grown bigger and that he would have been happier had his father treated his workers as he had treated his customers – John Spedan Lewis developed his ideas of industrial democracy. He evolved a partnership system which he implemented with much success, between 1914 and 1928, at Peter Jones, the Sloane Square store in which he had been given a controlling interest. He went on to improve, extend and formalize it, as he inherited the Oxford Street store and as, in due course, he went on to acquire other businesses.

His objective for the Partnership was quite clear. It was to be the happiness of its members: 'The supreme purpose of the John Lewis Partnership is simply the happiness of its members. True happiness requires a sense of honest service to the general community, a sense of being of some use in the world.'[1] 'The Partnership', he wrote, 'would give its members something to live for as well as something to live by.'[2]

The happiness he had in mind was more than what we would call today 'job satisfaction'. He wanted democracy in the workplace and for the employees to share in the advantages of ownership, sharing fairly in the trinity of reward, knowledge and power. In this way, the business would in effect be a partnership and the employees partners in the enterprise.

I must say that, in my early days in the Partnership, imbued from my previous work with the usual legal meaning of partner and partnership, I found it difficult to refer to myself as a 'partner', to think of the others as 'partners'. However, the apparent inappropriateness of the term soon wore off. I quickly came to appreciate that the Partnership, properly understood, meant just that: that all workers in it, both managers and managed, were members of the same team, partners in the business. This made the job of managing more demanding but also more productive and more fun.

Its organization: three of its principles

By the mid-1930s, as the Partnership grew into many separate and different outlets, the founder had to flesh out the detail of the organization best capable of combining effective business performance with industrial democracy. Over time, adjustments have been made to strengthen the democratic arrangements and to meet the evolving needs of the business but the present system is, in substance, that which became established by the late 1940s.

It is not possible, in this short piece, to cover the whole of the Partnership system, by way of institutions and management structure and their intermeshing relationships, in place to ensure both effective democratic governance and successful business management. I have to limit myself to those three principles of the Partnership's organization which impulsed the creation of the registrar's function.

Devolution of power
As between centralization and decentralization, Spedan Lewis had no doubt. Decentralization was the only means of achieving best business results and implanting democracy in the workplace. Executive power had to move to the local level, to devolve to the 'Man on the Spot'. Thus it is that the managing director or the general manager is 'the Man on the Spot' (or today

it can be 'the Woman on the Spot') running the branch with a large measure of autonomy. For my part, having run my own small accountancy practice and never having worked before in a large organization, I did not feel that, as head of branch, I had such a large degree of autonomy. But other heads of branches, coming to the Partnership from large companies, were delighted with the much greater freedom of action allowed them in the Partnership.

Two-sided management: executive and critical
On central management, already much earlier, Spedan Lewis had worked out that it had to be split into two sides: the Executive Side and the Critical Side. In a memorandum written in July, 1920, he had explained:

> The Board will gradually develop into two wings – an executive wing which does things and a critical wing which does what the Army calls 'Staff Work' and of which the function, broadly, is to make theoretical investigations for which executive officials generally lack the time *and also to prevent the executive officials from being blind to any of the facts of their own affairs'* (emphasis added).[3]

The Critical Side was not only to make 'theoretical investigations' but was also to have teeth *and* pinpoint any one thing they should have known about their business but did not. The system has stood the test of time, is still in place and flourishing. The two sides work well together and the result is very good overall performance.

Accountability of the managers to the managed

Managers are appointed by the central management. Their job is to manage but it is a fundamental Partnership precept that they are accountable to the managed:

> If the business is to succeed and to continue, the power to settle policy and to take executive decisions at the highest level must be concentrated in the hands of a few people . . . But both the Chairman and the rest of management hold themselves fully accountable to the general body of partners through the Partnership's systems of communication and of representative institutions.[4]

The accountability of the managers to the managed, through regular reporting, *inter alia*, to councils and committees remains a cornerstone of the Partnership system. An important means to accountability is the Partnership's journalism which has been taken to a very professional standard.

At central level, there is the weekly, *The Gazette* (considered the Partnership's national press), which publishes trading results, appointments, changes in rules and regulations, reports from the various central boards and so on. It also has a 'Readers' letters' section. Anyone can write to the editor, anonymously if preferred, criticizing any part of the Partnership's operations or institutions, demanding explanation and correction. And the managers, from the chairman downward, have to reply in full detail immediately. In each branch there is, weekly, the branch *Chronicle* (all together forming the Partnership's local press) fulfilling a similar function to that of *The Gazette*.

The readers' section in *The Gazette* reflects public opinion in the Partnership: what the partners are thinking about, agreeing with, anonymously complaining about; how one apparently innocuous letter can lead to a series of letters over the weeks from either the original complainant or other partners dissatisfied with the answer given by the relevant manager. It is avidly read and much commented upon. Top officials know there is no hiding place for one's actions. Full, honest and fast disclosure is the best answer. The possibility of being suddenly subjected to public examination is most effective in keeping one to the straight and narrow.

THE BRANCH REGISTRAR

The questions to be resolved were: How to avoid 'The Man on the Spot', in his eagerness, say, to produce highest bottom-line profits, getting carried away and neglecting to share with his rank-and-file partners the trinity of reward, knowledge and power? How to ensure, at every point, accountability of the managers to the managed? How could devolution of power to local level be combined with consistent implementation of Partnership philosophy there?

The concept

For Spedan Lewis, the answer was simple. If the mountain would not come to Mahomet, Mahomet would go to the mountain. Thus, he invented the role of the Registrar:

> If we are to give to numerous officials this degree of freedom, we must in the interest of the rank and file take care to have a certainly fairly full knowledge of the use that is made of those powers and, apart from that motive, we must, for the sake of the general efficiency of our business, secure due consistency and coordination between the work of all the little separate teams into which our business will now be in a certain sense be broken up.[5]

To ensure this, there would be, at local level, a representative of the central management, 'a registrar'. This registrar, with her own registry office, would be responsible for the secretarial work relating to the partners. As 'secretaries are necessarily cognisant of the contents of the papers that pass through their hands', the Registrar would thus know every material thing about the partners. This registrar would be trained at the centre and would accordingly also have 'a proper knowledge of the letter and understanding of the spirit of the Partnership's regulations'. Combining her detailed knowledge both of the Partnership rules and of what is going on in the branch, the Registrar can tell 'the Man on the Spot' where he may be deviating from the Partnership ethos. In this way, 'things cannot go far wrong'.

The Chief Registrar and her representatives in the branches would belong to the Critical Side, without any executive power. But to emphasize their importance, the local registrars were to be responsible 'to the Chief Registrar who herself will be a member of the Central Management and in due course a member of the board of directors of our controlling company'.[6]

Spedan Lewis thought everything right through and provided for most eventualities. Thus, to avoid the local registrar getting too settled in the ways of the branch and losing her critical edge, she had to move every few years. As he put it:

> The registrars may and should become congenial and valuable advisers to the executive officials but the Registrars will be moved from time to time so that there may not grow up inexpedient relations between these representatives of the Central Management and the officials upon whose procedure they are intended to hold for the Central Management a watching brief.[7]

Thus was Spedan Lewis explaining in minute detail the role of the registrars to a possible candidate for the Chief Registrarship, way back in mid-1939.

Why a woman as the Registrar?

How come that the registrars in the branches have been to date invariably women? When he introduced the function in the late 1930s, John Spedan Lewis thought that women would be better than men for the job. This was still his view in 1946:

> The Registry system was set up to secure that, however big the Partnership became, there would be still . . . a proper coherence of all its parts, proper touch between each particular section and all the others, including the Principal Management. This is, I think, work peculiarly suitable for women with well trained minds and with certain natural abilities, certain powers of understanding, attention to detail and general helpfulness that are pretty common feminine gifts. Many and many a man owes a very great deal of success in life to the counsels of his wife. Without her, he would be more or less lost. But it does not follow that she could do his job.[8]

John Spedan Lewis did not, as he put it, 'undervalue the potentialities of women for important work' and he was a pioneer in promoting women to senior commercial positions. But, *in the running of a branch*, he felt that men and women had complementary contributions to make. There was obviously some dichotomy in his thinking. One can see him working through it. By 1948, in *Partnership for All*, he had moved a little forward:

> I suspect that the Partnership will find that really high efficiency in managerial work will be attainable much more easily by letting a zealous, energetic and forceful but not very clever or perhaps very experienced man in a Managership work with a really intelligent and well informed woman Registrar than it would be by trying to find their joint qualities combined in one man or one woman.[9]

By 1954, he had integrated all of his thinking on the subject. In *Fairer Shares*, he was painstakingly heading his chapters about the Chief Executive 'A chief executive: his or her limitations'; 'A chief-executive: his or her powers and rights'.

Currently, the advertisements for registrars are of course non-gender specific. In 1988, one such advertisement attracted 248 applications, 191 from men and 57 from women; although some of the men were short-listed, two women were finally recruited. The Chief Registrar, himself a man, said the two women were chosen because 'they were the applicants felt to be best suited to the job and most likely to remain with us' and that 'there could be no reason to suppose necessarily that a man would not qualify or compete'.[10]

The Registrar's function today

Over time, the function of the Registrar has evolved, in tandem with the growth of the Partnership. But in essence it has not changed much. It comprises five main components.

To keep the personal records of the partners in her branch

The Registry keeps the records up to date, passing the information only to those authorized to receive, and take action on, it. This is fulfilling the secretarial bit specified by Spedan Lewis, the bit that enables her to be 'cognisant of the papers' that pass through her hands, and to ensure they are within the law, within Partnership policy and fair to the partners concerned.

By keeping the partners' records, the Registry is doing some of the work which, in other companies, is invariably done by the personnel department. The Partnership has also a well established Personnel Department, with a Director of Personnel sitting at board level, but the personal records of the partners continue to be the responsibility of the Registrar. There is inevitably some duplication of work between personnel and Registry departments; there is inevitably confusion in the minds of some partners as to what falls within one or the other's province. But, whenever the matter has been investigated, it has been found essential for the Registry to keep this recording component, so that the Registrar be directly in touch with the personal details of the partners. (Currently, an experiment is being carried out to transfer some of the administrative work to staff offices.)

To secure in the branch consistency in the operation of the partnership system, its constitution, rules and regulations

At the local level, the Registrar represents the central management, with all knowledge of the democratic institutions, rules and regulations of the Partnership. It is her responsibility to explain and ensure that these are followed in the branch. She advises the head of branch, not usually well versed in her field of partnership knowledge, what he or she can or cannot do. She has of course no authority over him or her but no wise head would consistently ignore her advice. She interprets central policy to the partners in the branch and is available to advise them or their rights; she tries to solve their problems at local level but, where necessary, will take up the cases for consideration and adjudication at the centre.

To interpret the branch to the central management

The Registrar is an important channel of communication between the branch and the centre. Although the head of branch reports to the centre, such reporting is on the trading operations but . . . in the Partnership our trading operations are a means to an end and Registrars have the advantage over the Executive Side of being concerned not primarily with the means but wholly with the end. Therefore as a channel of communication from the Branch to the Centre, you are more important in many ways than the Executive Management.[11]

She reports monthly to the Chief Registrar, concentrating on the intangibles: Are the partners in the branch being treated fairly, in accordance with the Partnership rules? What is the morale in the branch? What do the partners in her branch feel about the new arrangement, say the working hours over Christmas, promulgated by central management?

To act as internal communicator in the branch

In addition to being the connecting thread between branch and centre, the registrar also acts as link between managers and managed in the branch itself. Just as she passes information about the branch to the central management, so can she keep the executive management on the spot informed of the underlying tone and morale of the partners in the branch. This is not in place of direct communication between rank-and-file partners and their managers but in addition to it. I found this of real value. In the hurly-burly of managing, one does not always fully appreciate how one's actions are being seen by, or are affecting, the others. To have someone keeping one in touch with the feeling in the branch was invaluable. This gave me the opportunity to explain or adjust decisions, as appropriate. Thus, misunderstandings were nipped in the bud and mistakes corrected.

To edit the Chronicle

As the editor of the *Chronicle* of the branch, the weekly collection and publication of all news concerning the branch, from the general manager's trading report to the anonymous letter from the disgruntled partner, fall within her province. This, too, makes her the hub of knowledge which enables her to feel exactly the pulse of the branch and understand its every change.

THE VALUE OF THE REGISTRAR TO THE PARTNERSHIP

The Registrar represents most of the Critical Side of central management in the branch. As the holder of the personal details of the partners, she knows exactly their individual positions. as the fount of knowledge of the Partnership constitution, of its rules and regulations, she ensures that these are followed in her branch and, importantly, that the local management operates within the framework of the Partnership system. As the channel of communication between the branch and the centre, she interprets central policies to the partners in the branch and conversely keeps the central management *au fait* with their feelings and views. As the internal communicator in the branch, she facilitates relations between the 'Man on the Spot' and the rank and file. As Editor of the *Chronicle*, she sees to it that the managed are fully informed and their voices fully heard.

The Registrar does other things besides, but these five components of her job combine to ensure that the powers devolved to the operating outlets are exercised, always, within the letter and the spirit of the Partnership philosophy. Thus, is the philosophy secured in every corner of the Partnership's activities.

Those concerned with the ombudsman function will note that the Registrar is always *in situ*, on a par with the head of branch but independent of him or her and that the organizational arrangements enable her to know everything. It is that combination of knowledge and of independence of the operating manager in charge that enable her to guide him or her to act according to the Partnership rules and regulations.

The Registrar makes sure that the right things are done *ab initio*, preventing things from going far wrong. There is no need to correct large mistakes, *ex post facto*. To use the currently fashionable concepts, she ensures 'zero defect production first round', 'total quality management' from start to finish, in so far as the treatment of the partners is concerned.

Of course, human nature being what it is, things never go always according to plan. Some heads of branches may think their registrar an interfering busybody. (I found mine a great support and comfort; she was much more than my Partnership conscience; an impartial and disinterested observer, she became a confidante whose business advice I valued highly.) Some rank-and-file partners may not even realize that the registrar is independent of the local management and would not consider confiding to her their worries or complaints. Misunderstandings and conflicts are part of the stuff of life. What Spedan Lewis put in place is the organizational set-up of checks and balances to ensure implementation of the Partnership philosophy in all its outlets. The rest is up to the partners, all of them, with much greater responsibility on those at the top to see that it is done.

There have been, and there will continue to be, changes in the arrangements of the registrars, to meet evolving different conditions. In future, some of the registrars will undoubtedly be men, as now some heads of branches are women. Parts of the work of the registrars may be taken over by one or other department. But their essential function – of ensuring that the Partnership ethos is implemented at grassroot level – will remain at the heart of Partnership affairs.

NOTES

1. Lewis, J. S. (1954) *Fairer Shares*, Staples Press, London, p. 127.
2. *Ibid.*, p. 11.
3. Quoted in Flanders, A., Pomeranz, R. and Woodward, J. (1968) *Experiment in Industrial Democracy*, Faber & Faber, London, p. 40.
4. *Ibid.*, p. 17.
5. Lewis, J. S. (1939) *The Gazette of The John Lewis Partnership*, 29 July, Vol. 21, no. 26, p. 692 (33).
6. *Ibid.*, (38).
7. *Ibid.*, (36).
8. Lewis, J. S. (1946) *The Gazette of the John Lewis Partnership*, 29 June.
9. Lewis, J. S. (1948) *Partnership for All*, Kerr-Cros, London, p. 430.
10. Alexander, I. D. (1990) *The Gazette*, 17 March, p. 157.
11. Miller, Sir B. (1956) *The Gazette of The John Lewis Partnership*, 5 May, p. 300.

4

What does it mean to be a committed employee?*

Christopher Mabey and Carolyn Hooker

INTRODUCTION

While the concept of organizational commitment has been consistently re-searched since the early 1970s, it has been the focus of intensified interest in recent years. This is because much of the analytical writing on human re-source management (HRM) has stressed the benefits of a loyal and com-mitted workforce and the central role HRM practices may play in creating and maintaining such commitment (Guest, 1987; 1989; Storey, 1989). Early attempts to model the impact of HRM upon organizational outcomes stressed employee perceptions of advancement opportunities and the fair-ness of staffing decisions (Beer *et al.*, 1984), and linked this with the critical capability of the organization to achieve sustainable competitive advantage over the long term (Tichy, Fombrun and Devanna, 1982; Fombrun, Tichy and Devanna, 1984). Alongside other organizational benefits, like strategic integration, high-quality performance, low morale, absenteeism and griev-ance, and high flexibility, which all have been cited as the outcomes of enlightened HRM (Guest, 1987), high employee commitment remains a cen-tral goal. The supposed rationale is that staff who believe they are, and perceive they will be, treated fairly will remain committed to their employer: 'committed employee behaviour rather than mere observance of formal pro-cedures is, in many ways, at the heart of HRM' (Storey, 1987, p. 22).

Despite the apparent desirability of organizational commitment, the con-cept is not unproblematic. What factors, or combination of factors, bring about commitment, and can these processes be managed? Even if such factors can be identified and encouraged, to whom or what are employees expressing their commitment? Is such commitment always favourable, and to what other organizational outcomes is it linked? Finally, even if such

---

* An earlier version of this chapter was presented by the authors at the British Academy of Management Annual Conference, Bradford, September 1992.

outcomes are positive, does commitment remain stable over time? Most of us could happily speculate about the answers to these questions, but in this chapter we scan the considerable research into commitment in order to reach more reliable conclusions.

WHAT BRINGS ABOUT ORGANIZATIONAL COMMITMENT?

Studies seeking to identify the reasons for organizational commitment fall into two broad categories: those investigating personal demographic predictors and those assessing the impact of organizational practices and characteristics. There is some evidence that advancing age and tenure is linked to commitment (Angle and Perry, 1981; Meyer and Allen, 1984), possibly due to the incremental accrual of organizational investments as proposed by Becker's side-bet theory (1960). Perhaps for associated reasons, married respondents have been found to express higher commitment (Alutto, Hrebiniak and Alonso, 1973; Meyer and Allen, 1988), whereas those with better formal education, and those with more professional commitments, are less committed than those with less formal education (Hrebiniak and Alutto, 1972; Angle and Perry, 1981; Morris and Sherman, 1981; Meyer and Allen, 1988) and those in generalist managerial careers (Nicholson and West, 1988).

Even before an employee commences employment, the perceived autonomy and irrevocability of job choice has been found to correlate with subsequent commitment to the chosen organization (O'Reilly and Caldwell, 1981; Kline and Peters, 1991). This can be attributed to retrospective justification theory whereby individuals continue to act in ways consistent with the implication of their past behaviours, especially if such action – like job choice – is freely chosen, public and irrevocable (Salancik, 1977). While most of these factors are beyond the organization's control, there is a growing body of research linking specific HRM practice to enhanced organizational commitment. For instance, confirmation of pre-entry expectations (Arnold and Feldman, 1982; Mabey, 1986, Meyer and Allen, 1988), the perceived fairness of promotion practices and the accuracy of the merit system (Ogilvie, 1987; Folger and Konovsky, 1989), and performance feedback followed by goal-setting (Tziner and Latham, 1989), have all been shown to correlate positively with organization commitment. Caldwell, Chatman and O'Reilly (1990) also found realistic recruitment practices, clear-cut career paths and the articulation of strong, clear organizational values to be significantly correlated with organizational commitment. All such variables are readily influenced by the policies and practices chosen by an organization to manage its human resources. However, the tendency with this approach is to assume that the recipients of such HRM initiatives will respond in a uniform and positive manner, when this is patently not the case. It is also possible, although less usually considered, that individuals will make an impact on the organization, particularly if a cohort join at the same time. For instance, a longitudinal study by Kohn and Schooler (1978) found that people who were more intellectually flexible enhanced the complexity of their work over time. Clearly then, any assessment of organizational commitment needs to account not only for the predictive influence of individual characteristics and organizational policies but also for the crucial and subjective interplay between the two, and this is particularly the case where the nature of commitment being analysed is the area of cultural norms and personal values.

COMMITMENT TO WHAT?

An assumption of the discussion so far is that organization commitment is a unidimensional concept. Again this is overly simplistic – partly because 'commitment' can mean different things for different people and, indeed, may not always be a desirable state (Iles, Mabey and Robertson, 1990), and partly because 'organizations' are pluralist entities within which individuals can have multiple and competing commitments (Coopey and Hartley, 1991). It is possible for employees to be committed to their work in general, perhaps because they have a greater propensity towards commitment than others (Blood, 1969), and yet remain uncommitted to their actual job because it is failing to met salient intrinsic and extrinsic needs (Kanungo, 1982). Similarly, the notions of career commitment (Blau, 1988; Arnold, 1989) and professional commitment (Morrow and Wirth, 1989) have been shown to be conceptually distinct from organizational commitment, with different impacts upon turnover via career withdrawal cognitions. However, organizational psychologists have focused mainly on the term *organizational* commitment, which indicates the affective attachment of employees to their organizations, implying loyalty, involvement and the willingness to expend effort on behalf of their employer (Buchanan, 1974). This has been operationalized in the form of a 15-item questionnaire developed by Porter *et al.* (1974) and widely employed in research studies. It is predicated upon a matching hypothesis: if individuals perceive the job and organization to be as anticipated (Premack and Wanous, 1985; Mabey, 1986) or they feel the social exchange of personal effort given and positive experiences received to be a fair one (Goode, 1960), then they will register commitment. A quite different process and type of attachment is implied by behavioural commitment. Here it is the circumstances of job choice, particularly the degree of autonomy, and, once employed, the perceived revocability and costs of subsequently changing organizations that are believed to 'bind' an individual to his or her employer (Becker, 1960; Salancik, 1977). This notion of attitudes forming on the basis of prior behaviour is rooted in theory concerning cognitive dissonance, and has received continued empirical support (O'Reilly and Caldwell, 1981; Kline and Peters, 1991).

It is important to distinguish these types of commitment because, while attitudinal commitment is likely to result in high affective, psychological attachment to the employer concerned, behavioural commitment will probably lead to a more instrumental and compliant involvement. While most research has intended to examine one or other of these types of commitment, some studies have sought to measure both. For instance, Allen and Meyer

(1990) developed three scales tapping affective commitment, behavioural (or what they called 'continuance') commitment, and normative commitment – which was intended to reflect employees' loyalty and sense of moral obligation to remain. The authors acknowledge that 'more evidence is required before the Normative Commitment Scale can be used with as much confidence' as the others (*ibid.*, p. 15). Even these studies do not capture the aspect of commitment that refers to values congruence between the individual and the organization, yet it would seem that, especially in the non-profit sector of employment, this dimension is crucial to understanding why individuals remain loyal to organizations.

DOES COMMITMENT REMAIN CONSTANT?

Even when organizational commitment has been operationally defined, and its antecedents identified and measured, a question still remains about the constancy of commitment over time. The literature provides two ways of assessing this: a limited number of longitudinal studies that have tracked organization commitment as a dependent and independent variable over time, and studies which have measured the moderating influence of career stage. In both categories there is sufficient evidence to suggest that a static, or cross-section correlation of commitment with other variables is inadequate. For instance, in a five-year longitudinal follow-up to graduate entrants, Lydka (1991) found a strong correlation between job satisfaction and attitudinal commitment, and this relationship was sustained over time. The correlation with behavioural commitment, however, was weaker and decreased over time. Some tentative conclusions about causality can be drawn from another study of newcomers (at one, six and eleven months) by Meyer and Allen (1988): work experiences in the first month of employment influenced commitment measured later in the first year; also commitment registered at six months was predictive of subsequent perceptions of work experience. This partially supports the findings of Arnold (1989), who studied the first year's training for a sample of nurses. Although he used a measure of career – rather than organizational – commitment, unmet expectations had significantly negative impact on commitment at four months and one year, the influence of job choice variables was initially strong but waned, and the experience of training itself was initially unimportant but became increasingly determinative of commitment by the end of the first year.

Career-stage studies also suggest organization commitment to be a non-static concept. When career stage was operationalized in terms of age, organizational and positional tenure, Morrow and McElroy (1987) found in a large sample of public agency employees that those in their last career stage were the most committed, irrespective of occupational group. This concurs with other studies which have found positive correlations between age/ organizational tenure and organizational commitment (Angle and Perry, 1981; Morris and Sherman, 1981; Meyer and Allen, 1984). Furthermore, a meta-analysis of 41 samples dealing with relationships between organizational commitment and outcomes found the correlation between commitment and turnover (actual and intended) to be greater in early career stages, and the correlation with performance and absenteeism to be strongest in the later career stage (Cohen, 1991).

Clearly then it is important when studying the process of how employees become committed, and what other outcomes this results in, to account for such factors as tenure and age and, if possible, to track the evolution of commitment over time.

DOES COMMITMENT VARY DEPENDING ON THE SECTOR OF EMPLOYMENT?

The majority of studies which have been carried out to date, including many of those already mentioned, have largely sought to investigate the concept of commitment in commercial sector organizations. Since Kanter's work on utopian communities, when she studied the nature of attachment to religious sects in the USA, the amount of research which deviates from the commercial sector 'norm' has been remarkably small (Kanter, 1968; Oliver, 1984; Cornforth *et al.*, 1988; Glisson and Durick, 1988; Wetzel and Gallagher, 1990). In this respect organization commitment research differs very little from the main thrust of organizational and behavioural theory: organizations are often taken to be homogeneous and what is assumed of one may be assumed, however incorrectly, of all of them. However, there is an enormous number of alternative organizational contexts worth investigating, many of which could be said to lie between Kanter's utopian communities and the average commercial company. Some of this ground is occupied by non-profit organizations and by voluntary and charitable organizations in particular.

Interest in non-profit/charitable organizations is growing in the USA, and the focus is largely being driven from a management perspective. The membership of lay management boards, the commitment to constructing a vision for the organization and the clarity with which employees as well as volunteers regard their commitment, could be said to be the envy of the average commercial organization. As it happens, just as the NPOs (non-profit organizations) struggle to learn conventional management techniques from the commercial sector, so the management gurus are beginning to turn their attention to what commercial organizations can learn from NPOs (Drucker, 1989). Fortunately, this is somewhat tempered by sensitive analyses of some of the unusual and complex operating problems of NPOs (such as their lack of a 'bottom line' in performance terms), as well as some of their advantages (Walker, 1983; Kanter and Summers, 1987).

Over 170,000 voluntary organizations/charities are registered with the Charity Commissioners in the UK, they represent a turnover of 16 billion pounds, employ over 250,000 staff and include many well-known household names (such as Oxfam, Save the Children Fund, Christian Aid, RNIB, and so on). They share some similarities with the public sector but differ from it quite considerably (Paton, 1991; Paton and Cornforth, 1991), and are believed to be subject to quite separate pressures in sustaining the commitment of their employees (Young, 1984; Glisson and Durick, 1988).

Why be interested in voluntary and charitable organizations? One reason is that they represent a largely forgotten segment of organizational life, in which the need to engage in managing values or norms can occupy a large part of the organization's time. It is often assumed that they have strong cultures (although they are again neglected by the mainstream organizational culture literature), high employee commitment and that individuals experience a high degree of value congruence between themselves and their organization (Drucker, 1989; Butler and Wilson, 1990). It is certainly a fact that such organizations combine the unusual practice of engaging paid employees alongside voluntary staff at all levels, including management. However, empirical research and discussion of the non-profit commitment phenomenon is so far limited to co-operatives (Oliver, 1984; Cornforth *et al.*, 1988; Wetzel and Gallagher, 1990). The results, nevertheless, lend credence to some of the above assumptions, as higher organizational commitment scores have been found when compared to employees from other sectors.

WHAT WOULD A NON-PROFIT PERSPECTIVE BRING TO BEAR ON THE ORGANIZATIONAL COMMITMENT DEBATE?

An investigation of organizational commitment which compares and contrasts the profit and non-profit sectors would begin to establish whether differences exist between the sectors and, if they do, what the implications/outcomes are in behavioural terms. First, it has already been recognized that the way in which commitment is translated into behaviour is very under researched (Meyer and Allen, 1991). The behavioural outcomes of absenteeism and turnover have long been the focus of conventional commitment research but, more recently, 'prosocial' or 'extra-role' behaviour (positive behaviour resulting from high commitment carried out over and above what is normally expected of an employee) is beginning to attract attention (O'Reilly and Chatman, 1986; Chatman, 1989). The non-profit sector becomes an ideal context in which to research prosocial behaviour because the expectations regarding what an employee will do for the organization are that much higher than in conventional organizations (Butler and Wildon, 1990).

Second, if there is a link between high levels of affective and/or normative commitment and performance, which may have consequences for the organization, then the experience of employees within NPOs in this area will be illuminating. It has long been assumed that the desired state of high commitment, which the average commercial organization wishes to achieve in its employees (if the HRM literature is to be believed), is already apparent in the non-profit sector and this alone deserves investigation. Or it may be the case that anecdotal evidence disappears when subjected to empirical research. Whatever the outcome, it would be fortuitous to examine many of the so-called advantages of high commitment and the potential disadvantages for organizations, which are only just beginning to be subjected to speculation (Randall, 1987; Coopey and Hartley, 1989).

CAN THE 'FIT' BETWEEN ORGANIZATIONS AND INDIVIDUALS BE MEASURED?

The interplay between an individual's characteristics and the organization's policies or culture has already been briefly alluded to. One aspect of this is the degree of 'fit' between the individual's values and the norms current within the organization. In the scale Meyer and Allen (1991) have developed, they attempted to measure a form of normative commitment underpinned by a belief in loyalty. However, normative commitment may be extremely variable from one context to another and for the individual the antecedents may lie in a variety of factors (personality, upbringing, education, and so on). The link between individual norms and organizational culture is also very complex. For instance, a norm may be held by an individual prior to joining an organization, or it can be a strong characteristic of the organizational culture which, over time, affects the individual's values.

Issues such as these are relevant to another strand of existing research, which is represented in psychology by the 'person–environment' debate, and differences over the degree of influence that one has on the other have intrigued researchers for some time. The emphasis seems to have shifted to the interaction taking place between the individual and the environment, rather than one or the other taking precedence (Pervin, 1989; Chatman, 1989). Work in this field has led to the development of a model of 'person–organization fit' (the OCP),* in which individual value profiles are compared to organizational value profiles (Chatman, 1989; O'Reilly, Chatman and Caldwell, 1991). Previous research in this field has been hampered by the tendency for individuals to be described with one set of measures or characteristics and situations with another, but the OCP is believed to have removed these problems. By drawing on a Q-sort methodology (which is both nomothetic and idiographic), the OCP allows *individual* and *organizational* values to be captured simultaneously. Hence 'person–organization fit' becomes the congruence between the norms and values of organizations and persons.

Attempting to assess individual values against the values or norms of an organization, using quantitative measures, is not easy. The concept of organizational culture is immensely complex, and academic approaches to the

---

* The organization culture profile (OCP), as it is known, assesses 'person–organization fit' by asking respondents to place 54 value statements about themselves and their organizations into 9 categories. The value statements generically capture individual and organizational norms and values. To compare the individual respondent's characterization of their organization with a reference point, a broad representation of other organization members is also asked to sort the same statements. Member profiles are then combined by averaging each time to form an organizational profile and the 'crystallization' of organizational values is assessed by calculating a reliability coefficient for the mean organizational profile (Chatman, 1989).

study of it are many and varied (see Smircich, 1983, for an overview). Nevertheless, the methodological problems associated with its measurement have been reviewed (Rousseau, 1985; Cooke and Rousseau, 1988; Rousseau, 1990). The evidence suggests that, first, their needs to be clarity concerning the parameters of research because culture is not a unidimensional concept. Second, when tackling the complexity of culture research, a multilevel and multimethod approach should be employed. In this respect, the OCP has been seen as an appropriate measure and significant relationships have been found between organizational and individual norms, thus leading to it being an appropriate measurement of 'person–organization fit' (Rousseau, 1990).

SUMMARY

Further development of our understanding of organizational commitment and its links with behaviour is required. Despite the fact that the concepts of attitudinal and behavioural commitment are now well established, this review of studies in the field has shown that there is scope for further refinement and investigation. There are, in particular, three promising lines of inquiry. The first is to utilize the concept of normative commitment. As this construct seeks to tap the values of the individual as well as the link between these and the values or culture of the organization, it is central to organizational commitment research. The second is to pursue the measure of 'person–organization fit' which will enable research at the level of organizational culture and individual values to be undertaken. Third, if we recognize that organizational commitment is not a unidimensional construct, and that it cannot be assumed to be static over time, this points to the need for research that is multidimensional and longitudinal.

REFERENCES

Allen, N. J. and Meyer, J. P. (1990) 'The measurement and antecedents of affective, continuance and normative commitment in the organization', *Journal of Occupational Psychology*, Vol. 63, pp. 1–18.

Alutto, J. A., Hrebiniak, L. G. and Alonso, R. C. (1973) 'On operationalizing the concept of commitment', *Social Forces*, Vol. 51, pp. 448–54.

Angle, H. and Perry, J. (1981) 'An empirical assessment of organizational commitment and organizational effectiveness', *Administrative Science Quarterly*, Vol. 26, pp. 1–13.

Arnold, H. and Feldman, D. (1982) 'A multivarative of the determinants of job turnover', *Journal of Applied Psychology*, Vol. 81, pp. 350–60.

Arnold, J. (1989) 'The career commitment of learner nurses during their first year of training'. Unpublished manuscript, Manchester School of Management.

Becker, M. (1960) 'Notes on the concept of commitment', *American Journal of Sociology*, Part 66, pp. 32–40.

Beer, M., Spector, B., Lawrence, P., Quinn Mills, D. and Walton, R. E. (1984) *Managing Human Assets*, Free Press, New York.

Blau, G. J. (1988) 'Further exploring the meaning and measurement of career commitment', *Journal of Vocational Behaviour*, Vol. 32, pp. 284–97.

Blood, M. R. (1969) 'Work values and job satisfaction', *Journal of Applied Psychology*, Vol. 53, pp. 456–9.

Buchanan, B. (1974) 'Building organizational commitment: the socialization of managers in work organization', *Administrative Science Quarterly*, Vol. 19, pp. 533–46.

Butler, R. J. and Wilson, D. C. (1989) *Managing Voluntary and Non-Profit Organizations: Strategy and Structure*, Routledge, London.

Caldwell, D., Chatman, J. and O'Reilly, C. (1990) 'Building organizations' commitment: a multifirm study', *Journal of Occupational Psychology*, Vol. 63, pp. 245–61.

Chatman, J. A. (1989) 'Improving interactional organizational research: a model of person–organization fit', *Academy of Management Review*, Vol. 14, no. 3, pp. 333–49.

Cohen, A. (1991) 'Career stage as a moderator of the relationship between organizational commitment and its outcomes: a meta-analysis', *Journal of Organizational Psychology*, Vol. 64, pp. 253–68.

Cooke, R. A. and Rousseau, D. M. (1988) 'Behavioural norms and expectations: a quantitative approach to the assessment of organizational culture', *Group and Organization Studies*, Vol. 13, no. 3, pp. 245–73.

Coopey, J. and Hartley, J. (1991) 'Reconsidering the case for organizational commitment', *The Human Resource Management Journal*, Vol. 1, no. 3, pp. 18–32.

Cornforth, C., Thomas, A., Lewis, J. and Spear, R. (1988) *Developing Successful Worker Co-operatives*, Sage, London.

Drucker, P. F. (1989) 'What business can learn from non-profits', *Harvard Business Review*, July/August.

Festinger, L. (1957) *Theory of Cognitive Dissonance*, Row Peterson, Evanston, Ill.

Folger, R. and Konovsky, M. A. (1989) 'Effects of prodedural and distributive justice in reactions to pay rise decisions', *Academy of Management Journal*, Vol. 32, no. 1, pp. 115–30.

Fombrun, C. N., Tichy, M. and Devanna, M. A. (1984) *Strategic Human Resource Management*, Wiley, Chichester.

Glisson, C. and Durick, M. (1988) 'Predictors of job satisfaction and organizational commitment in human service organizations', *Administrative Science Quarterly*, Vol. 33, pp. 61–81.

Goode, W. J. (1960) 'Norm commitment and conformity to role-status obligations', *American Journal of Sociology*, Vol. 66, pp. 1246–58.

Guest, D. (1987) 'Human resource management and industrial relations', *Journal of Management Studies*, Vol. 24, no. 5, pp. 503–21.

Guest, D. (1989) 'Personnel and HRM: can you tell the difference?, *Personnel Management*, January, pp. 48–51.

Hrebiniak, L. G. and Alutto, J. A. (1972) Personal and role related factors in the development of organizational commitments, *Administrative Science Quarterly*, Vol. 18, pp. 555–73.

Iles, P., Mabey, C. and Robertson, I. T. (1990) 'HRM practices and employee commitment: possibilities, pitfalls and paradoxes', *British Journal of Management*, Vol. 1, pp. 147–57.

Kanter, R. (1968) Commitment and social organization: a study of commitment mechanisms in utopian communities, *American Sociological Review*, Vol. 33, pp. 499–517.

Kanter, R. M. (1972) *Commitment and Community*, Harvard University Press, Cambridge, Mass.

Kanter, R. M. and Summers, D. V. (1987) 'Doing well while doing good: dilemmas of performance measurement in non-profit organizations and the need for a multiple-constituency approach', in W. W. Powell (ed.) *The Non-Profit Sector Handbook*, Yale University Press, New Haven, Conn.

Kanungo, R. N. (1982) 'Measurement of jobs and work involvement', *Journal of Applied Psychology*, Vol. 67, pp. 341–9.

Keisler, C. A. (1971) *The Psychology of Commitment*, Academic Press, New York.

Kline, C. J. and Peters, L. H. (1991) 'Behavioural commitment and tenure of new employees: a replication and extension', *Academy of Management Journal*, Vol. 34, no. 1, pp. 194–204.

Kohn, M. and Schooler, C. (1978) 'The reciprocol effects of the substantive complexity of work and intellectual flexibility: a longitudinal assessment', *American Journal of Sociology*, Vol. 84, pp. 24–52.

Lydka, H. (1991) 'Organizational commitment and job satisfaction: a longitudinal study of the UK graduates'. Paper presented to the British Academy of Management Annual Conference, Bath, September.

Mabey, C. (1986) *Graduates into Industry*, Gower, Aldershot.

Meyer, J. and Allen, N. (1984) 'Testing the "side-bet theory" of organizational commitment: some methodological considerations', *Journal of Applied Psychology*, Vol. 69, pp. 372–8.

Meyer, J. and Allen, N. (1988) 'Links between work experiences and organizational commitment during the first year of employment: a longitudinal analysis', *Journal of Occupational Psychology*, Vol. 61, pp. 195–209.

Meyer, J. P. and Allen, N. J. (1991) 'A three-component conceptualization of organizational commitment', *Human Resource Management Review*, Vol. 1, no. 1, pp. 61–89.

Morris, J. H. and Sherman, J. D. (1981) 'Generalizability of an organizational commitment model', *Academy of Management Journal*, Vol. 24, pp. 512–26.

Morrow, P. C. and McElroy, J. C. (1986) On assessing measures of work commitment, *Journal of Organizational Behaviour*, Vol. 7, pp. 139–45.

Morrow, P. C. and Wirth, R. (1989) 'Work commitment among salaried professionals', *Journal of Vocational Behaviour*, Vol. 34, pp. 40–56.

Nicholson, N. and West, M. (1988) *Managerial Job Change: Men and Women in Transition*, Cambridge University Press.

Ogilvie, J. R. (1987) 'The role of human resource management practices in predicting organization commitment', *Group and Organization Studies*, Vol. 11, no. 4, pp. 335–59.

Oliver, N. (1984) 'An examination of organizational commitment in six workers' cooperatives in Scotland', *Human Relations*, Vol. 37, no. 1, pp. 29–46.

O'Reilly, C. A. and Caldwell, D. F. (1981) 'The commitment and job tenure of new employees: some evidence of post-decisional justification', *Administrative Science Quarterly*, Vol. 26, pp. 596–616.

O'Reilly, C. A. and Chatman, J. (1986) 'Organizational commitment and psychological attachment: the effects of compliance, identification and internalization of prosocial behaviour', *Journal of Applied Psychology*, Vol. 71, no. 3, pp. 492–9.

O'Reilly, C. A., Chatman, J. and Caldwell, D. F. (1991) 'People and organizational culture: a profile comparison approach to assessing person–organization fit', *Academy of Management Journal*, Vol. 34, pp. 487–516.

Paton, R. (1991) 'The social economy: value based organizations in the wider society', in J. Batsleer, C. Cornforth and R. Paton (eds) *Issues in Voluntary and Non-Profit Management*, Addison-Wesley, Wokingham.

Paton, R. and Cornforth, C. (1991). 'What's different about managing in voluntary and non-profit organisations?', in J. Batsleer, C. Cornforth and R. Paton (eds) *Issues in Voluntary and Non-Profit Management*, Addison-Wesley, Wokingham.

Pervin, L. (1989) 'Persons, situations, interactions: the history of a controversy and a discussion of theoretical models', *Academy of Management Review*, Vol. 14, no. 3, pp. 350–60.

Porter, L. W., Steers, R., Mowday, R. and Boulian, P. (1974) 'Organizational commitment, job satisfaction and turnover among psychiatric technicians', *Journal of Applied Psychology*, Vol. 59, pp. 603–9.

Premack, S. L. and Wanous, J. P. (1985) 'A meta-analysis of realistic job preview experiments', *Journal of Applied Psychology*, Vol. 70, pp. 706–19.

Randall, D. M. (1987) 'Commitment and the organizational man revisited', *Academy of Management Review*, Vol. 12, no. 3, pp. 460–71.

Rousseau, D. M. (1985) 'Issues of level in organization research: multi-level and cross level perspectives', in L. L. Cummings and B. M. Staw (eds) *Research in Organization Behavior*, JAI Press, Greenwich, Conn., pp. 1–37.

Rousseau, D. M. (1990) 'Assessing organizational culture: the case for multiple methods', in B. Schneider (ed.) *Climate and Culture*, Jossey Bass, San Francisco, Calif.

Salancik, G. P. (1977) 'Commitment and the control of organizational behavior and belief', in B. Staw and G. R. Salanck (eds) *New Directions in Organizational Behavior*, St Clair Press: Chicago, Ill.

Smircich, L. (1983) 'Concepts of culture and organizational analysis', *Administrative Science Quarterly*, September, pp. 342–58.

Snow, C. C. and Hrebiniak, L. G. (1980) 'Strategy, distinctive competence and organizational performance', *Administrative Science Quarterly*, Vol. 25, pp. 317–36.

Storey, J. (1987) 'Human resource management in the public sector', *Public Money and Management*, Autumn, pp. 19–24.

Storey, J. (ed.) (1989) *New Perspectives in Human Resource Management*, Routledge, London.

Tichy, N. M., Fombrun, C. J. and Devanna, M. A. (1982) 'Strategic human resource management', *Sloan Management Review*, Vol. 23, Winter, p. 2.

Tziner, A. and Latham, G. P. (1989) 'The effects of appraisal instrument, feedback and goal setting on worker satisfaction and commitment', *Journal of Organizational Behaviour*, Vol. 10, pp. 145–53.

Walker, J. M. (1983) 'Limits of strategic management in voluntary organizations', *Journal of Voluntary Action Research*, Vol. 12, no. 3, pp. 39–55.

Wetzel, K. W. and Gallagher, D. G. (1990) 'A comparative analysis of organizational commitment among workers in the co-operative and private sectors', *Economic and Industrial Democracy*, Vol. 11, pp. 93–109.

Young, D. (1984) *Performance and Reward in Non-Profit Organizations: Evaluation, Compensation and Personnel Incentives* (Yale University PONPO Working Paper 79), Yale University Press, New Haven, Conn.

5

Codes of ethics and whistleblowing*

George C. S. Benson

In recent decades American corporations have been improving their whole outlook on business ethics. There have been reform movements in American business before; the early nineteenth-century states slowly adopted provisions requiring reports to shareholders and making directors responsible to shareholders. Another reform came in the progressive movement, 1890 to 1930, in which state regulation of security sales began, and commercial bribery was sharply limited by industrial codes of ethics. A third came when Franklin Roosevelt secured passage of the Securities and Exchange Commission Acts in 1933–4. But the Securities and Exchange Commission had difficulty in enforcing its decrees, and books criticizing corporations for many illegal acts have often been published in recent decades.[1]

Laws regulating corporate action are today being enforced more than in President Reagan's first term, but to this writer the greater hope is that of the corporations reforming themselves. A Conference Board review in 1987 found a high proportion of major corporations paying more attention to employee health, quality control of products, prohibiting misuse of inside information, and other ethical problems.[2] The Corporate Roundtable in 1988 issued a substantive study of ethics, reviewing ethical procedures of a dozen major corporations.[3]

A major characteristic of the current reform movement has been the adoption of codes of ethics by corporations. Those in the defence industries have been pressured to adopt codes by a Defense Department which was rightfully angry at a number of ethical violations. Prosecution of violations under the Foreign Corrupt Practices Act of 1978 has stimulated other corporations to writing codes. Approximately 90 per cent of Fortune 500 corporations and half of all corporations today have codes.[4]

Especially in the case of defence industry corporations, but also in many other concerns, administrative machinery has been devised to enforce codes,

* Reprinted by permission of MCB University Press Ltd, from *Managerial Auditing Journal*, Vol. 7, no. 2, 1992, pp. 37–40, where it appeared under the title 'Codes of ethics, whistleblowing and managerial auditing'.

or a better phrase, to educate executives and employees to codes. Codes and accompanying instructions are delivered to all employees; many are asked annually to sign a statement certifying to reading of the code. Seminars in business ethics are held for many employees.

General Dynamics, largest or next to largest of defence corporations, has an ethics training programme which has been supervised by an able Vice-President, Ethics. Instructional ethics programmes are largely assigned to line supervisors to convince staff that the corporation intends to view ethics as a major part of its work programmes. There are ethics programme directors in various divisions. A Board Committee on Corporate Responsibility has been appointed; policies and procedures were reviewed to test their conformity to ethical standards; 'hotline' communications to designated ethics officers have been set up (discussed in the next section on whistleblowing); and ethics workshops were held for all employees. A 'no-reprisal' policy for critical communication to ethics management has been established.

In 1988, discharges on ethical grounds by General Dynamics were interesting. Sixteen employees had misused timecard records of their own work. Two had accepted large gift certificates; three had falsified quality standards. Three were dropped for falsification of test data and two for forgery; three for misuse of company and customer resources; four for drug trafficking; two for false statements against others; and also dismissals for sexual harassment, racial discrimination and extortion. Some lessons learned by ethics management included:

> Most employees want to do what is right and appreciate direction and support.
> Persons in leadership positions play pivotal roles in establishing ethics and setting examples.
> Ethics programs need to be positive and to be integrated within existing organization structures and practices.
> The ability to foresee consequences of actions and a willingness to accept responsibility are very difficult lessons to teach.
> Appearance is often as important as fact in ethical judgements.
> Enforcement is necessary for credibility.
> Most everyday questions of ethics involve fair treatment of others.[5]

Later correspondence with the director of the programme on the knotty problem of conflicts of interest led to this interesting remark: 'We daily encounter conflict situations where no wrongdoing has occurred or is likely to occur. Nonetheless we often seek to break up these situations in order to avoid problems of fact or appearance down the road.'[6]

Other methods of ethical education have been used. Several institutions including Ethics Resource Center in Washington, and Wharton School of the University of Pennsylvania, have prepared for sale audio visual presentations of frequent ethical problems with suggestions as to means of securing discussion. This writer is not aware of studies of the effectiveness of such audio visual presentations. They lead to an ethically thoughtful approach to management but there is also a need for instruction in ethical values established by higher religions and great philosophers.

Other corporate codes follow different lines of approach. International Business Machines publishes *Business Conduct Guidelines* which includes very well written accounts of what salespersons and other employees should and should not do in connection with purchasers, suppliers and competitors. This emphasis is probably a result of IBM's many years of fighting off a very expensive anti-trust prosecution.

Caterpillar Tractor with a worldwide business code includes wishes to 'help improve the quality of life' in every country in which it works, and the necessity of obeying the laws of each country. All executives and managers are asked to report to the General Counsel in Peoria (Illinois) of any events indicating that the code has not been closely followed.

Hewlett-Packard's 1983 policy statement outlines obligations to 'HP', to customers, to competitors and to suppliers in careful well written paragraphs. McDonnell Douglas has carefully written five standards, with questions and answers regarding product quality, customer, supplier and buyer relationships, hiring former government employees, conflicts of interest, company records, government data, and important company data.

Tandem Computers Inc. published in 1984 a corporate policy statement which makes an effort to give the reason for the rule in connection with each rule. Other corporations do this in connection with some rules but not all. Tandem is to be commended. Johnson and Johnson (J and J) has for several decades had a 'credo' which briefly outlines its objectives for staff, shareholders, consumers and company. The credo is displayed in offices of J and J's 150 subsidiaries over the world. The credo was helpful to J and J executives in their decision to spend over $30 million in withdrawal of Tylenol after murderers had 'laced' a few packages with cyanide.

The nature of these corporate ethical codes naturally varies with the business. As noted above, one of IBM's biggest problems has been anti-trust. Computer industries in the recent past have had troubles of intercorporate stealing of plans. The defence contractors have worries about illegal shifting of funds by their own executives between government projects.

Very special ethical problems exist in large retail establishments where enticing articles for sale tempt both customers and sales staff. Codes of ethics can meet only a part of these problems. In America the problem of stealing is worse because the public schools rarely teach any ethics. If retailers have made special efforts to persuade public schools to teach ethics, including the ethical arguments against stealing, this writer is not aware of it.

WHISTLEBLOWING

Accompanying the development of what might be called code of ethics administration in the last two decades in America, there has been a remarkable change of attitude about 'whistleblowing' in American industry and government. All defence industries code-education machinery now include some opportunity for critical employees to tell their story to a higher-level employee, often to a staff committee, usually with a guarantee against recriminatory action. The General Dynamics employee incidents listed above are mostly the result of employee whistleblowing – at times as many as 3,000 a year. A federal statute enables defence industry employees to sue for damages against a contractor policy or decision which has cheated the government. If damages are won, not more than 30 per cent goes to the whistleblower; the balance includes fees for the complainants' lawyers and the remainder is returned to the government. Several cases have already resulted in transfer of substantial funds from contractor to whistleblower, his or her law firm and the Department of Defense.

Several state governments and state courts have moved towards legal protection of whistleblowers. In 1981 a Michigan Act provided that employers cannot discharge, threaten or discriminate against an employee who reports a violation of federal, state or local laws, rules or regulations to a public body. A Florida bill creates a legal third party who has power to look at poor construction reported by employees. A Kentucky law 'protects from reprisal a miner who reports or refuses to operate unsafe equipment.'[7] Connecticut passed a law protecting private sector employees from discharge for exercising First Amendment rights of free speech.

In California in 1985 the federal Occupational Safety and Health Administration (OSHA) was probing the state OSHA because of '104 cases in which employees of private companies and public agencies were disciplined or fired after filing complaints with Cal-OSHA about unsafe working conditions'.[8]

Whistleblower programmes are not always in favour of all employees. A four-year-old programme in California led to the disciplining – even the firing – 'of state workers who made hundreds of dollars of personal long distance calls, operated private businesses on that line, or falsified expense accounts'.[9]

This article would become far too long if it attempted to review all the American literature on whistleblowing. It is probably fair to say that the more thoughtful writings have been in favour of some protection of whistleblowers. It is part of the general trend in America of more regard for the rights and independence of women, of children, of racial minorities. There are occasions where the attempt to secure these ends by legal means may become cumbersome or damaging to quality of performance. Whistleblowing to date seems to be a reasonable effort to secure greater safety for all and higher-quality work.

As the world moves towards more general acceptance of democracy and freer economic systems, there may be greater demand for whistleblowing. Perhaps corporations should try better ethical instruction of engineers and executives as a partial substitute for whistleblowing which must have some unfortunate effects on organizational morale. Until American schools and colleges decide to view ethics as an important part of their curriculum, whistleblowing seems to be a necessary device.

There has not been great public opposition to the recent spread of whistleblowing. An exception is the comment of my much admired friend and colleague, Peter Drucker, who likened the idea of whistleblowing to odious 'informer' systems set up by monarchs or dictators.[10] There is an apparent parallel between these two processes, but a well run whistleblowing system need not resemble a dictatorial system of informers if well educated, responsible corporate employees review and research the complaints.

THE ROLE OF MANAGERIAL AUDITORS IN RAISING BUSINESS ETHICS

How great a role in development of corporate ethics is being made or will be made by managerial or internal auditors? The question is important since twice as many American CPAs are internal auditors as are on the staff of outside auditing firms. Important steps in enforcement of intra-company ethics should be made by the internal auditor.

Examination of the *Internal Auditor* magazine issues over half-a-dozen years discovered many articles which dealt with the edge of ethical problems. In February 1982 (Vol. XXXI, p. 35) two Canadian Comptroller General officers commented that their national accounting standards paid too little attention to 'senior management support, organizational climate, management style, and attitudes', an observation which perhaps indicated their feeling that internal auditors should be interested in organizational ethics. Another article (pp. 44–5) alludes to Chester Barnard's view that 'managing is a *moral* job of setting the tone of organizations'.[11] An article in December, 1982, Vol. XXXIX, pp. 26–8, 'Think like the president', however, omits ethics as a goal of the president except in mentioning 'the worth of each new product or service' as one of the president's thoughts. In a June article (p. 42) of *Internal Auditor* there is an excellent outline of the problems which may trouble the CEO but on which information from internal auditors would help him. But Barnard's CEO job of morality of the organization is not mentioned.

In April, 1986 (pp. 37–42) the writers describe a case in which a company's top marketing director had ordered some cost data manipulated so that cost plus billings to the defence department were greatly inflated. The Certified Internal Auditors Code provides auditors should not knowingly be a party to any illegality or improper activity. The discussion concludes that it would be illegal for them not to report the marketing director's action. The ethics of not doing so is barely discussed. In June 1986 (pp. 29–35) an Internal Revenue Service auditor discusses the difficulties of placing an audit agency within a government department and does refer to the need for 'honesty' (p. 35).

In October 1986, an interesting article compares the examination for Certified Public Accountants (CPA), for Certified Internal Auditors (CIA), and for the National Association of Accountants (CMA); all three examinations refer to some ethical standards. Certified Internal Auditors have a code of ethics. So do CPAs, but the examinations in ethics seen by this writer are easily passed with little thought.

In the later 1980s and 1990 articles in the *Internal Auditor* about the profession searched more deeply into management problems. One uncertainty was whether CIAs or CMAs should strive to work with management or be 'independent'. This writer had met a similar problem in the personnel field at America's beginning of World War Two. He was personnel director of a rapidly expanding war agency, and constantly battled with the Civil Service Commission, at that time the central personnel agency, to get things done. The magazine *Public Personnel Administration* published his article on how personnel should fit into management, but it took decades before the federal government followed the advice. Effective staff service must be a part of management.

Perhaps a majority of the latter *Internal Auditor* articles reviewed here incline towards the view that CIAs should try to help management if its actions were 'good auditing', which means ethical although that word was little used.[12] If internal auditors are to be in the management channel and help develop the ethical atmosphere which modern administration is increasingly demanding, internal auditors must try to share the problems of management and convince management that accounting must be ethical. My own experience with internal auditors in government and education, which has always been co-operative, leads me to think that this position is workable. The ethics vice-president of a very large corporation assures me that his staff and the internal auditors view themselves as co-workers in a common cause.

The fourth issue of the *Managerial Auditing Journal*, in 1989, has some excellent articles on the internal audit function which seem to indicate a slightly greater emphasis on the ethical aspects of internal auditing. An amusing article on 'Naming the auditor' confirms the judgement of my accounting professor friends that their chosen field is not highly regarded by some fellow workers. 'Wimpy', 'meddlers', 'critics', 'undercover' and 'Gestapo' are examples (Wilson and Wood, 1989).[13] Then there is the criticism of the internal auditors 'who come in after a management battle and shoot all the wounded'.

Thoughtful executives simply smile at this exaggerated nomenclature but internal auditors cannot be blamed for resenting it. Perhaps an educational campaign is needed to let fellow employees realize how basic the internal audit is to corporate success. Professor Vinten (1989) wisely[14] comments that the auditor by his behaviour should show that he is not to be feared. The auditor's efforts for quality assurance are a part of what should be the ambition of all corporate employees, to increase their corporation's ethical service to the whole community.

A thorough report on *Fraudulent Financial Reporting* was made in 1987 by the National Commission on Fraudulent Financial Reporting, commonly called the Treadway Report after its chairman, James C. Treadway jr.[15] This report fairly clearly defines a position that this writer has been groping towards in his discussion of the *Internal Auditor* articles. According to the commission, auditors need very thorough accounting training, but also an ethical education. In America, public schools generally do not teach ethics except as an ethical teacher may incidentally pass to the student his or her own way of doing things. The Treadway Commission is very specific in its comments on ethical education for auditors, both independent and internal. The commission endorses the corporate codes of ethics discussed above and comments that all codes should have specific lists of prohibited conflicts of interest between employees or executives and the company. Internal auditors should consider non-financial audit findings, a position which coincides with the vice-president's ethics suggestion noted above that internal auditors and ethics staff are allies. Professors and students of accounting should learn how to find the causes of the fraud and how to prevent fraud. Faculties should convey ethical values to their students.

Internal or managerial auditors may be pleased to learn that a summary of the various research reports submitted to the Treadway Commission found that the Internal Auditors Association report of fraud was broader than that of the American Institute of Certified Public Accountants.[16]

Some readers may wish to know more about the 'ethics' which the Treadway Commission and this writer believe should be taught to all auditors. A wide variety of books on ethics and compilations of ethics problems exist. Much of it is not particularly relevant to business problems. Following the pattern of C. S. Lewis in *The Abolition of Man*, here are some of the ethics generally accepted in the civilized world which accounting students might well discuss:

'Do unto others as you would be done by' (all higher religions).
'Love your neighbour as yourself' (Old and New Testaments).
'Do not steal' (Ten Commandments).
'Do not kill' (Ten Commandments).
'So act that your action would have been a result of universal law' (Immanuel Kant).
'Act as if every individual was an end in himself' (Immanuel Kant).
'Complete what you have promised to do' (business ethics).
'Obey the law' (general).
'Honour your parents, care for your children' (most religions).
'Do not deliberately mislead or cheat anyone with whom you have dealings' (business ethics).
'Tell the truth. Let your customer know about the difficulties they may encounter with your product' (business ethics).

Future accountants could easily be overloaded with many volumes of philosophical discussions, some of it useful only for discussion with philosophy professors. Perhaps a final treatise on ethics in auditing will never be written. But if professors of accounting and auditing would bring the more perceptive thoughts of ethics into their classrooms the level of corporate morality could be greatly improved.

NOTES

1. M. B. Clinard (1983) *Corporate Ethics and Crime*, Sage, Beverly Hills, Calif.; (1990) *Corporate Corruption*, Praeger New York; and M. B. Clinard and P. C. Yeager (1980) *Corporate Crime*, Free Press, New York, are three of the better ones.
2. The Conference Board (1987) *Corporate Ethics*, New York.
3. Corporate Roundtable (1988) *Corporate Ethics: A Prime Business Asset*, New York.

4. P. E. Murphy (1988) 'Implementing business ethics', *Journal of Business Ethics*, Vol. 7, pp. 907–15.

5. The General Dynamics Ethics Program, 1988.

6. Letter by Kent Druyvesteyn, Vice-President, Ethics, General Dynamics, reprinted with permission.

7. *Los Angeles Times*, 16 December 1982, p. 4.

8. *Los Angeles Times*, 4 June 1985, p. 3.

9. *San Gabriel Valley Tribune*, 18 March 1985, editorial page.

10. *The Public Interest*, no. 63, Spring, 1981, pp. 18–36.

11. *The Functions of the Executive*, Harvard University Press, Cambridge, Mass., 1983.

12. D. Shaw (1986) 'Internal audit and quality improvement', *The Internal Auditor*, December, pp. 50–3.

13. Wilson, J. A. and Wood, D. J. (1989) Naming the Auditor, *Managerial Auditing Journal*, Vol. 4, no. 4, pp. 7–13.

14. Vinten, G. (1989) The Rottweiler Auditor, *Managerial Auditing Journal*, Vol. 4, no. 4, pp. i–ii.

15. Available from the American Institute of Certified Public Accounts, New York.

16. Treadway Report and appendices, p. 116.

Part II

PROFESSIONAL PERSPECTIVES

6

US law, whistleblower protection and the Office of the Special Counsel*

Bruce D. Fong

INTRODUCTION

In 1979, Congress established the Office of the Special Counsel (OSC) under the Civil Service Reform Act of 1978 (CSRA or Act)[1] as an independent investigative and prosecutive arm of the United States Merit Systems Protection Board (MSPB or Board).[2] The CSRA enumerated eleven specific prohibited personnel practices[3] and empowered OSC to investigate and prosecute these prohibited practices for corrective and disciplinary action.[4] Without doubt, the protection of employees from reprisal for protected activity, in particular 'whistleblowing', was a primary purpose of the Act.[5] Although Congress intended each of the agencies to protect the merit system[6] against prohibited personnel practices, it made OSC the system's chief enforcer.

The impetus for statutory protection for whistleblowers derived from a variety of developments, experiences, and events. These include the changing nature of federal government,[7] emerging first amendment doctrines concerning the public employee,[8] a growing public distrust of government,[9] increasing attention to the plight of the federal whistleblower,[10] the ineffectiveness of existing remedies and protection mechanisms to protect whistleblowing,[11] the enactment of the federal Freedom of Information Act, and widespread political support for whistleblower reform. In response to these converging forces, the 95th Congress, for the first time, adopted comprehensive legislation protecting specifically identified employee speech and related activity from reprisal.[12] Although the administration's initial whistleblower protection proposal called only for the protection of allegations of violations of law, rules, or regulations, Congress expanded whistleblowing activities to include disclosures which evidenced mismanagement, a gross waste of funds, an abuse of authority, or a specific danger to public health and safety.

* Reprinted by permission of *The American University Law Review*, 1991, Vol. 40, no. 3, where it appeared under the title, 'Whistleblower protection and the Office of Special Counsel: the development of reprisal law in the 1980s'.

In addition to the protection given to whistleblowing activities, the CSRA protected employees from reprisal for the exercise of any lawful appeal right. During the first decade under the Act, the two protected activities, whistleblowing and the exercise of a lawful appeal right, were the mainstay of the Special Counsel's enforcement program, with whistleblower protection occupying the office's highest priority.[13]

To accomplish the goal of enforcing the CSRA's protections against prohibited personnel practices, Congress provided OSC with investigative and prosecutive authority and authorized the United States Merit Systems Protection Board to hear and adjudicate such prosecutions.

Since its inception, OSC's role in the enforcement of the CSRA's protections for whistleblowers has been the subject of intense debate, scrutiny, and controversy.[14] Much of the early controversy centered on the perception that OSC had not succeeded before the MSPB in its mission to obtain relief for employees complaining of whistleblower reprisal and sanctions against managers committing reprisals. Contrary to this perception, the record indicates that OSC has tried to develop a body of administrative law – although, as will be discussed, not always successfully – which maximizes protection for federal employees who engage in protected activity, facilitates OSC's ability to bring successful corrective and disciplinary actions when reprisals occur, and upholds the safeguards of the merit system Congress envisioned. This Article analyzes the first ten years of federal reprisal law under the CSRA. The analysis traces the law's development, explores the impact of that development on federal whistleblower protection policy, and describes the OSC's role in the development of this unique body of law. The Article also describes the recent changes in the federal reprisal law that result from the passage of the Whistleblower Protection Act of 1989 (WPA). The Article concludes that although the Whistleblower Protection Act amendments to the CSRA have enhanced protection for federal employees from reprisal, this legislation may have been unnecessary had there been greater receptivity to OSC's efforts to shape the law into a reasonable and workable tool for promoting whistleblowing and deterring retaliatory activity in the federal workplace.

I. *IN RE FRAZIER*: THE BASIC REPRISAL MODEL

The Board's first opportunity to apply the new statutory protections of the CSRA against reprisal came in the case of *In re Frazier*, OSC's first corrective action case.[15] In *Frazier*, four deputy marshals employed by the United States Marshals Service received directed geographic reassignments allegedly in reprisal for whistleblowing and for exercising their lawful appeal rights.[16] After an OSC investigation and an MSPB order temporarily staying the reassignments, OSC moved to half the reassignments permanently by filing a corrective action with the Board alleging violations of section 2302(b)(8) and (9).

The *Frazier* corrective action was a matter of first impression for the Board. The Board not only had to establish a substantive standard for determining whether the reassignments had violated the statute's proscriptions, it had to define the procedural ground rules for the action.

A.   The corrective action provisions of the CSRA

From the start, OSC took an aggressive, pro-whistleblower stance. In the absence of any statutorily mandated hearing, OSC advocated the adoption of a streamlined dispute-resolution process to be based on the results of OSC's investigation and whatever comments the agency or Office of Personnel Management (OPM) submitted to the Board for consideration under the statute's right-to-comment provision. OSC argued that a full evidentiary hearing was neither required by Congress nor necessary for the Board to determine whether corrective action was appropriate, since the Board had the benefit of the entire fact-finding record of OSC's investigation and the agency's and OPM's comments on the investigation and recommended action.

Nowhere in the 1978 legislation did Congress provide for an evidentiary hearing in cases brought by OSC for corrective action. Congress' only requirement was that the Board give the agency and OPM an opportunity to comment on OSC's findings and recommendations before determining what corrective action was appropriate. Congress' legislative approach in corrective actions was fundamentally different from its approach in disciplinary actions and employee-initiated appeals before the Board. In those procedures, Congress explicitly provided for the right to a hearing. OSC believed it was proposing a procedure that was consistent with congressional intent and would enhance its ability to enforce the law. Such a streamlined process would permit OSC to bring more corrective action cases more quickly, obtain expedited relief for complainants, allocate its limited resources to investigation rather than litigation, and expand the influence of the office. Under the circumstances, OSC argued, a hearing would only prolong the violation, delay the determination and order for relief, require government resources to be expended needlessly, and duplicate the fact-finding process that OSC had already performed pursuant to its statutory mandate.

In addressing the issue, the Board interpreted the statute's right-to-comment provision as establishing only a minimum requirement. The Board reasoned that it could, in its discretion, permit the agency and OPM an even greater opportunity for persuasion than the statutory right-to-comment requirement. Finding that both OSC and the agency were entitled to a presumption that they were 'acting in good faith and according to the law', the Board ordered that a hearing be held to resolve conflicts in testimony. The Board based its ruling on its inherent power under the CSRA to 'hear, adjudicate, or provide for the hearing or adjudication, of *all* matters within the jurisdiction of the Board . . .'.

B.   Reprisal for whistleblowing

On the principal issue of whether the Marshals Service had retaliated against the deputies for their disclosures to members of Congress, the Board agreed with OSC on the definition of whistleblowing but resolved the reprisal issue against OSC and the deputies. The OSC contended and the Board agreed that the disclosures, which had prompted the Marshals Service to look into the deputies' situation, were protected under section 230(b)(8). The agency had argued that the deputies' disclosures were not protected because the deputies had blown the whistle in order to insulate themselves from legitimate disciplinary action. Rejecting the Marshals Service's premise, the Board held that the statute specifically protected disclosures if the discloser 'reasonably believes' that his disclosure evidences one of the subjects identified in the statute.[17] If this condition precedent was satisfied, the Board held, the personal motives of the deputies were not relevant to whether their disclosures were protected. In determining whether disclosures qualified for protection, the Board chose an objective standard of review based on reasonableness, rather than a subjective standard of review based on individual motivation.[18]

Under this standard, the Board found the deputies' disclosures to be reasonably based and, therefore, protected. On the merits of the reprisal allegation, however, it held that OSC had failed to establish that Director Hall, the official who ordered the reassignments, or that the management review team, which recommended the action, had actual or constructive knowledge of the deputies' disclosures to their elected representatives in Congress.[19] In making these factual findings, the Board rejected the testimony of the deputies who claimed that they had discussed their disclosures with the review team. The Board also declined to infer knowledge from circumstantial evidence that other management officials, including the United States Marshal in Atlanta, had knowledge of the deputies' disclosures. Instead, the Board found credible the testimony of Hall and the team members who had denied any knowledge of the deputies' whistleblowing to members of Congress. Finding the requisite element of knowledge to be missing, the Board held that there could be no reprisal for whistleblowing.

Because lack of actual or constructive knowledge is fatal to an allegation of whistleblower reprisal, the Board could have based its finding solely on the absence of this element of proof. However, the Board chose instead to analyze the merits of the agency's justification for the reassignments in order to show further that the reassignments had not been made in reprisal for the deputies' disclosures. After validating the agency's finding that the deputies were 'hostile, frustrated, disruptive and demonstrably unable to function effectively in Atlanta', the Board concluded that the management team's recommendations to reassign the deputies were 'based upon sound management considerations' and made 'to accommodate the competing needs of the dissident deputies and those of the Atlanta office'.[20]

Based on the Board's findings that knowledge was lacking and that the reassignment actions had been based on legitimate managerial decisions, the Board delayed discussion of the broader issues concerning what quantum of proof would be required to establish retaliatory motivation and how the burden of proof would be allocated in reprisal cases until its evaluation of OSC's alternative theory for prosecution under section 2302(b)(9).[21]

C.   Reprisal for the exercise of lawful appeal rights

In *Frazier*, OSC had proposed that for reprisal cases under sections 2302(b)(8) and (b)(9), the Board adopt the Supreme Court's model for allocating burdens of proof used in discrimination cases under Title VII of the Civil Rights Act of 1964. The Court's discrimination model placed the initial burden on the party seeking relief to establish a prima facie case of discrimination.[22] Thereafter, the burden shifted to the employer to establish a non-discriminatory justification for the action. If the employer established a non-dicriminatory justification, the burden shifted back to the plaintiff to demonstrate that the justification was pretextual. In proposing that this model be applied in reprisal cases under the CSRA, OSC argued that in order to account for congressional policy favoring the protection of employees from reprisals and the inherent disparity of power between agency and employee, the Board should evaluate the legitimacy of the employer-agency's justification under a 'clear and convincing evidence' standard of proof, which had been applied by some federal circuit courts in Title VII cases.

OSC further proposed that the Board apply an 'any part' test in evaluating whether retaliation had tainted the action. If reprisal for protected activity played any part in the decision to take the challenged action, OSC argued, the antireprisal provisions of the statute had been violated and required a remedy. OSC's argument was premised on the assumption that the CSRA had no tolerance for reprisals and was supported by a line of analogous Title VII discrimination cases that had applied the 'any part' test. OSC reasoned that retaliation, even if only a partial motivating factor, should be presumed to have a broad chilling effect on other employees who wished to exercise their protected rights under the CSRA. In order to remove the threat of that effect and to maintain a federal work environment that encouraged rather than discouraged protected activity, OSC contended that the Board could not permit actions motivated even partially by reprisal to stand. If protected activity, especially whistleblowing, was to be promoted effectively, neither the agency nor the Board should endorse actions based, even in part, on retaliatory motivation.

Admittedly, the 'any part' test could result in the retention of employees whose poor performance or misconduct justified, in the abstract, the agency's action. This was the inevitable result of conflicting purposes within the CSRA. The CSRA's goal of promoting whistleblowing conflicts with its objective of furthering efficiency in government through discretionary management-directed personnel actions. In cases where retaliation was only a partial motivating factor for the personnel action, there was no easy method to achieve fully both objectives. OSC urged the Board to adopt a test for causation in dual motivation cases which would err, if at all, on the side of protecting employees from reprisal.

Without clear congressional guidance, the Board had to make a policy decision. On one side weighed the importance of protecting whistleblowers whose efforts Congress determined would make the government more efficient. On the other side weighed the importance of removing unnecessary obstacles to legitimate management actions which Congress determined had impeded the efficiency of the government prior to the reformation of the Civil Service. The Board struck the balance in the middle. It held that it would reverse actions only where OSC could establish that reprisal was a significant factor in the decision to take the action. Thus, the Board construed the CSRA as tolerating some reprisal motivation in the adverse personnel action as long as the motivation was not significant to the decision. In adopting this significant factor test, the Board specifically reserved judgment on whether it would adopt the defense articulated in *Mt. Healthy City School District Board of Education v. Doyle*[23] as a barrier to remedial action in future cases and held that the facts of *Frazier* did not require it to decide this issue.[24]

To establish reprisal, the Board announced a four-part test that incorporated the significant factor standard. The Board held that OSC must show: (1) the employee engaged in protected activity; (2) the official responsible for the action had actual or constructive knowledge of the activity; (3) the employee was treated in an adverse fashion; and (4) a sufficient causal connection existed between the protected activity and the adverse action to establish that retaliation for the protected activity was a significant factor in the challenged action.[25] The Board in *Frazier* emphasized that proof of reprisal need not depend on direct evidence of the offending official's retaliatory state of mind. Instead, the Board held, the causal link between the protected activity and the adverse action 'merely consists of an inference of retaliatory motive for the adverse employer action'. As the Board further emphasized, '[retaliatory] motive must in almost all situations be inferred from circumstantial evidence'.

The Board did adopt some of the points advocated by OSC under section 2302(b)(9). For example, OSC urged the Board to consider not only participation in one's own lawful appeal as an 'exercise' of an appeal right, but also participation in the lawful appeal of another. In opposition, the agency argued that mere 'participation' as a witness or counselor in an appeal process of another did not constitute an 'exercise' of an appeal right which section 2302(b)(9) protected. The Board sided with OSC on this issue and concluded that participation in a lawful appeal by another fell within the protective ambit of the CSRA. The Board wrote:

> Protection against reprisal is necessary to prevent employer intimidation of prospective complainants and witnesses, which would dry up the channels of information and undermine the implementation of the statutory policy which the administrative process was established to serve. Thus section 704(a) of Title VII (42 U.S.C. § 2000e–3(a)) makes it unlawful for an employer to discriminate against an employee 'because he has made a charge, testified, assisted, or participated in any manner in an investigation, proceeding, or hearing under this subchapter'.

As it did in defining the protected activities under section 2302(b)(8), the Board construed the CSRA broadly in determining whether the activities qualified for protection from reprisal.

Turning to the merits of the reprisal allegations based on equal employment opportunities activities, the Board found a violation concerning one of the employees.[26] To correct the violation, the Board permanently enjoined the employees' pending reassignment. Consistent with its broad authority to address individual and systemic merit system abuses, the Board also ordered the Marshals Service to cease retaliating against the employee for his EEO activities and directed the Marshals Service to correct noted EEO problems in its Atlanta office.

Unlike employees adversely affected by decisions of the Board OSC lacks authority to appeal adverse Board decisions. The employees who had intervened in the administrative proceeding did appeal the Board's decision to the United States Court of Appeals for the District of Columbia. OSC's attempt to file an *amicus curiae* brief in that appeal, however, was successfully opposed by the Department of Justice and the Board, effectively precluding OSC from further participation in the case. The court eventually upheld the Board's decision on every issue affecting OSC prosecutions.

II.   THE BOARD ADOPTS THE *MT. HEALTHY* TEST

The next significant Board decision concerning reprisal for protected activity came in December 1981, in *Gerlach v. Federal Trade Commission. Gerlach* arose through the Board's employee appeal procedures after the Federal Trade Commission (FTC) had removed Gerlach for alleged poor performance. Gerlach prevailed at the initial decision stage where the Board's presiding official reversed the agency's action, finding that the agency had removed the appellant in part for the grievance she had filed against her supervisor. The agency petitioned the Board to review the initial decision, arguing that the presiding official's finding of reprisal had been in error. Because the case arose from the Board's appellate procedures, OSC was not a party in the case.

As a starting point, the Board succinctly recited the four-part test for reprisal announced in *Frazier*. Applying this four-part test, the Board 'agree[d] with the presiding official's holding that the protected conduct was a significant factor in the decision to remove appellant'.

Next, the Board confronted squarely the issue it had declined to resolve in *Frazier*, namely, how to deal with a personnel action that may have been taken for both prohibited and legitimate reasons: the so-called 'dual motivation' or 'mixed motive' case. The Board expressed concern that, as a policy matter, it should not reverse actions unless the most important basis or real motivating factor for the action was a prohibited personnel practice. After reviewing analogous areas of law for guidance, the Board adopted the Supreme Court's causation standard announced in *Mt. Healthy* for use in dual motivation reprisal cases under the Board's appellate jurisdiction. The Board paraphrased the Supreme Court's two-part *Mt. Healthy* test as follows:

> First, the employee has the burden of establishing by a preponderance of the evidence that the protected conduct was a 'substantial' or 'motivating' factor. If the employee carries that burden, the burden shifts to the employer to prove by a preponderance of the evidence that it would have taken the same action even if the protected conduct had not taken place.

The Board's purpose in adopting this test was to preclude demonstrably incompetent employees from using their protected activities to shield themselves from valid personnel actions. After consulting the legislative history of the CSRA, the Board concluded that Congress 'sought to protect employees from prohibited personnel practices, but at the same time not to insulate them from legitimate conduct or performance-based adverse actions'. Acknowledging that it was not compelled to adopt the *Mt. Healthy* test, the Board nevertheless concluded that it was the best available test for resolving the conflicting purposes of the CSRA in dual-motivation cases. The Board quoted a passage from *Mt. Healthy* which stated that the test was not intended to preclude the 'borderline' or 'marginal' employee from being vindicated because of a protected activity.

III.   EXTENSION OF THE *MT. HEALTHY* TEST TO OSC CORRECTIVE ACTIONS

In 1981, while *Gerlach* was pending before the Board, OSC filed two corrective action cases charging reprisal for protected activity, *Special Counsel ex rel. Rohrmann v. Department of State*[27] and *Special Counsel ex rel. Mortensen v. Department of the Army*.[28] *Rohrmann* involved the suspension and geographic reassignment of a passport officer by the Department of State after the officer had written a series of memoranda to his supervisors, the Secretary of State, and the President, accusing the State Department of incompetence and indifference in the management of its fraud detection program. After considering Rohrmann's removal, the State Department finally imposed a fourteen-day suspension and reassigned him from New York to Boston for failing to return fraud case files that he had removed from his office in order to expose what he believed to be mismanagement.

Mortensen involved the proposed removal of an Army chemist for insubordination and unsatisfactory performance. An OSC investigation revealed reasonable grounds to believe that the Army wanted to remove Mortensen because she had filed EEO complaints against the Army and had made communications concerning the Army's treatment of her outside EEO channels, activities protected by section 2302(b)(8) and (9). In both *Rohrmann* and *Mortensen*, the facts raised the possibility that management officials may have acted out of a combination of legitimate and illegitimate motives. The presence of dual or mixed motives prompted the Board in *Rohrmann* and *Mortensen* to consider whether the *Mt. Healthy* test adopted in *Gerlach* should be applied to cases brought by the Special Counsel for corrective action.

The cases were assigned to an administrative law judge (ALJ) for a recommended decision. *Rohrmann* was first to reach the Board for final decision and was the case in which the Board decided to extend the tests of *Gerlach* and *Mt. Healthy* to corrective action cases brought by the Special Counsel. In *Rohrmann*, the ALJ found a prima facie case of reprisal. The ALJ, however, upheld the agency's action by concluding that the agency would have taken the action regardless of the employee's protected activity. OSC filed exceptions to the recommended decision, challenging the ALJ's application of the *Mt. Healthy* test to deny corrective action. *Rohrmann* went to the Board for consideration prior to the issuance of the *Gerlach* decision. The issue before the Board was a narrow one: whether, in an action brought by OSC pursuant to its enforcement responsibilities, an agency should be allowed to take a personnel action against an employee whose protected activity was a significant factor in the agency's action, when the agency would have taken the same action for legitimate reasons.

Once again the Board confronted the fundamental conflict between the employee's right to engage in protected activity and the agency's authority to manage its work force, with OSC advocating a tilt toward employee rights. As a threshold matter, the Board found in both *Rohrmann* and *Mortensen* that the personnel actions were motivated in significant part by protected activity sufficient to establish a prima facie case of reprisal. OSC argued that as a matter of public policy, employees should be protected from adverse personnel actions once retaliatory animus had been shown to be a significant factor in the action, even if this meant that some misconduct or poor performance would be overlooked. This was necessary, OSC asserted, because decisions motivated by both retaliatory and legitimate reasons had a detrimental effect on the merit system. OSC reasoned that if promotion of protected activities like whistleblowing was Congress' intent, retaliatory action should not be condoned regardless of whether the agency had established an alternative, legitimate motive for the decision. OSC warned that, if adopted, the *Mt. Healthy* test could invite agencies to engage in *post hoc* rationalizations and make it more difficult for OSC to protect employees from reprisal.

One of the practical dangers of adopting the *Mt. Healthy* test was that the 'could have' and 'would have' distinction would easily blur. Although the *Mt. Healthy* test required the employer to establish by preponderant evidence that it would have taken the same action regardless of the employee's protected activity, in practice, evidence that it could have taken the action would become the only available means to meet circumstantially the 'would have' burden, absent unusual circumstances.

In fact, in December 1981, while *Rohrmann* and *Mortensen* were pending before the Board, an MSPB presiding official, purportedly applying the *Gerlach-Mt. Healthy* test, used a 'could have' standard in *Spadaro v. Department of the Interior*, a dual motivation employee-appeal case. In *Spadaro*, OSC exercised its independent intervention authority in support of the employee who alleged that his thirty-day suspension was a reprisal for whistleblowing. The presiding official who heard the initial appeal applied *Gerlach* to conclude that a reprisal motivation had been a significant factor in the decision to suspend. The presiding official, however, upheld the suspension because he found that the agency could have imposed the suspension for insubordination and misuse of a government telephone, as the agency had charged, even if the protected activity had not occurred. OSC asked the Board to reverse the presiding official's decision, arguing that the standard was erroneous, and urged the Board to instruct its presiding officials on the type and quality of proof necessary to satisfy the 'would have' standard under the *Mt. Healthy* test. OSC expressed particular concern that presiding officials and the Board would accept as dispositive the self-serving statements of officials shown to have used prohibited motives to influence their decisions. These officials were likely to testify that they would have taken the same action regardless of whether the employee engaged in the protected activity.

The Board in *Spadaro* ultimately rejected the presiding official's interpretation of *Mt. Healthy* and concluded that the agency had not established by preponderant evidence that it would have taken the same action absent the protected activity. Recognizing the 'highly individualized' nature of dual motivation cases, the Board stated that the agency's burden was not merely to establish that it could have taken the action, but that 'this appellant, in this branch of this agency, with its own history of disciplining employees for similar infractions, would, in fact, have received the discipline imposed absent the protected conduct'. The Board then listed several examples of ways in which agencies might satisfy the 'would have' standard. This decision not only instructed the Board's adjudicators on the proper application of the *Mt. Healthy* test, but also signalled agencies that the Board would strictly review personnel decisions infected with consideration of protected conduct.

In the OSC corrective action cases of *Rohrmann* and *Mortensen*, the Board, spurred by its reasoning in *Gerlach* and the advocacy of OPM and the agencies to apply *Mt. Healthy* in OSC corrective actions, ultimately adopted the *Mt. Healthy* standard over OSC's objection. The Board relied on the legislative history of the CSRA to support its assertion that the statute was not intended to protect employees who engaged in misconduct.

Using the *Mt. Healthy* test, the Board easily upheld the actions taken by the agencies in *Rohrmann* and *Mortensen*. In both cases, the agencies established that the employees had engaged in misconduct warranting discipline. Having established this, the agencies prevailed on the ultimate issue of whether they would have taken the action regardless of the retaliatory animus by merely demonstrating that the actions were otherwise justified. Without access to judicial review, OSC could not challenge the Board's decision to apply *Mt. Healthy* in corrective action cases. Nevertheless, the Board's clear directions in *Spadaro* on the application of the *Mt. Healthy* test ensured that the doctrine would not be misconstrued to the detriment of employees who engaged in protected whistleblowing. Indeed, since the Board's clarification of the *Mt. Healthy* test in *Spadaro*, OSC has encountered little resistance from agencies in response to OSC requests for corrective action in individual cases. This, in turn, has produced a significant improvement in OSC's success rate at obtaining relief for victims of reprisal and other prohibited personnel practices.

IV.   DISCIPLINARY ACTION CASES AND THE *MT. HEALTHY* TEST

Special Counsel v. Cummings 1984 was the first case prosecuted by OSC for disciplinary action of a supervisor because of reprisal for protected activity.

OSC alleged that Cummings, a Regional Administrator for the Department of Housing and Urban Development (HUD), reassigned two employees in reprisal for disclosures made prior to Cummings' appointment. Before going to HUD, Cummings had been a management agent for a HUD-insured non-profit housing project. The disclosures were of particular significance to Cummings because they contained information which opposed his use of tenant security deposits to repay debts incurred through repairs on property under his management. In addition, the disclosures led to the cancellation of HUD contracts with two associates of Cummings.

In *Cummings*, OSC, for the first time, departed from its opposition to the *Mt. Healthy* test and supported its extension to OSC disciplinary actions. The Board, however, found it unnecessary to reach that issue, holding that OSC had failed to establish a prima facie case that the reassignments had been taken in reprisal for protected activity. In making its determination, the Board issued only a brief decision, adopting the administrative law judge's recommended decision in the case.

In August 1983, OSC filed a series of disciplinary actions charging federal officials at various agencies with reprisal for protected activity. The first, *Special Counsel v. Hoban*, eventually became OSC's first contested disciplinary action for reprisal to result in the Board's imposition of sanctions against a retaliating official.[29] The Board's decision in *Hoban* failed to reach the *Mt. Healthy* issue, however, and did not alter the existing status of reprisal law. Nor did it indicate what the Board's position on the *Mt. Healthy* issue might be in a disciplinary action reprisal case.

With the filing of two more disciplinary cases charging reprisal for protected activity, *Special Counsel v. Harvey* and *Special Counsel v. Starrett*, OSC successfully placed before the Board the issue of what test for reprisal would be used in disciplinary actions. In both cases, OSC argued for the adoption of an 'any part' test.

Harvey was the first of the two cases to be decided. In addition to sustaining the allegations of reprisal and imposing disciplinary measures against the supervisor, the Board made two significant rulings in *Harvey* which promoted OSC's enforcement of the CSRA's reprisal protections. First, the Board agreed with OSC that a draft of a letter, an unsent appeal for help addressed to OSC, constituted protected activity. The Board held that even though OSC could not establish that Harvey knew at the time of the reprisal that the employee had sent the letter to OSC, the fact that he had knowledge of the employee's intention to send it was sufficient to protect the employee from reprisal for having written the letter.

Next, the Board rejected the *Mt. Healthy* defense in OSC disciplinary actions. In doing so, the Board endorsed OSC's argument that disciplinary actions did not involve the same concerns that had prompted the Board to adopt *Mt. Healthy* in corrective actions. The Board noted that in *Gerlach, Rohrmann*, and *Mortensen*, it had been concerned with the prospect that failure to apply the *Mt. Healthy* defense might result in possible unjust enrichment for employees whose conduct or performance justified the actions taken against them. In the Board's view, disciplinary cases did not present the same concern. The Board wrote:

> [O]ur concern here is not whether the actions taken against [the employee] were effected on legitimate grounds, would have been taken despite protected activity, and should be allowed to stand. Our concern in a disciplinary action . . . is whether a respondent should escape discipline for a prohibited personnel practice even if there is a lawful reason for taking the personnel action.

The Board observed that the absence of the concern about unjust enrichment removed the basic premise for the adoption of the *Mt. Healthy* defense in corrective actions.

However, the Board refused to adopt the 'any part' test advanced by OSC. Instead, the Board employed the significant factor standard that it had been using in various incarnations since *Frazier*: a prohibited causal connection is established if the protected activity is a significant factor in the decision to take the action.

The Board in *Harvey* announced its rejection of the *Mt. Healthy* defense for all OSC disciplinary actions in a separate portion of its decision discussing discrimination based on the employee's performance of his duties, activity prohibited by section 2302(b)(10) of the statute. Consequently, the Board's rejection of the *Mt. Healthy* test and adoption of the significant factor test for all forms of prohibited reprisal was dicta. The Board in 1985 applied this significant factor test to section 2302(b)(8) whistleblower reprisals in *Starrett*. In *Starrett*, the Board held that three Defense Contract Audit Agency (DCAA) officials, including the Director, had committed the prohibited personnel practice of reprisal for whistleblowing.

Significantly, the Board in *Harvey* analogized the alleged section 2302(b)(9) violation to prohibited retaliation based on the filing of a discrimination complaint under Title VII of the Civil Rights Act of 1964. The Board cited approvingly a federal district court decision which had imposed a presumption of reprisal in a Title VII retaliation case where the natural consequence of the personnel action was to discourage the protected activity. That court created a presumption that an employer intended to discourage employees from exercising their Title VII rights when retaliation occurred. Finding that the personnel action was 'based' in significant part on protected activity, the Board held that reprisal had occurred. In this manner, the Board construed the antireprisal statute as if it were an antidiscrimination statute.

With victories in *Hoban, Harvey*, and *Starrett*, OSC appeared to be on its way to establishing a viable enforcement program.[30] The Board decisions in those cases increased the likelihood that OSC would prevail in future reprisal cases. As in *Frazier*, the Board explicitly acknowledged that reprisal could be established by inference where a significant causal connection between the protected activity and the challenged action existed.

V.   REVIEW BY THE COURTS

The disciplined officials in *Harvey* and *Starrett* appealed their Board decisions to the United States Court of Appeals for the District of Columbia

Circuit and the United States Court of Appeals for the Fourth Circuit, respectively. Subsequently, the D.C. Circuit and the Fourth Circuit reversed Harvey's demotion and Starrett's removal, respectively. *Starrett* was decided first. In that decision, the Fourth Circuit overturned the Board's disciplinary sanctions for Director Starrett on the facts. Although the court agreed with the Board that Starrett had 'considered' protected activity in making his decision to deny the employee's request for a waiver of the agency's rotation policy, the court held that such consideration did not establish improper retaliatory motive. The court noted that '[t]here is simply no evidence that Starrett had improper motives or that [the employee's] whistleblowing, *qua* whistleblowing, entered into his decision not to grant [the employee] a waiver to DCAA policy'. Thus, the court's decision turned on insufficient proof of subjective retaliatory motivation.

Although the court's decision in *Starrett* turned on the facts of that particular case, it revealed an unwillingness to infer retaliatory motivation from the established causal connection between the protected activity and the personnel action. Thus, the court's approach was at odds with the Board's observations in *Frazier* that '[retaliatory] motive must in almost all situations be inferred from circumstantial evidence'.

In *Harvey*, the D.C. Circuit also reversed key factual determinations that had formed the bases for the Board's findings of prohibited personnel practices, including reprisal for protected activity. In doing so, the court rejected the Board's finding of fact that reprisal had been established through the existence of a causal connection between the protected activity and the personnel actions. Citing *Starrett*, the D.C. Circuit endorsed the notion that consideration of protected activity in the course of making a management decision was not alone sufficient to establish the particular retaliatory motivation which Congress intended to proscribe. The court wrote:

> Harvey's action in not recommending [the employee] for the SES opening was not in retaliation for [the employee's] exercise of his appeal rights or an attempt to deter him from exercising those rights, but was a management decision about [the employee's] qualifications, both technical and personal. To be sure, that management decision was based on an opinion that Harvey formulated of [the employee] based in part on [the employee's] allegations in his draft complaint [to the Special Counsel] and his efforts to use the draft to preserve his job. In that regard, of course, there is some link between Harvey's actions and [the employee's] protected conduct. But it is not the type of prohibited link covered by the Act. . . . Formulating an adverse opinion of an employee, based upon what he has written and thereby not recommending him for certain jobs, is not the same as taking action against an employee in an attempt to thwart his exercise of his protected rights. If it were, it would mean that one in an executive position can never exercise his considered judgment in making personnel recommendations when asked to do so when that judgment is based on anything even tangentially related to the exercise of protected conduct.

Unstated, but nevertheless at the heart of these two appellate court decisions, was the courts' predilection to uphold federal managers' 'business judgments', even where such judgements are proven to be significantly linked to protected activity. This is clear from the courts' criticism of the significant factor test. The Fourth Circuit wrote:

We observe that such difference, [between corrective action and disciplinary cases] valid as it may be in some contexts, may not support the use of a standard of causation which inadequately protects personnel, like Starrett, who are forced to make scores of personnel decisions which may peripherally or incidentally involve situations where employees have engaged in protected practice. The Act was designed to prohibit retaliation or reprisals by personnel because of *improper* consideration of protected actions. The standard of proof used must insure that the *motivation* for the adverse action was an improper one. There is no support in the legislative history of the Act for any particular standard of causation, but the standard used by the Board for any action under the Act . . . must not be so loose or weak as to punish those not motivated by improper purposes.

These decisions are more likely to discourage, rather than to encourage, whistleblowing and other protected activities by their endorsement of adverse management decisions that are based significantly on protected activity. For the courts to remove such decisions from the reach of the law because the official purportedly believed he or she was acting for legitimate purposes undermines the plainly stated whistleblower protections of the CSRA. Prior to *Harvey* and *Starrett*, it had not been apparent that supervisors, who acted to the disadvantage of an employee based in significant part on that employee's protected conduct, could successfully defend their decisions by arguing that they thought they were acting 'reasonably'.

VI.   BOARD REACTION TO UNITED STATES COURTS OF APPEALS DECISIONS

The judicial rejection of the Board's factual conclusions in *Starrett* and *Harvey* was not an endorsement of the Board's more expansive view of reprisal. The Board's reaction to the appellate decisions would be crucial to OSC's prospects for bringing successful disciplinary and corrective actions based on reprisal for protected activity.

In *Special Counsel v. Mongan* 1987, a disciplinary case filed prior to and decided after *Harvey* and *Starrett*, the Board applied the significant factor test in spite of the reservations of the D.C. Circuit and the Fourth Circuit. The Board, however, displayed sensitivity to those concerns by specifically noting that if it had applied *Mt. Healthy* to the facts of *Mongan* it would have found the defense unavailing. In *Special Counsel v. Zimmerman* 1988, another disciplinary case filed prior to and decided after *Harvey* and *Starrett*, the Board again applied the significant factor test to find reprisal based on the filing of an EEO complaint. In a footnote, the Board again stated, in deference to the Fourth Circuit's concerns in *Starrett*, that it would have reached the same conclusion under *Mt. Healthy*.

VII.   RESTATEMENT OF THE *GERLACH-MT. HEALTHY* TEST

While the Fourth Circuit and the D.C. Circuit were reviewing the Board's rulings in *Harvey* and *Starrett*, the Federal Circuit embarked on a restatement of the elements of a reprisal case. Development of the Federal Circuit standard occurred in the Board's appellate jurisdiction cases without input from OSC. Under the Federal Circuit standard as articulated in *Warren v. Department of the Army* 1986, the party claiming reprisal must establish that: (1) a protected disclosure was made; (2) the accused official knew of the claimant's disclosure; (3) the adverse action under review could, under the circumstances, have been retaliation; and (4) after careful balancing of the intensity of the motive to retaliate against the gravity of employee misconduct or poor performance, a nexus is established between the adverse action and the motive.

In *Warren*, the Federal Circuit noted that the four elements were drawn verbatim from *Hagmeyer v. Department of Treasury* 1985 and that the authority for them was *Frazier*. In describing this approach to reprisal cases, the court in *Warren* stated that:

> The wording there found [in *Frazier*], though different, in essence is the same, but more elaborate and analytical, which was to be expected as the Board was writing on a clean slate in interpreting a statute then new. The conclusion must follow that this court in . . . *Hagmeyer* was not undertaking to reassign to the four tests exactly the tasks they were to perform, but simply to identify them so the employee's success in invoking them could be ticked off and weighed according to *Frazier*.

Contrary to the court's assertion, part four of the *Warren* test departed from the Board's decisions in *Frazier* and *Gerlach*. The Federal Circuit's new test required the Board to refocus the inquiry from the search for the significance of the protected activity in the challenged personnel action to the balancing of competing interests which were defined, respectively, as evidence of an employer's specific motive to retaliate and evidence of the gravity of the whistleblower's alleged misconduct. Under *Warren*, the court would find a prohibited nexus only if the whistleblower could prove that the intensity of the motive to retaliate against him was greater than the seriousness of his alleged misconduct. Thus, the court introduced in mid-decade a new analytical approach to the developing body of administrative law.

In addition to this restatement, the Federal Circuit also began to insinuate first amendment principles into cases alleging reprisal for whistleblowing. In 1986, the Federal Circuit held in *Fiorillo v. Department of Justice*, that 'in the context of an adverse action against a public employee, the rights under section 2302(b)(8)(A) (prohibition of reprisal) and the First Amendment's right to free speech have been considered coextensive rights'.[31] In fact, up until that time, the opposite had been considered true. In 1982, the Board held that the right to engage in whistleblowing under section 2302(b)(8) was independent of the right to free speech. This distinction was implicit in the Board's application of the 'reasonable basis' test to determine whether a disclosure is protected. Under traditional first amendment analysis, determination of whether a disclosure is protected turns, not on whether a reasonable basis exists for the disclosure, but on whether the disclosure involves a matter of public concern and whether the legitimate interests of the government to take the action outweighs the interests of the employee as a citizen to make his disclosures.

To the extent that *Fiorillo* applied the balancing test from *Pickering* to reprisal for whistleblowing, it moved the focus of the law even further from the causation test of *Gerlach-Mt. Healthy* than had the retaliatory-motivation balancing test of *Warren*. Although *Warren* represented a new approach in federal reprisal law, it did not depart significantly from the prior case law's analytical objective of determining the existence of a prohibited connection between the whistleblowing and the personnel action. *Fiorillo*, however, departed significantly from this analytical approach. *Fiorillo's* interest-balancing test minimized the importance of a causal connection by concerning itself with the relative weights of the government's interest to take the personnel action and the employee's interest to blow the whistle. Under *Fiorillo*, the party with the more compelling interest at stake would prevail. A *Fiorillo-Pickering* balancing test theoretically permits an agency to prevail even where retaliatory motivation outweighed the gravity of the employee's misconduct or poor performance as long as the interests of the government outweighed the interests of the whistleblower. This would probably occur where the disclosure itself was trivial or where the disruption caused by the disclosure was so great that the interests of the government could overcome the interests in protecting the disclosure. Nevertheless, under a first amendment balancing test, an agency could base its action solely on the protected activity and still not violate the statute.

In addition to introducing the first amendment calculus into reprisal law, *Fiorillo* undermined the Board's reasonable basis test for protected activity in another important way. Whereas the Board had held consistently that reasonableness, not personal motivation, was to be the determinative factor in evaluating whether a disclosure qualified for protected status under section 2302(b)(8), *Fiorillo* held that 'to be given "whistleblower" status and thus the protections under 5 U.S.C. § 2302(b)(8), the *primary* motivation of the employee must be the desire to inform the public on matters of public concern, and not personal vindictiveness'. This, of course, echoes the whistleblower-as-model-citizen arguments which the Board had seemingly rejected in *Frazier*. In two broad strokes, *Fiorillo* significantly altered the landscape of federal reprisal law by introducing the first amendment balancing-of-interests test to weigh the relative importance of an employee's whistleblowing against management's discretionary authority to take personnel actions, and by introducing a subjective motive test to measure the civic-mindedness of the whistleblower's intentions.

Post-*Fiorillo* Federal Circuit decisions have not applied its first amendment analysis to claims of reprisal for whistleblowing. Even so, *Fiorillo* suggests that future reprisal cases in the Federal Circuit may produce additional anomalies, thereby making federal reprisal law even more unsettled.

VIII. BOARD ADOPTS FEDERAL CIRCUIT *WARREN* TEST IN EMPLOYEE APPEAL CASES

In a significant 1987 case, the Board applied the Federal Circuit's four-part test announced in *Warren*. The case, *Oliver v. Department of Health & Human Services*,[32] was an employee appeal in which OSC did not participate. Oliver, a mid-level manager at the National Institutes of Health (NIH), appealed her removal for misconduct to the Board. Oliver's misconduct concerned a series of memoranda she had written to high-level officials at NIH. In her memoranda, Oliver expressed great dismay over low minority and female participation in an agency grant program intended to promote affirmative action, and over certain changes in the program that she believed were detrimental to her career. She charged her supervisors with discriminatory treatment of program participants, improper program practices, and racist hiring practices, which she believed evidenced mismanagement. She also charged her supervisors with having mistreated her on matters concerning her performance evaluation, office space, and travel schedule. The agency removed her for disrespectful conduct and insubordination after she disobeyed instructions to use only the employee grievance procedures to express her discontent and after she refused to provide information to an advisory board reviewing her program.

Oliver argued that her removal was based on her memoranda, which, although strongly worded and highly critical of her superiors, should have been protected as whistleblowing under section 2302(b)(8). The Board rejected the argument, comprehensively reexamining CSRA reprisal law and adopting the *Warren* standard. Applying this standard, the Board concluded that the agency's motive to retaliate did not outweigh the gravity of the employee's misconduct and, therefore, the agency's removal action did not constitute a reprisal for whistleblowing.

In discussion whether Oliver's memoranda met the threshold test of protected activity under section 2302(b)(8), the Board, without explanation, cited the first amendment test in the 1984 *Osokow v. Office of Personnel Management*, that disclosures must touch matters of public concern to qualify for protection. While the Board in *Oliver* did not specifically reject the utility of the traditional reasonable basis test in whistleblower reprisal cases, its reference to *Osokow* was surprising given its previous position that the first amendment 'd[id] not establish the standard for protected conduct under 5 U.S.C. § 2302(b)(8)'. The Board's resort to first amendment law as an appropriate analytical model for section 2302(b)(8) cases recurred when the Board discussed the protective scope of section 2302(b)(8). The Board wrote:

> The Board is not alone in employing this kind of analysis to determine whether conduct which might appear to be protected loses that status for any reason. For example, even when dealing with paramount constitutional issues, the Supreme Court has recognized in first amendment cases to which we analogize, that whether an employee's speech addresses a matter of public concern, and is therefore protected, is circumscribed, and must be determined by the content, form and context of a given statement, as revealed by the whole record. . . . While the case presently before the Board was not argued in the first amendment context, the analogy is nevertheless apt, and supports the notion that in determining whether speech is protected, it is necessary to carefully scrutinize the facts surrounding the employee's declaration.

In addition to its use of first amendment law, the Board followed the course taken by the Federal Circuit in *Fiorillo* when it analyzed Oliver's conduct under an ethical standards test similar to the model citizen test of *Fiorillo*. The Board wrote:

> In enacting 5 U.S.C. § 2302(b)(8)(A), Congress sought to protect whistleblowers whose 'dedication to the highest moral principles' helps create 'a more effective civil service . . .'. It recognized that this protection was not absolute, however, by providing certain exceptions, *e.g.*, employees who claim to be whistleblowers in order to avoid an otherwise meritorious adverse action. . . . Thus, in deciding whether certain types of conduct should be immunized from sanction because of the law, the Board has held that the relevant inquiry is whether expanding the protections of the law to include the conduct under review would effectuate the purposes of 5 U.S.C. § 2302(b)(8). . . . We conclude, for the following reasons, that protecting appellant's diatribe would not further the purpose of the law.

The *Oliver* decision represents a discernible shift away from the objective reasonable basis test and towards a more fluid balancing-of-interests test more characteristic of first amendment and, in general, constitutional law. Under this new approach, disclosures which do not touch matters of general public concern and employees who do not blow the whistle out of 'the highest moral principles' may not be found deserving of protection from reprisal under section 2302(b)(8), even if there is a reasonable basis for the disclosures. In this sense, statutory protection from reprisal risks become a privilege accorded to those who act for 'the highest moral principles' on matters of public concern, instead of a right granted to all federal employees who reasonably believe that the information they disclose evidences one of the enumerated improprieties in the statute. Such a standard changes the emphasis of the statute from one which promotes reasonably based disclosures of wrongdoing under an objective standard of review, to one which promotes only morally principled disclosures under a subjective standard of review. Arguably, it simply mirrors existing first amendment protections. For federal employees trying to decide whether or not to blow the whistle, this shift makes predetermination of the protected status of an intended disclosure less predictable. Emphasis on the ethical quality of the whistleblower's motivation and the public-interest nature of the disclosure as outcome-determinative factors in the establishment of parameters for protected activity may deter employees from whistleblowing rather than encouraging them. Furthermore, a first amendment approach may be too narrow and lead to the punishment of a protected disclosure which is not in the general 'public interest' and which causes disruption. Such an approach could also lead to the blending of broad policy disagreements publicly articulated by federal employees on the one hand with protected disclosures of wrongdoing on the other. Congress, however, intended the former to be subject to a first amendment balancing test and the latter to be absolutely protected if reasonably believed.

The implications of *Oliver* to whistleblower protection reach beyond the facts of that case. The Board concluded in *Oliver* that the general content of Oliver's disclosures concerning affirmative action policies qualified for protection either as matters of public concern or as matters of a more personal nature which satisfied the reasonable basis test. It also concluded that the agency removed Oliver because the tone and wording of her disclosures, some of which were of a personal nature, were 'abusive', 'insolent', 'caustic', and 'insubordinate'. The Board then measured Oliver's personal motives in making her disclosures against the newly adopted 'highest moral principles' standard. Under this test, the Board found that the offensive tone of the disclosures required it to strike the *Warren* balance in favor of the agency.

It can reasonably be argued that section 2302(b)(8) protections could not have been meant to apply to statements which were so inflammatory in tone and style that they constituted misconduct under a subject-neutral standard. *Oliver*, then, could have been decided by finding that the inflammatory parts of Oliver's charges had been unreasonable and were not, therefore, protected by section 2302(b)(8) under the reasonable basis test. Instead, the Board granted qualified protection to Oliver's disclosures in their entirety and then stripped them piecemeal of their qualified protections under the first amendment, model-citizen, and *Warren*-balancing tests. If the Board had found Oliver's highly inflammatory language not reasonably based, it could have sustained the agency's disciplinary action as easily under the existing standards of *Gerlach-Mt. Healthy* without having to inject moral and first amendment principles into the *Warren* reprisal equation.

IX.   A TEN-YEAR SUMMARY OF FEDERAL REPRISAL LAW

The past ten years have witnessed the beginnings of the development of federal reprisal law created by the CSRA. Thus far, the law has struggled to resolve the inevitable conflict between two distinct congressional policies of the CSRA that have sometimes been at cross purposes with each other. One of those policies promotes and encourages the disclosure of waste, fraud, abuse of authority, and mismanagement. It accepts as necessary the attendant disruption that such disclosures may engender. The other promotes management's discretionary authority to eliminate disruptions caused by inefficiency by encouraging management to discharge employees 'who cannot or will not improve their performance to meet required standards'. The Board and the few federal courts which have confronted this conflict have attempted to devise analytical models to accommodate both competing interests. However, the balance these models have struck has not been consistent and has sometimes created ambiguous and elusive standards which offer only marginal guidance to the two million civil service employees who must conform their conduct to these standards.

The record demonstrates the OSC, recognizing that an effective whistleblower protection program may require the vindication of a few marginal employees because of their protected disclosures, has advocated interpretations of the law which would favor whistleblowers and encourage whistleblowing activities. Response by the Board and the courts to OSC's advocacy has been decidedly mixed. Initially, the Board rejected OSC arguments for an expansive interpretation of the substantive and procedural safeguards for whistleblowers under the CSRA. However, by mid-decade, OSC had made some progress before the Board in expanding the law's protection. More recent judicial interpretations have indicated that on the tenth anniversary of the CSRA, the pendulum had swung back in favor of management discretion to the detriment of whistleblower protection, making it more difficult for OSC and whistleblowers to prevail in litigation before the Board.

X. THE WHISTLEBLOWER PROTECTION ACT OF 1989: A RENEWED COMMITMENT TO PROTECT WHISTLEBLOWERS FROM REPRISAL

As early as 1986, Congress began to move in earnest to draft legislation to toughen the CSRA protections against reprisal for whistleblowing. That year, the House passed H.R. 4033 which provided, among other things, the right of any individual who may have suffered a prohibited personnel practice to appeal directly to the MSPB, regardless of the significance of the personnel action suffered, and to obtain judicial review of the Board's decision in the federal district courts. The bill would have lowered the standard of proof for whistleblower reprisal from preponderant evidence to substantial evidence and would have required OSC to represent all alleged victims of prohibited personnel practices before the Board. H.R. 4033 further proposed to permit agencies to defend against a prima facie case of reprisal by showing that the challenged action had been based solely on legitimate management reasons.

In 1987, Congress returned to the issue of whistleblower protection with renewed commitment to enhance the existing protections for victims of whistleblower reprisal. Both the House and the Senate drafted versions of the 'Whistleblower Protection Act of 1987'. Both bills contained a private right of action, expanded judicial review options, and a lower burden of proof for employees in whistleblower reprisal cases. By 1988, Congress passed S. 508, a modified version of the Senate bill from the previous year, only to see it pocket-vetoed by outgoing President Reagan.

However, in March 1989, a compromise was reached between the Congress and the new administration which resulted in S. 20, the Whistleblower Protection Act of 1989 (WPA). This reform bill contains most of the pro-whistleblower features of earlier proposals with the exception of authority for the Special Counsel to seek judicial review of a decision of the MSPB, a prominent feature in earlier proposals. The most significant change to the substantive law was the deletion of the word reprisal from sections 2302(b)(8) and (9) and the substitution of the phrase 'because of'. Congress made these changes in direct response to what it perceived to be the unduly restrictive decisions of the Board and the courts which had made it difficult to prove reprisal. The legislative history of this amendment reveals that congressional reformers were critical of the *Starrett* and *Harvey* courts for having misinterpreted the CSRA's protection for whistleblowers in section 2302(b)(8) with their punitive-intent requirement, a criticism the Special Counsel had advanced in congressional hearings. The change expressed Congress' intent that the statute prohibited actions that are based on protected conduct, regardless of the personal motivation of the responsible officials. If a causal link can be established between the protected conduct and the personnel action, the statute has been violated.

The new law goes even further. It defines precisely what quantum of proof is required to justify corrective action in section 2302(b)(8) cases. Believing that the existing law required proof that the protected disclosure be a significant or substantial factor in the action taken, Congress lowered the threshold burden of proof by establishing a 'contributing factor' test in corrective action cases under section 2303(b)(8). Based on the explanatory discussion in the enactment history of the WPA, it seems clear that the new contributing factor standard was intended to make corrective action the norm whenever a protected disclosure, alone or in connection with other factors, tended to affect in any way the outcome of the decision. With these two important changes, Congress returned the focus of whistleblower protection inquiry to the factors considered by the employer in making a personnel decision and away from the particular motivations of the employer. The WPA amendments ensure a whistleblowing-neutral decision-making process that is more consistent with the CSRA goals of promoting and encouraging federal employees to disclose evidence of waste, fraud, and abuse of authority than the prevailing motivation-based inquiry established by case law.

CONCLUSION

With the recent passage of the WPA amendments, the federal civil service begins its next decade under the CSRA with new standards designed to ease the burden on employees and the OSC to prove that employees have been disadvantaged by their whistleblowing. The congressional creators of whistleblower protection firmly rejected the law's development at the Board and in the courts during the first decade under the CSRA. The WPA returns us to 1979, when the law of reprisal began its development. Where the WPA amendments will lead in the next ten years is, of course, unknown. What is clear from this survey of the OSC's role in the development of reprisal law in the first decade of the CSRA is that OSC efforts to expand the legal protections for whistleblowers through the MSPB have had mixed results. Some of these efforts have succeeded. When they did not, the OSC has been constrained, as it must be, to operate within the framework of the law as interpreted by the Board and the courts. The adoption of the WPA amendments, however, reflects to a large extent OSC's historical advocacy in the development of federal reprisal law.

NOTES

1. Pub. L. No. 95–454, 92 Stat. 1111 (codified as amended in scattered sections of 5 U.S.C.) (effective Jan. 11, 1979). The CSRA represented the first comprehensive reform of the federal civil service system since the Pendleton Act of 1883. *See* Frazier v. Merit Sys. Protection Bd., 672 F. 2d 150, 153–54 (D.C. Cir. 1982) (discussing shortcomings of Pendleton Act and events leading to enactment of CSRA).

2. 5 U.S.C. § 1206 (1988), *repealed by* Whistleblower Protection Act of 1989, § 3(a)(8), 103 Stat. 18 (current version at 5 U.S.C.A. § 1212 (West Supp. 1990)).

3. The prohibited personnel practices are set forth at 5 U.S.C. § 2302(b)(1)–(11) (1988), *amended by* Whistleblower Protection Act of 1989, § 4, 103 Stat. 32 (current version at 5 U.S.C.A. § 2302(b)(1)–(11) (West Supp. 1990)). They cover unlawful discrimination; soliciting or considering recommendations not based on personal knowledge; coercing political activity; reprisals for refusing to engage in political activity; obstructing the right to compete for employment; influencing applicants to withdraw from competition; granting unauthorized preferences; nepotism; reprisals for whistleblowing and exercising appeal rights; discrimination for conduct not adversely affecting performance; and violations of law, rules, or regulations which directly concern merit system principles. *Id.*

4. 5 U.S.C. § 1206(b)(4)(A)–(E) (1988), *repealed by* Whistleblower Protection Act of 1989, §3(a)(13), 103 Stat. 19 (current version at 5 U.S.C.A. § 1212(a)(2)(A)–(B) (West Supp. 1990)). In addition, OSC enforces provisions of the Hatch Act governing employee participation in partisan political activities, serves as a secure channel through which employees may disclose waste, fraud, and abuse in the federal government, and investigates allegations of other personnel activities prohibited by civil service law, rule or regulation. *Id.* § 1206(b)(2)–(3) (1988), *repealed by* Whistleblower Protection Act of 1989, § 3(a)(13), 103 Stat. 19 (current version at 5 U.S.C.A. § 1212(a)(3)–(5) (West Supp. 1990)).

5. *In re* Frazier, 1 M.S.P.R. 163, 165 n.1 (1979); *see infra* note 17 and accompanying text (noting statutory definition of protected whistleblowing activities). According to Senator Patrick Leahy's ground-breaking report on federal whistleblowers, the term whistleblower was coined as 'a catch-all word used to describe almost any case involving a federal employee who encounters career problems after bringing information to public light'. SENATE COMM. ON GOV'T AFFAIRS, THE WHISTLEBLOWERS: A REPORT ON FEDERAL EMPLOYEES WHO DISCLOSE ACTS OF GOVERNMENTAL WASTE, ABUSE, AND CORRUPTION, 95th Cong., 2d Sess. 10 (Comm. Print 1978) [hereinafter *Leahy Report*]. The Senate committee report accompanying the Civil Service Reform Act defined whistleblowers as federal employees 'who disclose illegal or improper government activities'. S. REP. No. 969, 95th Cong., 2d Sess. 8, *reprinted in* 1978 U.S. CODE CONG. & ADMIN. NEWS 2723, 2730 [hereinafter S. REP. No. 969].

6. The merit system or merit employment system refers to those civil service laws, rules, and regulations that provide for open competitive examinations to test and evaluate the relative merit and fitness of applicants for positions in the competitive service consistent with the basic principle that appointments to and personnel actions within the civil service be based solely on merit and fitness. *See* 5 C.F.R. §§ 300.102, 330.101 (1990) (noting policy that competitive hiring practices be based on merit). Existing merit system safeguards ensure that appointments and other personnel decisions are made for proper and lawful reasons and protect against the improper use or abuse of personnel authorities which may tend to undermine the integrity of the merit system. *See* 124 CONG. REC. 27,538 (1978) (noting that thrust of CSRA is to assure the federal employee's career prospects are directly tied to performance and to ensure that employee's rights are protected) (statement of Sen. A. Ribicoff). After several unsuccessful attempts at reform, the merit system was introduced to the federal civil service in 1883 by the Pendleton Act of 1883, ch. 27, 22 Stat. 403, to create politically neutral personnel management and to replace a spoils system which had become ingrained in the fabric of American politics. 124 CONG. REC. 27,543–44 (statement of Sen. T. Stevens) (1978). Among the sweeping changes ushered in by the Pendleton Act was the establishment of a three-member, bipartisan Civil Service Commission to provide for competitive examinations, ensure political neutrality, and condition job tenure on actual performance. *Id.* at 27,544.

7. For a general discussion of the factors that engendered whistleblower protection in the Act, see Vaughn, *Statutory Protection of Whistleblowers in the Federal Executive Branch*, 1982 U. ILL. L. REV. 615, 616–18 [hereinafter Vaughn, *Statutory Protection*]. Perhaps nowhere was the justification for statutory whistleblower protection made more apparent than in the seven-month study of whistleblowers and whistleblower problems conducted by Senator Leahy and his staff in 1977. The *Leahy Report* identified a number of different justifications for whistleblower protection. The report accepted as its premise the goal of greater efficiency and the elimination of waste, misfeasance, and malfeasance in government. *Leahy Report, supra* note 5, at 10. The report recognized, however, that as the federal government grew 'larger and more complex, the opportunities for inefficiency, corruption, mismanagement, abuse of power, and other inappropriate activities bec[a]me more frequent'. *Id.* The report found that when employees revealed incidents of such activities and conditions, the bureaucracy tended to react not to the

revelations themselves but to the employee who had revealed them. *Id.* at 12. It concluded that in the modern bureaucracies, certain built-in incentives naturally produced this phenomenon. The report stated:

The acid test for an agency is whether it is recognized as a smooth running organization providing a useful public service. As such, federal employees are not encouraged to be on the lookout for waste or inefficiency, as are their private sector counterparts [whose motivation is to maximize profit]. The key to success in the bureaucracy is to be quiet, to do competent work, and to move slowly up the hierarchy.

An employee who makes known instances of governmental waste, misfeasance, or malfeasance upsets the standard operating procedure. His or her questioning of agency patterns and practices may upset the cohesion a large organization needs in order to operate. Any evidence of wrongdoing hurts the agency's image, reflecting poorly upon the officials in charge and possibly jeopardizing its appropriations.

Id. at 11–12. In addition, the report noted that concurrent with the growth in the federal bureaucracy, policy makers in the executive agencies were becoming further removed from the information readily accessible to the 'policy implementors', those 'front line' employees providing government services to the public. *Id.* at 7. This phenomenon, the report concluded, made it even more imperative that lines of 'vertical communication' be kept open and protected from interference, which the report found often had not been the case. *Id.* at 16–21.

8. *See* T. EMERSON, THE SYSTEM OF FREEDOM OF EXPRESSION 563–81 (1970) (discussing emerging first amendment protection for federal employees during 1960s); *see also* Vaughn, *Statutory Protection, supra* note 7, at 637–41 (discussing first amendment and CRSA whistleblower protections); *Leahy Report, supra* note 5, at 40–47 (discussing first amendment and weaknesses of protection that it provides to federal whistleblowers). In 1968, the Supreme Court decided that the first amendment did protect the speech of government employees, rejecting out of hand the notion that government employment was an unprotected privilege. Pickering v. Board of Educ., 391 U.S. 563, 574 (1968); *see* VAN ALSTYNE, *The Demise of the Right-Privilege Distinction in Constitutional Law*, 81 HARV. L. REV. 1439 (1968) (discussing development of first amendment protections for government employees prior to *Pickering* decision). Prior to the CSRA, the first amendment right to free speech and right to petition in whistleblower or grievance-type activities, as delineated in the Supreme Court's decisions in *Pickering* and New York Times v. Sullivan, 376 U.S. 254 (1964), figured prominently in judicial decisions. *See, e.g.,* Burkett v. United States, 402 F.2d 1002, 1007–08 (Ct. Cl. 1968) (citing *Pickering* and *New York Times* and discussing constitutional protection of free speech); Swaaley v. United States, 376 F.2d 857, 863 (Ct. Cl. 1967) (holding petition by federal employee to be covered by first amendment); *cf.* Meehan v. Macy, 392 F.2d 822, 831–35 (D.C. Cir. 1968) (balancing first amendment protection with disharmony produced by unrestrained public speech of government employee), *vacated on other grounds,* 425 F.2d 472 (D.C. Cir. 1969).

9. The Vietnam War and the Watergate scandal contributed to a public mind set that was suspicious of government, accustomed to the expression of dissent, and desirous of more controls to prevent government wrongdoing. Vaughn, *Statutory Protection, supra* note 7, at 618.

10. The *Leahy Report* examined 70 whistleblower cases and provided extensive documentation on 15 sampled whistleblower experiences, an unprecedented effort in this area. *Leahy Report, supra* note 5, at v. In addition, the case of Ernest Fitzgerald, a civilian employee who in 1968 had revealed to Congress mismanagement and billion-dollar cost overruns in a defense contractor's development of the C5A transport program, had attained public notoriety not only for the extent of Fitzgerald's disclosures, but also for the extent to which the United States Air Force retaliated against him for those disclosures. *Id.* at 6. Fitzgerald brought suit against the United States Air Force for damages claiming unlawful discharge. The case ultimately reached the Supreme Court where it was the subject of two precedent setting decisions on executive immunity. *See* Nixon v. Fitzgerald, 457 U.S. 739, 749 (1982) (holding President has absolute immunity from damages arising from his official acts); Harlow v. Fitzgerald, 457 U.S. 800, 813 (1982) (holding presidential aides enjoy only qualified immunity from damage suits).

11. The *Leahy Report* documented numerous cases in which the law and the Civil Service Commission were inadequate to protect whistleblowers from reprisal and the threat of reprisal. *Id.* at 36–47. The report found that whistleblowers had been 'fired, transferred, reprimanded, denied promotions, RIFFED, . . . harassed through the misuse of formal discipline procedures', and subjected to informal harassment 'designed to neutralize [them]'. *Id.* at 1. It found that the employee grievance procedures, rather than helping whistleblowers, had served 'to significantly weaken their position[s]' and had become 'actually a frustrating and biased exercise'. *Id.*

at 3. It further found that the Commission had been ineffective in protecting whistleblowers and that Congress had not offered real assistance to these employees. *Id.* at 4. Finally, the report concluded that the courts had been 'reluctant to play an active role in the whistleblower problem'. It stated that '[a]lthough statutes do exist which might be interpreted as applicable to whistleblower cases, the Courts appear to be waiting for Congress and the Executive Branch to resolve this problem.' *Id.*

12. The CSRA also included protections for all the rights of the first amendment which include the freedoms of speech, expression, and religion, and the right to petition the government for grievances.

13. *See* M. Wieseman, *Remarks of the Special Counsel Before the MSPB Practitioner's Forum*, 87 F.M.S.R. 47, 49 (Nov. 30, 1987). In an audit of the OSC, the Comptroller General of the United States found as of December 1984 that although whistleblower reprisal allegations constituted only 13% of all matters received by OSC, whistleblower reprisal allegations constituted 42% of the cases under active investigation. COMPTROLLER GENERAL OF THE UNITED STATES, WHISTLEBLOWER COMPLAINTS RARELY QUALIFY FOR OFFICE OF THE SPECIAL COUNSEL PROTECTION 18 (1985) [hereinafter WHISTLEBLOWER COMPLAINTS]. Furthermore, the General Accounting Office auditors found that although OSC had referred all new matters after initial intake and inquiry for some fuller investigation at a rate of only 8%, the agency had referred a disproportionate 41% of all whistleblower repirsal allegations for more comprehensive investigation. *Id.* at 20. That OSC employed an initial screening process to identify employee complaints of prohibited personnel practice with potential merit was consistent with Congress' intent that OSC prevent frivolous or unmeritorious cases from clogging the appeals system. *Id.* at 9–10.

14. WHISTLEBLOWER COMPLAINTS, *supra* note 13, at 3–4, 35, 49–50. GAO summarized this controversy in the following terms:

> In its 6-year history, OSC has been the object of criticism from federal employee representatives, GAO, and the Congress. OSC has been described as administratively inept, ineffective in prosecuting violations, and of little benefit to federal employee complainants such as whistleblowers alleging management reprisal for their disclosures. As a result, questions have been raised in the Congress as to whether OSC should continue to exist, and if it should, whether alterations are needed in its powers or in its statutory authorization.

Id. at 35. After a lengthy investigation, GAO concluded that by 1984 OSC had overcome earlier administrative deficiencies and reported that OSC was effectively handling allegations of reprisal for whistleblowing. *Id.* at 36. In fact, GAO concluded that based on its review of closed files, it 'could not disagree with OSC's decision to close these cases'. *Id.* at 25.

15. 1 M.S.P.R. 163 (1979).

16. *In re* Frazier, 1 M.S.P.R. 163, 166 (1979). The deputies disclosed information critical of management to two members of Congress and filed or participated in various complaints and grievances concerning race discrimination, work-place harassment, supervisory incompetence, inefficient office procedures, and an incident in which deputies were permitted to play cards and drink alcohol during a morale-building outing on official time, all matters which they reasonably believed evidenced mismanagement and violations of agency regulations. *Id.* at 170–71. The congressional disclosures, which were made after the deputies received no relief through the agency's equal employment opportunity (EEO) and grievance appeal processes, prompted a congressional inquiry to the agency. *Id.* at 171–73. Ray Lora, special assistant to the Director of the Marshals Service, had been sent to the Atlanta office, site of the controversy, to investigate. *Id.* at 172–73. Within a day or two of Lora's investigation, the local United States Marshal, Ronald Angel, recommended to William Hall, Marshals Service Director, that three of the four deputies who had made disclosures be reassigned from the Atlanta office. *Id.* at 173. Anmogel's recommendation, the deputies alleged, was in reprisal for their disclosures. *Id.* at 166. Hall did not act on Angel's request. *Id.* at 180. Instead, he appointed a management review team to look into the situation at Atlanta and make recommendations to him. *Id.* During the review, the team interviewed each of the complaining deputies and listened to their criticisms. *Id.* at 181. Based on the review, the team concluded, among other things, that there had been a breakdown in communication within the Atlanta Office, that office morale was very low, and that the office was being poorly managed. *Id.* at 181–82. The team made a number of specific recommendations to Director Hall concerning the problems they had discovered, including geographic reassignments for the four whistleblowers and one management official. *Id.* at 182. Hall implemented only the recommendation that the whistleblowers be reassigned. *Id.* at 170. The issue presented was whether Hall or the team members had acted in reprisal for any of the deputies' protected activities. *Id.* at 187.

17. The relevant sections of the Act identify the following subjects as within the ambit of protected whistleblowing: '(i) a violation of any law, rule or regulation, or (ii) mismanagement, a gross waste of funds, an abuse of authority or a substantial and specific danger to public health or safety.' 5 U.S.C.A. § 2302(b)(8) (West Supp. 1990).

18. The Board wrote:

It is true, as the Marshals Service has emphasized, that Congress has expressed great concern that the whistleblower provisions not be abused by dissident employees who have no legitimate basis for disclosures, but rather are bent upon disruption or upon creating smoke screens to obscure their own wrongdoing. This, however, does not mean that there can never be an element of self-interest in whistleblowing activities protected by section 2302(b)(8). Indeed, since the matters complained of by the deputies in this case directly affect the deputies themselves, their interest is quite consonant with the public interest in improving the management and operations of the Marshals Service.

The Board's decision left open the question of whether reasonably based disclosures might not be protected where the discloser's intent in making the disclosure was not consonant with public interest. Both the Board and the Court of Appeals for the Federal Circuit would later revisit this issue in employee-appeal cases with mixed results.

19. *Id.* at 189. The Board considered OSC's argument that it apply the 'small plant' doctrine, as used by the National Labor Relations Board in certain unfair labor practice cases, to infer knowledge on the part of Director Hall. *Id.; see* A. T. Krajewski Mfg. v. NLRB, 413 F.2d 673, 676 (1st Cir. 1969) (finding inferences from circumstantial evidence as to employer's knowledge permissible when employee engaged in in-plant activity and plant is relatively small). The Board concluded, however, that the 'small plant' doctrine was not applicable to the facts in *Frazier* because the work force for which Director Hall was responsible was not small because it included 1,400 employees nationwide. *In re* Frazier, 1 M.S.P.R. at 189.

20. In reaching its conclusion, the Board credited the testimony of three team members whose assessments of the deputies were summarized in the opinion:

The team determined that four deputies, Frazier, Morris, Reilly and Love, were totally alienated and distrustful of district management and had become so embittered that they could no longer present rational arguments to support their concerns. Moreover, in their testimony before the Board, the team members reiterated some of their findings and the bases upon which they were reached. Gary Mead testified that deputy Frazier was 'paranoid' with respect to district management, and was unable to support his general complaints. Mead testified that Love was extremely contemptuous of the district management staff to whom he referred in extremely crude terms. Russell testified that Deputy Reilly was 'totally polarized' and made unfounded allegations that district management took kickbacks from airlines used to transport prisoners.

Id. at 181–82.

21. Section 2302(b)(9) provides:

Any employee who has authority to take, direct others to take, recommend, or approve any personnel action, shall not, with respect to such authority . . . take or fail to take any personnel action against any employee or applicant for employment as a reprisal for the exercise of any appeal right granted by any law, rule, or regulation. 5 U.S.C. § 2302(b)(9) (1988), *amended by* Whistleblower Protection Act of 1989, § 4(b), 103 Stat. 32 (current version at 5 U.S.C.A. § 2302(b)(9) (West Supp. 1990)).

22. McDonnell Douglas Corp. v. Green, 411 U.S. 792, 802 (1973) (outlining steps necessary for plaintiff to prove prima facie case). The four steps are: (1) the plaintiff belongs to a protected class; (2) the plaintiff applied and was qualified for a job the employer was trying to fill; (3) though qualified, the plaintiff was rejected; and (4) thereafter the employer continued to seek applicants with plaintiff's qualifications.

23. 429 U.S. 274 (1976).

24. *In re* Frazier, 1 M.S.P.R. 163, 195–96 (1979). The *Mt. Healthy* defense derives from a first amendment infringement case decided by the Supreme Court. Mt Healthy City School Dist. Bd. of Educ. v. Doyle, 429 U.S. 274 (1976). The *Mt. Healthy* defense permits an employer to defend successfully against a claim of violation of protected rights by demonstrating with preponderant evidence that it would have taken the same action regardless of the protected activity. *Id.* at 287. In *Mt. Healthy*, the Mt. Healthy School Board refused to renew the employment contract of an untenured teacher who was also the president of the local teacher's union. *Id.* at 281–82. The decision not to rehire the teacher was based on three incidents, the first of which involved the teacher's obscene gestures at students. *Id.* at 282. The second involved a physical altercation

between the teacher and a colleague that resulted in controversial suspensions for the two and eventually a walkout by a number of teachers. *Id.* at 281. The third, and most proximate in time, involved the teacher's release to a local radio station of an internal school district memorandum concerning the imposition of a teacher dress code. *Id.* After the lower courts granted the teacher relief based on the School Board's infringement of the teacher's first amendment right to release the dress-code memo to the media, the Supreme Court granted review to determine whether a remedy was constitutionally required in light of the apparent legitimate grounds for the action. *Id.* at 295. Although it recognized that the employee's first amendment activity had played 'a substantial part' in the decision not to rehire him, the Court nevertheless was concerned that providing the teacher a remedy could place him in a better position than he would be in had he not engaged in the protected activity. *Id.* Based on this concern, the Court remanded the case for a determination of whether the Board would have taken the same action regardless of the teacher's first amendment activity. *Id.* at 287. If the Board would have taken the same action, then, in the Court's view, the constitutional infringement had not caused the challenged action and no remedy was required. *Id.*

25. *In re* Frazier, 1 M.S.P.R. 163, 196 (1979).

26. The Board concluded that the reassignment of deputy Frazier was a reprisal for Frazier's long history of involvement in EEO activities. The Board found by preponderant evidence that the management review team considered Frazier's EEO complaints in recommending his transfer. Moreover, the Board found many instances in which Frazier's supervisors in Atlanta had taken actions against him immediately after he had engaged in protected EEO activities. Because of the number of incidents of reprisal, the Board inferred that the management team and Director Hall participated in the retaliation against Frazier.

27. 9 M.S.P.R. 363 (1982).

28. 16 M.S.P.R. 178 (1983).

29. Special Counsel v. Hoban, 24 M.S.P.R. 154, 161–62 (1984). In *Hoban*, OSC charged a Veterans Administration Chief of Police with having changed the duties of a subordinate in reprisal for the subordinate's disclosure of information evidencing mismanagement. *Id.* at 155–56. The reprisal charged was sustained both by the administrative law judge and the Board.

30. In *Hoban*, the Board orderd the offending official's demotion from GS–9, Chief of Police, to GS–5, Step 1, Police Officer. Special Counsel v. Hoban. In *Harvey*, the Board ordered the offending official's demotion from the Senior Executive Service to a nonmanagerial GS–14 position, for a period of three years from the date of demotion. In *Starrett*, the Board ordered Director Starrett's removal from federal service and fined him $1,000. It also ordered the demotion of two subordinate managers to nonsupervisory positions one grade below their previous grade for a minimum period of three years and fined them each $500.

31. Fiorillo v. Department of Justice, 795 F.2d 1544, 1549 (Fed. Cir. 1986). *Fiorillo* concerned whether a prohibited personnel practice had occurred in the termination of a prison guard's appointment for disclosures he had made to the press which had brought discredit to the agency. A stipulation between the parties that the removal action was based on the disclosures left the court to decide only whether the disclosures qualified for protection under section 2302(b)(8) and whether the nature of the causal connection between the disclosures and the termination action constituted prohibited reprisal.

32. 34 M.S.P.R. 465 (1987).

7

Whistleblowing in English law

Michael Cover and Gordon Humphreys

INTRODUCTION

Through the confines of employment law the UK courts are attempting to
protect those employees who 'blow the whistle' on the unconscionable behaviour of their employers.[1] Examples of such behaviour are manifold, but
essentially concern the commission of some form of civil wrongdoing or
illegality on the part of the employer. The whistleblower is the employee
who takes it upon himself[2] to report the offending behaviour to the
authorities.

While whistleblowing may be desirable from an ethical point of view it
can have disastrous consequences, not only on the employer but also on the
employee in question. Dismissal, victimization, demotion and other forms of
harassment can place serious stress on the complainant's private and working life, both medically and financially.[3]

In this chapter we examine the problems of whistleblowing from the
perspective of the US experience, and the existing UK case law and legislation before attempting to offer suggestions on how employers and employees could synchronize their efforts so as to minimize the need for
whistleblowing and use the aftermath of a whistleblowing situation to make
real changes in corporate efficiency and structure.

THE US EXPERIENCE

While the UK has yet to enact a specific statute dealing exclusively with
whistleblowing across the board, whistleblowing legislation in the USA is
not a particularly new phenomenon. The False Claims Act was enacted as
long ago as 1863 to combat fraud by defence contractors during the US Civil
War, by allowing private citizens the *locus standi* to bring an action on their
own behalf as well as for the US government[5] (the so-called *qui tam*

provision'). The modern-day *qui tam* action is not limited to suits filed by employees or federal fraudster tendering companies but will certainly act as a considerable incentive to 'blow the whistle' on wrong-doing in the government procurement sector.

Qui tam actions

The *qui tam* phenomenon seeks to strike a delicate balance between the prosecution of government fraud cases, in order to limit federal government losses, while at the same time attempting to prevent 'parasitic' private-citizen actions. The notion of 'parasitic' actions is still somewhat fluid, but includes: situations where the facts upon which action is based have already come into the public domain; or where a case is already pending on similar facts; or where a lawsuit is filed by military personnel in a military context; and, more controversially, where legal actions are commenced against the judiciary or senior members of the executive.[7] Arguably, any *qui tam* suit filed by government employees based on information obtained in the context of their employment is inherently parasitic, on the basis that Congress only ever intended the *qui tam* mechanism[8] to apply to private citizens.

The revolutionary aspect of *qui tam* actions is that they allow the person who has commenced a *qui tam* action (the 'relator') a percentage of the government's recovery under the False Claims Amendments Act 1986.[9] This is no minor incentive when one considers that the False Claims Act allows US federal government to recover treble damages and civil penalties from entities who knowingly make false claims for payment of government funds. In practice, the relator's award is typically in the order of 15 to 25 per cent if the Department of Justice intervenes or 25 to 30 per cent if the department declines to join the action.[10] Moreover, in the *qui tam* context every entity which does business with the US federal government can be a potential defendant in a legal action commenced by a private citizen.

Cynics may well agree with the remarks of Senator Howard in 1863, who suggested that *qui tam* actions appealed to natural human greed by 'setting a rogue to catch a rogue'.[11] These sentiments were echoed in the 1885 case of *United States* v. *Griswold*,[12] in which a district court noted that private persons would often act 'under the strong stimulus of personal ill will or the hope of gain'.[13] However, Congress has been at pains to reduce the risks of 'roguish' elements trying to avail themselves of the *qui tam* action by introducing an amendment to the False Claims Act in 1988, so that here the relator 'is convicted of criminal conduct arising from his or her role . . ., that person shall be dismissed from the civil action and shall not receive any share of the proceeds of the action'.[14]

Clearly, the incentive of personal gain can be dangerous if left completely unharnessed. It is for this reason that the US federal draughtsmen have attempted to limit claims by introducing the 'public disclosure' bar, while the courts have grappled with the thorny question of government employee *qui tam* actions.

The public disclosure bar essentially covers two problematic areas:

- the original source exception; and
- revelations obtained in the course of legal proceedings.

The original source exception

This was demonstrated in the recent case of *United States ex rel. Dick* v. *Long Island Lighting Co. (LILCO)*[15] where two employees of a nuclear power station commenced *qui tam* proceedings against the defendant, Lighting Co. The claim was on grounds of exaggerated construction costs estimated by the defendants and which had allegedly led to federal government being defrauded. However, the district court dismissed the claim on the basis that the suit had only been filed after the employees had read in the newspaper about an almost identical case against the defendants some months previously. In the district court's judgment, which was confirmed by the Second Circuit, the relators were not 'original sources' (i.e. the original source from which information to commence proceedings came) and, therefore, the action was dismissed.

Revelations obtained in the course of legal proceedings

The 'race to the court house' can take some quite unexpected turns. In *United States ex rel. Stinson* v. *Prudential Insurance (Stinson)*,[16] a law firm filed a *qui tam* action against the Prudential following the unearthing of internal Prudential memoranda – in the context of discovery proceedings – indicating fraud on the part of the defendant company against the USA. The Third Circuit held that discovery fell within the meaning of 'civil hearing' and as such constituted public disclosure, invalidating the *qui tam* action for want of an original source.

The *Stinson* case is perhaps especially shocking to European observers, since it appears to demonstrate just how far even professional advisers will go in the search for personal profit. Some doubt must remain as to how dedicated the attorney will be to his client's case when there is possibly greater reward to be had in using pretrial information for a *qui tam* action for his own ends. This concern was to some extent shown recently in *United States ex rel. Doe* v. *John Doe Corp. (Doe)*.[17] In this case an attorney, who had successfully negotiated immunity for his client from criminal procurement fraud charges, then commenced a *qui tam* action against his client's employer.

Although the attorney in *Doe* had asked his client's permission before filing suit and, in the event, the action was unsuccessful, the case shows that the client–lawyer relationship can be in serious danger of abuse if the lawyer is constantly on the lookout for information from his client which can be used for his personal gain rather than furthering the client's cause.

Government employees

In a similar vein is the thorny problem of *qui tam* suits filed by government employees. Just as the lawyer has an over-riding duty to uphold and defend the legitimate interests of his client, so the government employee owes allegiance to the state. Allowing government employees to commence *qui tam* actions is almost an invitation to untenable conflict of interest situations.

Although there is no specific statutory exclusion of government employees[18] from *qui tam* actions – and for this reason recent case law tends to support such actions[19] – a number of practitioners remain critical of this right.[20]

The *qui tam* suit damages are in some respects designed to compensate a private citizen who may become subject to informal blacklisting by prospective employers; expensive and harassing countersuits; and peer pressure not to report wrong-doing committed by the relator's fellow workers or company. These elements are not so prevalent in the case of a government employee who, in many instances, will have been specifically engaged to uncover fraud. To allow such government employees to bring *qui tam* actions could undermine public confidence in the fairness and objectivity of such officials.[21]

In addition, holding out the 'carrot' of personal financial reward could lead government employees to neglect their official duties in favour of more lucrative pursuits. This could undermine public confidence since private citizens would be wary about co-operating with government investigators prior to filing their *qui tam* suit for fear of the investigator pre-empting their action.[22]

Moreover, investigators would be disinclined to report planned fraud but would prefer to let it occur and then file a *qui tam* suit.[23] In other words, allowing such persons a right to commence *qui tam* proceedings could seriously jeopardize professional integrity.

Lessons for Europe

The *qui tam* mechanism has a number of advantages in an age when uncovering fraud and other forms of wrong-doing is increasingly complex, costly and time consuming. The utility of this system is especially poignant at a time when law-enforcement bodies are understaffed and overstretched.

However, the US experience shows that such rights of suit must not be allowed to get out of hand. In certain instances, the need to protect professional independence and integrity over-rides the desirability of increased prosecutions. Nevertheless, it must surely be one of the ironies of legal history that the *qui tam* suit finds its origins in England.[24] Perhaps there is a good case for history to repeat itself in this instance.

Protecting the US whistleblower otherwise than by *qui tam* reward

The False Claims Act contains the following general whistleblower protection clause:[25]

> Any employee who is discharged, demoted, suspended, threatened, harassed, or in any other manner discriminated against in the terms and conditions of employment by his or her employer because of lawful acts done by the employee on behalf of the employee or others in furtherance of an action under this section, including investigation of, initiation of, testimony for, or assistance in an action

filed or to be filed under this section, shall be entitled to all relief necessary to make the employee whole. Such relief shall include reinstatement with the same seniority, back pay, and compensation for any special damages sustained as a result of the discrimination, including litigation costs and reasonable attorneys' fees. An employee may bring an action in the appropriate district court of the United States for the relief provided by this subsection.

In other words, where an employee brings a *qui tam* action against his employer, the employer cannot take any reprisals against that employee. If he does retaliate he must make *restitutio in integrum* for the damages so caused.

As regards the federal employee whistleblower, such person will be protected under the Whistleblower Protection Act 1989 where he discloses information reasonably believed to evidence:

- 'A violation of any law, rule or regulation'; or
- 'Gross mismanagement, a gross waste of funds, an abuse of authority or a substantial and specific danger to public health or safety.'[26]

Moreover, protection is afforded to former employees and even job applicants.

The Whistleblower Act 1989 sets up an independent Office of Special Counsel to whom prohibited personnel practices (i.e. reprisals) may be reported and acted upon. Actions may then be commenced by the Special Counsel in front of the specially created Merit Systems Protection Board. The Merit Systems Protection Board is entitled to take 'corrective action'[27] and will have a wide discretion in this regard. An annual report is made to Congress regarding the Special Counsel's activities.

Numerous state whistleblower Acts exist. As with federal legislation, they attempt to curb 'prohibited personnel practices'. Whether on a practical level this legislation completely solves the problem is to be doubted.

Informal blacklisting and subtle discriminatory methods are difficult to legislate against. However, the extent of legal discussion over whistleblowing shows that US employers are very much alive to these issues and certainly tread cautiously. In the final section of this chapter we examine some of the guidelines used by US employers to minimize the risk of costly whistleblower litigation distracting management time. The fact that the issue is taken so seriously must surely be some indication of the success of the US legislation in this area.

FITTING WHISTLEBLOWING INTO UK EMPLOYMENT LAW

The legal context

In stark contrast to the USA, the UK is a virtual 'legislative desert' when it comes to whistleblower statutes. Almost the only piece of real statutory intervention in this area is the Offshore Safety (Protection Against Victimisation) Act 1992[28] which seeks to implement Lord Justice Cullen's recommendation, in the wake of the Piper Alpha Disaster Public Inquiry, that offshore employers be afforded protection against victimization when acting as safety representatives or as members of safety committees.[29]

It is to be regretted that this statutory protection is viewed from the perspective of the safety officer or committee member's union membership rather than purely his position *qua* employee. Moreover, even if the Act were to afford general protection to employees who 'blew the whistle', it would only do so in the limited sector of offshore installation employees. It is, therefore, of limited utility.

In view of this legislative lacuna, case law has a preponderant role to play. However, whereas statute may well serve to discourage infringement of the law by an employer, or at least clarify in the minds of both parties the consequences of such violation, case law is necessarily a somewhat stop-gap solution which is open to the vagaries of 'distinguished' decisions and particular sets of facts. The result is a rather piecemeal protection of employees, with courts and lawyers desperately trying to slot the facts of a particular case into some existing form of employment law.

Victimization

Perhaps the most obvious consequence of a whistleblower situation is that the employee undergoes some form of victimization as a result of his act. However, it does not follow that such victimization comes from the employer.

In *Wigan Borough Council* v. *Davies*[30] a junior manager of an old people's home has failed to support other assistants in a dispute with the employers (the local authority). As a consequence, the other membersof staff refused to co-operate with the junior manager and 'sent her to Coventry'. Despite assurances from the employers that attempts would be made to improve the situation, nothing was done. The Employment Appeal Tribunal upheld the decision of the industrial tribunal that the employer had an implied, and in the case in point, an express duty to provide support such that the employee could carry out her professional activities without harassment from her fellow employees. Furthermore, breach of this obligation on the part of the employer was considered as being fundamental and, therefore, justified the employee in terminating her employment and seeking damages for unfair dismissal.

The duty to lend reasonable support

The employer's implied duty to lend reasonable support in victimization of an employee by fellow employees has been upheld on a number of occasion in the context of strike breakers.[31] Although these cases primarily involve an employee who is not willing to support the wishes of his fellow workers, rather than one who actively seeks to report the acts of those he works with, they nevertheless provide a useful analogy with this latter situation.

In *Callanan* v. *Surrey Area Health Authority*,[32] the plaintiff, a student nurse at a psychiatric hospital, reported a senior charge nurse to the hospital nursing officer for having assaulted patients and having given them drug overdoses. Following an inquiry into the matter the charge nurse and colleagues refused to work with the plaintiff. Matters deteriorated to such an extent that the hospital management committee told Callanan to return to nursing school. He therefore resigned claiming constructive and unfair dismissal. On the same principles as in the *Davies* case the employee's action was upheld and he was awarded damages.[33]

The duty to give the employee reasonable support in the performance of his contract is a demonstration of the underlying obligation of mutual trust which exists as between employer and employee. To use the oft-cited words of Lord Denning, 'Just as a servant must be good and faithful, so an employer must be good and considerate'.[34] The law, therefore, implies observance of a basic degree of honesty in employer–employee relations.

The problem of participation in illegality

Requiring the employee to connive in acts of dishonesty removes the employer from the realms of being 'good and considerate' and thereby absolves the employee from his duty of loyalty. It, therefore, follows that an employee who refuses to drive untaxed vehicles,[35] or participate in falsifying company records over drawing petrol,[36] or co-operate in the concealment of the systematic loss of stock[37] will be entitled to resign and claim compensation for unfair dismissal.

Where the employee in question has in some way participated in the employer's illegality complained of, or is in a position of authority, the position is different from that stated above. In *Craig* v. *Engine Applications*,[38] an export clerk who had on one occasion collaborated in a false customs' declaration on behalf of his employer was estopped from claiming constructive and unfair dismissal when invited by his employers to make a similar false declaration on a subsequent occasion.

In fact, the clerk in the *Craig* case had already 'blown the whistle' on his employers, by reporting them to HM Customs and Excise *before* the subsequent incident occurred. Nevertheless, the duty to act honestly is of such importance that swift action is required on the part of the employee if he wishes to benefit from the full protection of English employment law. An employee cannot as in the *Craig* case co-operate in a fraudulent act on one occasion, then report the employer when a subsequent incident occurs and only resign on a third occasion.

This decision seems rather harsh given the wavering and somewhat uncertain nature of employment law protection for whistleblowers. Surely it cannot be unreasonable for an individual to ruminate over the issue of whether or not to report his employer or workmates rather than act with haste in what is necessarily an extremely traumatic situation for him. Clearly, the period for rumination must not be so long as to constitute acquiescence and a measure of reasonableness needs to be brought to bear in the light of the particular facts of the case.

The effect of seniority

Similarly, the seniority of the employee will be an important element in determining the importance of the obligation to report one's fellow workers as part of an overall duty to act honestly. In *Sybron Corporation* v. *Rochem Ltd*[39] the manager of European affairs of an American financial conglomerate was held to be under an implied contractual duty to report the involvement of a number of his fellow employees in the perpetration of a massive commercial fraud on the employer.[40]

Where the employee is less senior[41] than in the *Sybron Corporation* case, and takes it upon himself to report some form of wrong-doing, he may well find that the protection afforded at law is less than satisfactory.

In *Wild and Joseph* v. *Stephens and David Clulow Ltd*,[42] the personnel manager of the defendant firm complained to a supervisor of that firm about the unfair treatment of a receptionist, who had been moved because it was thought undesirable to have a black person in that job. However, no action was taken and the receptionist subsequently complained to the Commission for Racial Equality. She was then offered demotion or redundancy, a choice which the industrial tribunal considered to constitute victimization and unfair dismissal.

In contrast, in *Kirby* v. *Manpower Services Commission*,[43] an employee of a job centre informed the local Council for Community Relations that potential employers registered with the job centre were discriminating against non-white applicants. Neither the industrial tribunal nor the Employment Appeal Tribunal considered that the employee's ensuing demotion constituted discrimination under the Race Relations Act, since he had not been treated any less favourably than any other employee would have been who disclosed such information to an outside body.

This case underlines the inadequacy of English law in relation to whistleblowers. In the first instance, it is wholly unsatisfactory that an employee, who from the law report appears to have been white, was launched into a technical legal debate under the Race Relations Act. He had, of course, 'blown the whistle' on possible racial discrimination against job hunters by potential employers registered at the job centre. But surely the real issue concerned his demotion for reporting possible wrong-doing on the part of persons associated, albeit transiently, with his employers. This was not a racial issue but was forced to be treated as such because no relevant statute existed to regulate the specificity of the situation.

If, as appears to have been the case, the tribunal particularly objected to disclosure to an outside body, then again the issue was non-racial but rather one of balancing two potentially conflicting public interests. Those interests were, on the one hand, the arguable right of potential employers to have some guarantee of confidentiality in their dealings with a job centre and, on the other, a private citizen's right to bypass his employer in order to report wrong-doing to an outside body specializing in problems of the kind in issue.

Ironically, in a more recent case, *Re A Company's Application*,[44] Scott J ruled that the defendant's duty of confidence arising out of his employment was

not incompatible with him reporting his employer to the Financial Investment Management and Brokers' Regulatory Authority and the Inland Revenue, provided that the disclosures were within those bodies' investigative
prerogatives.

Public interest

Clearly, the important distinction with the *Kirby* case is that *Kirby* involved
disclosure over persons who were in contact with the employer rather than
the employer's wrong-doing *per se*. Nevertheless, the point about the importance of the prerogatives of the body to whom the report is made would
seem to be of relevance to both cases. It is arguably the function of such
bodies which are the true gauge of public interest.

However, the courts seem to have denied this logic – or at least interpreted it in somewhat surprising ways. For example, in *Thornley* v. *Aircraft
Research Association Ltd*[45] disclosure by an employee to a national newspaper
of research findings on Tornado aircraft was held by the Employment Appeal Tribunal to be a breach of trust. The fact of the employee having signed
a contractual undertaking not to disclose the results of the research was
deemed to outweigh the desirability of revealing accurate information to the
media on the performance of aircraft.[46]

Similarly, in the joined cases of *The Distillers Co (Biochemicals) Ltd* v. *Times
Newspapers Ltd* and *The Distillers Co (Biochemicals) Ltd* v. *Phillips*,[47] the court
considered that the public's interest in the proper administration of justice –
which required that the confidentiality of documents should be protected –
outweighed the public interest in a revelation to the newspapers of the
dangers of the Thalidomide drug.

On the other hand, the Court of Appeal[48] was willing to accept that a
liaison system between laundries to keep up their prices was a matter of
such public interest that it entitled a former employee of the plaintiff laun-
dry to disclose confidential information to the newspapers. However, the
court did add the qualification that such revelation should be made to a
body having the 'proper interest to receive it'.[49]

On occasion, courts have sought to add the notion of 'clean hands' to the
public-interest equation. An example of this was seen in *Hubbard and another* v.
Vosper and another.[50] In this case, Megaw LJ considered that the Church of
Scientology used such deplorable means in protecting their secrets that they
could not seek the equitable remedy of injunction against publication of a book
by a former member, since they did not come before the court with 'clean
hands'.[51]

It is interesting to note that in the *Putterill* case,[52] Lord Denning ruled that
the public interest exception to the duty of confidence extends to 'any misconduct of such a nature that it ought to be disclosed to others. . . . The
exception should extend to crimes, frauds and misdeeds, both those actually
committed as well as those in contemplation'. This list which was added to
in *Hubbard* v. *Vosper*[53] as including disclosure of activities that are 'dangerous to the public'.[54] This would seem to suggest that the Thalidomide
case[55] may not have been a correct decision.

Clearly, the notion of public interest may change over the years, as the 'mores' of a society develop. This may be one possible explanation as to why courts seem to have become increasingly sympathetic to the right of newspapers to publish matters of the utmost interest to a broad section of the general public. For example, in *Lion Laboratories Ltd* v. *Evans*,[56] it was held that the media had 'a right and even a duty to publish[57] information regarding the potential inaccuracy of the Intoximeter 3000' (a device used for 'breathalyser' tests). Significantly, the court considered that such right to publish would exist even where the information forming the basis of a press article had been obtained in 'flagrant breach of confidence and irrespective of the motive of the informer'.

There is an alternative explanation as to why the courts sometimes disregard, as in the *Lion Laboratories* case, the fact that the discloser of information may be acting for purely selfish motives (i.e. financial reward) and even illegally. This explanation may be that public interest is gauged in terms of what is of crucial relevance to the broadest possible cross-section of society. In the case of revelation of the Thalidomide drug story, it could, therefore, be argued that the facts were only of relevance to a relatively small section of the community (i.e. expectant mothers taking that drug), whereas 'breathalyser' tests can potentially effect every non-teetotal driver in the country.

Undeniably, the *Hubbard* case sits rather uncomfortably with this reasoning, unless one accepts that potential religious malpractice of a particular sect is of the utmost importance to the community at large. However, it should not be forgotten that members of the Church of Scientology had already been before the UK courts[58] and that the sect had attracted much media coverage all over the world by the time this case came to Lord Denning's court. The Thalidomide story was, on the other hand, a very new one at the time it came to be litigated. These factors may have had a part to play – albeit subconsciously – in the minds of those deciding the cases.

Duty to investigate

It is a well established principle of English employment law that where an employee makes a complaint regarding health and safety, the employer is under a duty to investigate. In *British Aircraft Corporation* v. *Austin*,[59] an employee who complained that she was unable to wear the standard safety goggles because she wore glasses did not receive any investigation or remedial action regarding her complaint on the part of her employer. It was held that this failure entitled her to claim constructive and unfair dismissal.

On the other hand, the courts have, on occasion, accepted that an 'innocent' failure to investigate by the employer will not automatically entitle the employee to treat the contract of employment as at an end and claim compensation. For example, in *Canning* v. *GLC*[60] an employee, Canning, was a housing officer with the Greater London Council. Following a visit to a particular property, Canning became convinced that fraudulent schedules of repairs and renovations were being submitted by an outside contractor. He reported the matter to the Director of Housing but heard nothing for four months and subsequently claimed that he had been constructively dismissed.

The Employment Appeal Tribunal confirmed the lower tribunal's decision that there had been no actionable failure on the part of the employer. The Employment Appeal Tribunal was influenced by the fact that Canning had not reverted to the matter during a four-month period. Moreover, it was held that no authority was cited to justify the existence of a contractual duty on the employer to report the outcome of an inquiry to the person who makes the complaint.

At first sight, the *Canning* decision seems to be in direct conflict with the judgment in the *Austin* case. However, the decisions deal with two different areas of concern: health and safety and financial irregularity. The physical endangering of an employee's eyesight is undeniably a matter of the utmost concern which warrants immediate attention. The same degree of urgency cannot usually be said to exist where financial matters are involved.

On the other hand, it should be remembered that case law to some extent reflects the priorities and values of a particular period in time. It may be legitimately questioned as to whether the spate of cases involving allegations of misappropriation or misuse of Liverpool City Council funds, together with the more recent pension and investment fund fraud cases would still lead courts to conclude, as in the *Canning* case, that employee's complaints did not necessarily have to be investigated.[61]

Compensation

The whistleblower employee who is dismissed (actively or constructively), victimized or otherwise discriminated against receives no special protection other than that given to employees at large. Classically, the common law considered that compensatory awards should indemnify the financial loss arising from unfair dismissal (i.e. the pure loss of wages element) without penalizing employers or 'comforting' sacked employees.[62]

On the other hand, courts and industrial tribunals have sometimes been prepared to accept rather more indirect elements of financial loss. In *Norton Tool Co* v. *Tewson*,[63] Sir John Donaldson ruled: 'We need only consider whether the manner and circumstances of his dismissal could give rise to any risk of financial loss at a later stage, for example making him less acceptable to potential employers or exceptionally liable to selection for dismissal.'

Sir John Donaldson went on to stress the need for an employee in these circumstances to mitigate his loss in so far as is possible. However, he emphasized that employees should not be compensated for injured feelings.

But where injury to feelings intervenes in a racial context the Court of Appeal has shown itself to be more sympathetic. In *NW Thames Regional Health Authority* v. *Noone*,[64] a doctor who was of Sri Lankan origin, and was shown to have been discriminated against in an application she made for a post as a consultant microbiologist, was awarded £3,000 specifically for injury to feelings. Moreover, in *Alexander* v. *Home Office*,[65] a prison inmate of West Indian extraction, who alleged discrimination on racial grounds, was held entitled to damages for injury to feelings. The Court of Appeal did, however, point out that such head of damages should be restrained but not minimal. In addition, the court considered that such damages should only be awarded where injury had resulted from knowledge of the discrimination; if the employee had been brought into 'hatred, ridicule or contempt', this would be a factor in assessing damages.

The *Noone* and *Alexander* cases show that injury to feelings can be a serious issue in employment disputes. However, it must be seriously questioned as to whether the court's willingness to entertain this head of recovery was primarily motivated by the racial discriminatory context of the claim. If this was the prime motivation then considerable doubt must subsist as to whether a straightforward whistleblower, reporting a party for wrong-doing which has no relation with racial discrimination, would enjoy similar protection for injury to feelings in a victimization situation.[66]

Finally, it should be noted that where the employee–employer relationship has not completely broken down then there may be the possibility of the court ordering reinstatement. However, where an employee is reinstated, there is only very limited scope for modest additional compensation.[67] In practice, the amounts of such additional compensation tend to be very restrained.

The final balance

If UK employment law were the only support whistleblowers received and, therefore, the sole obstacle for employers, it is unlikely that whistleblowing would be a highly controversial subject. Only the most principled or moralistic employees would 'blow the whistle'.

The law is inadequate so far as whistleblowers are concerned and unclear from the point of view of employers. Technical legal debates over such matters as the meaning of public interest, racial discrimination, combined with minimal damages for heads of claim, such as injury to feelings, does little to encourage employees to reveal wrong-doing. What is needed is specific legislation so that a greater degree of clarity is brought to bear on this subject.

In the meantime, self-regulation,[68] confidential internal reporting systems[69] and outside help organizations[70] are doing much to assist whistleblowers. The fact that employers are taking the issue seriously enough to set up their own in-house consultation groups shows that the current climate and legal situation is not considered as devoid of problems. Moreover, those in business realize – like the US statutory draughtsmen many years beforehand – that whistleblowing can have highly positive effects on the cashflow of a company or on unwelcome adverse publicity.

COPING WITH WHISTLEBLOWING

As far as employers are concerned, defending a whistleblowing action is likely to be expensive in terms of legal costs as well as distracted management time. Moreover, although many employers currently realize that the working systems which they continue to operate are inadequate, they lack the necessary resources to remedy these defects. For example, at present, British Rail simply cannot afford to implement the recommendations of the Hidden Report into the Clapham train crash relating to automatic train protection, because it does not have the necessary funds.

Nevertheless, there are a number of measures that employers can take to avoid or minimize the risks of whistleblowing:[71]

- Employers should ensure that their employees understand the company's commitment to acting legally, ethically and responsibly. Standards on safety, environmental compliance and ethics should be set and given wide publicity within the organization.
- The areas of business in which the employer is engaged should be subjected to constant risk analysis. Proper risk management in assessment will enable the right decisions to be taken about allocating scarce resources to improving systems and methods of working. In an effort to set up such internal procedures for potential whistleblowers to air their grievances, safe channels of communications should be created internally or, alternatively, a newsletter could be published regularly in which confidential and anonymous contributions can be made on safety, the environment and related topics.
- Employees should be assured that they will not face retaliation for voicing their concerns to management. Such assurance should be demonstrated by the employer being responsive to employee concerns and initiating inquiries wherever and whenever necessary.
- Employers should discuss the results of internal audits or investigations with employees who have expressed concerns over these matters.
- Employers should aim to achieve the highest possible standards of quality management, for example, by giving proper hierarchical recognition to managers responsible for safety and the environment.
- Consideration should be given to inserting confidentiality clauses into employees' contracts of employment and terms and conditions of employment. However, it should be recognized that these 'gagging' clauses will never be sufficient to prevent an employee bringing matters into the public domain where disclosure is justified in the public interest – for example, where fraud is involved.
- A document-retention policy should be implemented by employers so that all internal and external communications with employees, regulators or other administrative bodies are preserved as evidence in the wake of a potentially litigious incident.
- Employers should set up a review system to consider possible reprimanding action against a whistleblower employee. Such review should consider the seriousness of the wrong-doing alleged, together with all the relevant circumstances, and the truth of the matters alleged by the employee whistleblower. An overall assessment should be made by the employer as to how his corporate and commercial image has been tainted by whistleblowing.

- The employer should not be reticent to take appropriate disciplinary action against an employee who alleges wrong-doing without any reasonable cause, or simply out of malice.

Although the law governing whistleblowers is far less developed in the UK
than in the USA, it is none the less well worth employers taking heed of the
issues this topic raises and acting accordingly. Implementation of a structured approach to corporate management whistleblowing problems lays the
ground for proper defence to media pressure and, even, legal proceedings.
The establishment of a credible internal outlet for whistleblowers within the
corporate structure will also help potentially adverse energies to be chan-
nelled in a way which is beneficial to the company as a whole. Whistleblowing is not necessarily incompatible with the interests of an organization.
Apart from the possibility it presents for economy from the effects of fraud,
mismanagement and misappropriation of funds, it also could assist in pre-
serving a company from potentially ruinous publicity.

Whether whistleblowing will take on the same importance in the UK, as it
has enjoyed in the USA, remains to be seen. Nevertheless, the important
precedents which the US legal system has set in the field of racial discrimination and other areas of employment law, such as sexual harassment and
discrimination, means that only the unwisest of risk managers could ignore
the transatlantic developments in whistleblowing.

ACKNOWLEDGEMENT

Our thanks to Martin J. Golub, partner with the firm of attorneys, Seyfarth,
Shaw, Fairweather & Geraldson, for his generous assistance on the US section of this chapter.

NOTES

1. Whistleblowing can also be understood in its wider sense to include revelations
made by the press or any other private entity on matters falling within the scope of
public interest, such as the private lives of politicians. This chapter does not explore
this extended meaning, but instead focuses on the problems of the corporate and civil
service whistleblower.

2. All references to the masculine are purely made for the sake of brevity and are
not in any way intended to reflect the authors' views.

3. As regards the possible medical consequences, see Jean Lennane, K. (1993)
'Whistleblowing: a health issue', *British Medical Journal*, Vol. 307, 11 September, p. 667
ff., in which the following whistleblowing stress-related symptoms were noted
among a random 35-person sample study: difficulties in sleeping; anxiety; panic
attacks; depression; suicidal thoughts and feelings of guilt and worthlessness; nerv-
ous diarrhoea; trouble in breathing; stomach problems; loss of appetite; loss of
weight; high blood pressure; palpitations; hair loss; grinding of teeth; nightmares;
headaches; tiredness; weeping; tremor; and frequency of urination.

4. However, the Offshore Safety (Protection against Victimization) Act 1992 (1992
c. 24) does protect employees working on offshore installations against victimization
when acting as safety representatives or members of safety committees.

5. Vogel, R. L. (1992) 'Eligibility requirements for relators under *qui tam* provisions of the False Claims Act', *Public Contract Law Journal*, Vol. 21, no. 4, p. 596. See also Hanifin, P. (1991) '*Qui tam* suits by federal government employees based on government information' *Public Contract Law Journal*, Vol. 20, no. 4, p. 562, in which the author argues that 'qui tam statutes originated in England as a method of encouraging private enforcement of public laws at a time when public law enforcement organizations were minimal', and cites the case of *Marvin* v. *Trout*, 199 US 212, 225 (1905) in support of this proposition.

6. '*Qui tam pro domine rege quam pro sic ipso in hoc parte sequitur*' or 'who as well for the king for himself sues in the matter'. See Vogel, *op. cit.*, note 5, p. 594.

7. *Ibid.*, p. 599.

8. *Ibid.*, p. 611.

9. As amended in 1988 and 1990. See 31 U.S.C. § 3730.

10. Vogel, *op. cit.*, note 5, p. 594. See Hanifin, *op. cit.*, note 5, p. 557.

11. Cong. Globf., 37th Cong. 3d Sess. 955–56 (1863), cited in Vogel, *op. cit.*, note 5, p. 596.

12. 24 F. 361 (D. Ore 1885), aff'd, 30 F. 2d 762 (c.c. Ore. 1887).

13. *Ibid.* at 366.

14. 31 U.S.C. § 3730 (d)(3); cited in Vogel, *op. cit.*, note 5, pp. 600–1.

15. 912 F. 2d 13 (2d Cir.), cert. denied, 110 S. Ct 1471 (1990), cited in Vogel, *op. cit.*, note 5, p. 601 and Hanifin, *op. cit.*, note 5, p. 593.

16. 944 F. 2d 1149 (3d Cir. 1991), cited in Vogel, *op. cit.*, note 5, p. 604.

17. 960 F. 2d 318 (2d Cir. 1992), cited in Vogel, *op. cit.*, note 5, p. 605.

18. It should be noted, however, that military personnel, members of the judiciary and high-ranking members of the executive may not bring *qui tam* actions where the case involves the relator's specific sector.

19. See, for example, *Erickson ex rel. United States* v. *American Institute of Biological Sciences (Erikson)* 716 F. Supp. 908 (E.D. Va. 1989); *United States ex rel. Le Blanc* v. *Raytheon co. (Le Blanc)* 913 F. 2d 17 (1st Cir. 1990), cert. denied, 111 s. Ct 1312 (1991); *United States ex. rel. Hagood* v. *Sonoma County Water Agency (Hagood)* 929 F. 2d 1416 (9th Cir. 1991); *United States ex rel. Williams* v. *NEC Corp. (Williams)* 931 F. 2d 1493 (11th Cir. 1991). However, it should be noted that in the *Le Blanc* decision, the court considered that the apprehending of litigious information in the course of federal employment amounted to public disclosure.

20. See, for example, Hanifin, *op. cit.*, note 5, 573 ff., and Vogel, *op. cit.*, note 5, 608 ff.

21. *Ibid.*

22. *Ibid.*

23. *Ibid.*

24. See *ante*, note 5.

25. 31 U.S.C. § 3730 (h).

26. The Whistleblower Protection Act 1989, 103 STAT. 17, § 1213 (a)(1).

27. § 1221 (a) of the Act.

28. See *ante*, note 4.

29. Recommendation 30 of the *Report on the Public Inquiry into the Piper Alpha Disaster* (Cmnd 1310).

30. [1979] ICR 411 (EAT).

31. See, for example, *Adams* v. *Southampton & SW Hants Health Authority* COIT and *London Borough of Islington* v. *Richards EAT* 649/86.

32. [1980] IT.

33. For further examples of the duty of reasonable support, see *Robinson* v. *Crompton Ltd* [1978] ICR 401; *Carter* v. *Arnold & Golding* COIT 1729/193; and *Ferguson* v. *Henry Wigfall & Son Ltd* OIT 1550/141.

34. *Woods* v. *WM Car Services (Peterborough) Ltd* [1982] ICR 693 CA.

35. *Donnelly* v. *Renilson & Co* COIT 1414/143.

36. *Morrish* v. *Henly's (Folkestone) Ltd* [1973] ICR 482.

37. *Smith* v. *Youth Hostels Association (England and Wales)* [1980] IT.

38. [1978] EAT.

39. [1983] 2 All ER 707 (CA).

40. The court ruled that an employee 'may be so placed in the hierarchy as to have a duty to report either the misconduct of his superior . . . or the misconduct of his inferiors'.

41. The question of seniority is necessarily subjective and will depend upon the particular facts of the case and the hierarchical matrix of the company. The crucial factor would seem to be whether the employee can be said to be in a 'position of trust'. See, *Cooper* v. *Plessy Semi-Conductors* [1983] IT.

42. [1980] COIT 1031/35.

43. [1980] 1 WLR 725. See also *Aziz* v. *Trinity Street Taxis Ltd* [1988] 3 WLR 79, for a further instance of whistleblowing with racial overtones.

44. [1989] IRLR 477.

45. [1977] EAT 669/76.

46. However, in *Dunford and Elliot Ltd* v. *Johnson and Firth Brown Ltd* [1977] 1 Lloyd's Rep 505, Lord Denning considered that the courts will not enforce confidentiality in cases where the bounds of confidentiality are drawn wider than is reasonable, or if keeping information confidential would be contrary to the public interest, or if there is a just case for its disclosure.

47. [1975] 1 All ER 41.

48. *Initial Services Ltd* v. *Putterill and another* [1968] 1 QB 396.

49. See *ibid.* at 405. However, in *Francome* v. *Mirror Group Newspapers Ltd* [1984] WLR 892, the court rejected the contention that public interest demanded that a national newspaper was the appropriate forum for disclosing illegally taped telephone conversations showing breaches of the rules of racing.

50. [1972] 1 All ER 1023.

51. *Ibid.* at 1033.

52. See *ante*, note 44.

53. See *ante*, note 46.

54. The defence of public interest was likewise defined by Ungoed-Thomas J in *Beloff* v. *Pressdam* [1973] 1 All ER 241, as only relating to matters liable to breach the country's security, or law or otherwise harming the nation, including matters 'medically dangerous' to the public, and other equally serious misdeeds. It did not, therefore, extend beyond misdeeds of a serious nature, clearly recognizable as such.

55. See *ante*, note 47.

56. [1984] 3 WLR 539.

57. Per Stephenson LJ.

58. See, for example, *Van Duyn* v. *The Home Office* (41/74, 1974 ECJ, 1337).

59. [1978] 1 WLR 332 (EAT).

60. [1980] 1 WLR 378 (EAT).

61. The courts appear to be coming more supportive of whistleblowers in the financial sector as was demonstrated recently in *MacMillan Inc* v. *Bishopsgate Investment Trust PLC*, Times, 21 January 1993. In this case, the court underlined that it was important that witnesses asked to provide information to liquidators about their employer's affairs should be guaranteed confidentiality so as not to inhibit their disclosure of information.

62. See, for example, *Lifeguard Assurance Co. Ltd* v. *Zadronzny* [1977] EAT.

63. *Ibid.* at 188.

64. [1988] 3 ICR 813 (CA).

65. [1988] 1 WLR 968.

66. It should be noted that a former employer cannot seek to damage an employee's employment prospects by making imprudent or vindictive comments in any

references provided. If he does he will be liable for the financial loss so incurred. See *Lawton* v. *BOC Transhield Ltd* [1987] 2 All ER 608.

67. See, for example, *O'Laoire* v. *Jackel International Ltd* [1989] CA, in which the court discussed the provisions of the Employment Protection (Consolidation) Act 1978 in relation to reinstatement.

68. For example, the confidential systems of employee guardians established within the John Lewis Partnership.

69. Such as the 'near misses' system operated by the Royal Air Force.

70. For example, the recently created Public Concern at Work Organization, chaired by Sir Gordon Borrie, will provide free legal advice to potential whistleblowers. See *The Independent*, 15 October 1993, and *The Financial Times*, 15 October 1993.

71. The list which follows is largely inspired from *The Government Contract Compliance Handbook* (second Edn), Seyfarth, Shaw, Fairweather & Geraldson, pp. 407 ff. Federal Publications, Inc., Chicago.

8

Whistleblowing management accountants: a US view*

Michael K. Shaub and James F. Brown, jr

INTRODUCTION

The accounting profession finds itself in the midst of a rapidly changing ethical environment. In fact, all three branches of the US Government have been examining accountants' ethical decision-making processes. Congressional committee investigations are well documented; in recent years, Congressman John Dingell's House sub-committee investigating the role of the accounting profession has been outspoken on a number of issues, questioning auditors' failure to report fraud outside the company, their independence from companies for whom they perform significant management consulting services, and the commitment of American accounting bodies to implementing the recommendations of groups like the Treadway Commission.

The judicial branch has been confronted with front-page court cases involving audit failures and financial mismanagement such as the ESM Government Securities Inc. and ZZZZ Best cases. In the ESM case, an audit partner approved five years' worth of fraudulent financial statements while accepting $200,000 in loans from the company, which were never repaid. Initial losses to shareholders totalled $320 million. The ZZZZ Best case was a classic instance of staying one step ahead of the auditor. The carpet cleaning company that cost investors over $100 million never actually had any sales, despite the fact that unaudited revenues of $50 million were reported and the market value of the company exceeded $200 million at one point. Bogus renovation projects were shown to the auditors to keep them from discovering the fraud. Cases like these have been largely responsible for the high level of interest shown by Congress in the accounting profession.

The executive branch has applied pressure to revise accountants' ethical standards through US Justice Department investigations and threatened lawsuits for restraint of trade by the Federal Trade Commission. Several

* Reprinted with permission of MCB University Press Ltd from *Managerial Auditing*, Vol. 7, no. 2, pp. 30–6, where it appeared under the title 'A Case for updating management accountants' ethical standards'.

ethics standards enforced by groups such as the American Institute of Certified Public Accountants (AICPA) have been held by these agencies to inhibit the free exercise of market forces and to promote anti-trust activity. These standards included those prohibiting competitive bidding, advertising, solicitation of clients, and the acceptance of commissions and contingent fees. The accounting profession as a whole, including management accountants, is being evaluated by the public in light of these investigations.

Accountants are beginning to devote considerable time and resources to ethical issues. The AICPA recently restructured its *Code of Professional Conduct* (the AICPA code) based on recommendations made by its Special Committee on Standards of Professional Conduct for Certified Public Accountants (the Anderson Committee). This revision of the code broadened the applicability of a number of ethical rules, bringing under its more comprehensive guidelines almost half of all CPAs who are management accountants.

Accountants recognize a trichotomy of responsibilities in the corporate environment. Management accountants are responsible for maintaining an adequate system of internal accounting controls to ensure fair presentation of financial statements and accurate internal reporting. Internal auditors serve to assure that management accountants (among others) perform their duties in accordance with management's goals, evaluating both the technical accuracy of the recorded amounts and the operational effectiveness of the organization. Finally, external auditors are required to attest to the fair presentation of the financial statements. In the current ethical environment, co-operation among these three important functions has become increasingly important. This chapter will describe one means of achieving more effective integration of these functions – by establishing within the National Association of Accountants' code of ethics requirements that will encourage interaction among the parties.

The purpose of this chapter, then, is threefold. First, one of the primary reasons for restructuring the AICPA code was to increase management accountants' ethical responsibilities; this chapter explains the implications for management accountants of the changes brought about by the issuance of this new code. Second, it recommends revisions to the current management accounting ethical standards included in *Statement on Management Accounting No. 1C, Standards of Ethical Conduct for Management Accountants* that will enable management accountants to integrate more effectively their work with internal and external auditors. Finally, this integration is offered as a constructive alternative to whistleblowing by accountants.

ETHICS AND THE NAA

In 1981 the National Association of Accountants (NAA) published the research study *Towards a Code of Ethics for Management Accountants*. At that time the association realized a need for the adoption of a code of ethics for its general membership but more importantly for the holders of the Certified Management Accountant (CMA) certificate. Discussions took place, studies were completed, and finally in June 1983 the NAA published a code of ethics titled *Standards of Ethical Conduct for Management Accountants*. The four standards of ethical conduct identified were:

1. competence
2. confidentiality
3. integrity
4. objectivity.

In addition, the code suggested courses of action to be followed in resolving situations which resulted in ethical conflict within an organization.

Initially, the NAA relied on voluntary adherence to the code by the members of the organization. However, in October 1984 the NAA Executive Committee voted unanimously to amend the Association's by-laws to reflect the adoption of the *Standards of Ethical Conduct for Management Accountants*. The result of this action was to require compliance with the code as a condition for continuing membership in good standing in the association.

No additional changes have been made in the NAA code of ethics. However, recent efforts on the part of the AICPA to engage in a rigorous programme of self-examination have resulted in further revisions to *The Ethical Standards of the Accounting Profession* which was published in 1966. In 1988 the revised code was adopted. This code has implications for management accountants that will be discussed in the next section.

CURRENT DEVELOPMENTS IN ETHICAL GUIDELINES FOR ACCOUNTANTS

The NAA's *Standards of Ethical Conduct* consist of four standards covering competence, confidentiality, integrity, and objectivity, as well as guidelines for the resolution of ethical conflict. Similar rules exist in the AICPA code to the NAA's four standards. The resolution of conflict guidelines are covered under the 'Objectivity and independence' standard in the AICPA code.

The obvious difference in independence requirements between accountants employed in the public and private sectors has led many management accountants to believe that the old AICPA code has limited applicability for them. However, the new AICPA code makes most of its rules applicable to all AICPA members whether they are public accountants or management accountants.

THE ANDERSON COMMITTEE'S ROLE IN RESTRUCTURING ETHICAL STANDARDS

How did these changes develop? The AICPA appointed the Anderson Committee in 1983 to study the relevance of the current professional ethical guidelines 'to professionalism, integrity, and commitment to both quality service and the public interest' (p. 5).[1] This included not only an evaluation of the effects of current ethical standards on the rendering and marketing of professional services by public practitioners, but an assessment of their effect on the large number of CPAs in industry and government as well. One of the five primary means for improving the relevance of the code, in the committee's estimation, was by 'extending the application of standards to members not in public practice' (p. 20).[1] The Anderson Committee was explicit in indicating why they felt the need to expand the coverage of most ethical guidelines to encompass all CPAs:

> The professional activities of CPAs not in public practice are also a concern. The public views the CPA designation as an assurance of objectivity and integrity. As employees of others, CPAs serve as financial executives of business enterprises, as internal auditors, as government auditors, as educators, and in many other roles. In such roles, they may help to provide confidence in, among other things, the integrity of financial reporting, the efficient functioning of capital markets, and the integrity of government programs.
>
> (p. 12)[1]

This is certainly true of holders of both the CMA and CIA certificates.

In addition, auditors must rely on the integrity and co-operation of management accountants to ensure the fair presentation of financial statements and related disclosures. Management accountants are called on by their profession not simply to look out for the best interests of their employer, but for those of society. Integrity and objectivity are qualities that are at least as important for management accountants to possess as they are for auditors. The Anderson Committee attempted to create a *Code of Professional Conduct* that would recognize the importance of the professional accountant in corporations and government, and provide guidelines for those accountants to help them function ethically. Not all of their recommendations are easy to implement; however, they provide a basis for considering how ethical standards governing all management accountants might be expanded.

IMPLICATIONS OF NEW AICPA GUIDELINES FOR MANAGEMENT ACCOUNTANTS

The 'Principles of Professional Conduct'

One of the Anderson Committee's primary goals in reshaping the *Code of Professional Conduct* was to shift the emphasis away from a rule-oriented code towards a code which placed greater reliance on ethical principles. The final result in the code was the inclusion of six basic 'Principles of Professional Conduct':

1. responsibilities
2. the public interest
3. integrity
4. objectivity and independence
5. due care
6. scope and nature of services.

The purpose of these principles was to state ethical goals that professional accountants should strive to attain rather than primarily enforcing ethical rules when accountants fall below a minimum acceptable level of ethical behaviour. The Anderson Committee believed that the goal-oriented nature of the principles would still lead to enforceable tenets. The implications of these six basic 'Principles of Professional Conduct' will now be discussed.

The first article of the 'Principles of Professional Conduct' emphasizes the need for all members of the accounting profession to co-operate in building the public's confidence in the profession's ability to govern itself. Article II underscores the accountant's public interest responsibility and urges the accountant to act with integrity in resolving conflicting pressures from groups that rely on them. Professional accountants do not have the freedom simply to act in their employers' best interests, but must instead be committed to a higher standard of professionalism. Nor can they, according to Article III, place their own personal gain ahead of the public interest. Integrity, as demonstrated by an accountant's honesty and openness, is the basis for the public's reliance on professional accountants' ability to provide objectivity to the preparation and presentation of financial information.

Article IV of the principles concerns this objectivity, as well as the independence standard applicable only to providers of attestation services. Objectivity implies the professional accountant's ability to be impartial and intellectually honest in all situations. This article specifically addresses its applicability to management accountants in this way:

> Regardless of service or capacity, members should protect the integrity of their work, maintain objectivity, and avoid any subordination of their judgment. . . . Members employed by others to prepare financial statements or to perform auditing, tax, or consulting services are charged with the same responsibility for objectivity as members in public practice and must be scrupulous in their application of generally accepted accounting principles and candid in all their dealings with members in public practice.[2]

Thus, AICPA members who are management accountants are being held to the same standards in applying generally accepted accounting principles (GAAP) as the auditors reporting on the financial statements. Management accountants will also be held accountable for any failure to be open with the auditors, within the limits of confidentiality constraints.

Article V discusses the exercise of due care in the conduct of all professional services. The accountant must demonstrate both a competence derived from education and experience and a level of diligence in performing duties that ensures thoroughness, technical accuracy, and ethical forthrightness. In addition, all of the accountants' activities must be adequately planned and supervised. Article VI provides guidelines for those in public practice to determine what types of services they will be able to provide and has no applicability to the management accountant.

Changes in the 'Rules of Professional Conduct'

The AICPA deliberately purposed to broaden the applicability of most ethical standards to cover all of its approximately quarter of a million members, as can be seen from the discussion of the 'Principles of Professional Conduct'. However, the AICPA did not stop with broadening the applicability of the 'Principles of Professional Conduct', but expanded the coverage of the 'Rules of Professional Conduct' as well. This extension was accomplished in part by changing words such as 'engagement' in the old code to 'professional services' in the new code.

The Old Rule 102 covering integrity and objectivity barred all professional accountants from misrepresenting facts knowingly, but prohibited only those in public practice from subordinating their judgement to others. In the current AICPA code, the subordination of judgement rule is extended to management accountants as well. In other words, though management accountants are not independent, they are now required by the AICPA to maintain the same standards of integrity and objectivity as those in public practice. The NAA's *Standards of Ethical Conduct for Management Accountants* similarly require members to 'communicate unfavorable as well as favorable information and professional judgments or opinions' (p. 2).[3]

The Anderson Committee was explicit in its intention to expand the applicability of Rule 201, which covers the general standards of professional competence, due professional care, planning and supervision, and obtaining sufficient relevant data: 'Current Rule 201 applies only to members in practice. The proposed rule uses the term "professional services" instead of "engagements" to make the rule applicable to all AICPA members whether in public practice or not when they perform such services (p. 34).[1] This revised rule makes the professional competence standard parallel the NAA standard. Though due professional care is implied in the NAA's competence standard, the due care principle in the AICPA code goes beyond competence to incorporate a diligence requirement – the accountant must not only be able to do a good job, but must demonstrate that the work performed was that accountant's best effort. This can be accomplished only by fully documenting the thought process used to arrive at the accountant's decision regarding a financial statement amount or disclosure.

Adequate planning and supervision rules have not in the past been applied to management accountants. The AICPA's expansion of this rule to encompass professional accountants outside of public practice means that they will be required to demonstrate the same level of competence as auditors in planning their work and in providing supervision, when necessary, to those employees working for them. Though auditors may be required to prepare audit programmes as part of the evidence of their planning process, this cannot be realistically expected of management accountants for each assignment they confront. Instead, a planning memo or outline of the plan to accomplish a task may be the best means of meeting this requirement for management accountants who are AICPA members. This exercise will be in line with many companies' expectations of their professionals with regard to goal setting and planning. The current NAA ethical rules make no specific reference to planning and supervision.

Management accountants are now required by the new AICPA code to obtain sufficient relevant data to support their conclusions on any assignment. The practical outworking of this requirement for most management accountants will be that they should systematically document their thought processes during the completion of projects, particularly those having any relevance to financial statements or related disclosures. But the rule is evidently being interpreted in a broader sense by the AICPA to encompass any professional service provided by the management accountant. Consequently, documentation should become a habit for management accountants in any kind of decision-making.

The other rules in the AICPA *Code of Professional Conduct* primarily affect public practitioners and would affect the management accountant only if he or she provided those types of services. These include rules regarding confidential client information, contingent fees, advertising, commissions, and the form of practice utilized by the professional. The rule regarding the committing of acts discreditable to the professional continues to apply to management accountants as it always has.

RECOMMENDATIONS FOR CHANGES TO NAA ETHICAL STANDARDS

In light of the leadership position assumed by the NAA in providing direction to management accountants, as well as the changing expectations of society with regard to accountants' ethics, now is an opportune time for the NAA to consider the need to provide more specific ethical guidance to its membership. The first sentence of the NAA's *Standards of Ethical Conduct for Management Accountants* says: 'Management accountants have an obligation to the organizations they serve, their profession, the public, and themselves to maintain the highest standards of ethical conduct' (p. 2).[3] Management accountants are widely recognized for the professional services they provide to the organizations they serve. However, changes in public expectations have brought about changes in the accounting profession, and in the expected role of the accounting profession in society.

Users of financial statements, fairly or unfairly, expect that the auditor who attests to their fair presentation has conducted a thorough search for errors, irregularities, and weaknesses in the company's internal control structure. These same users expect management accountants to be not only people of integrity, but to maintain the same professional and ethical standards as the public auditors and to co-operate fully with them. When auditors' reputations are damaged by front-page revelations of wrongdoing, the reputation of the entire accounting profession is hurt as well. In fact, many financial statement users may hold management accountants even more responsible, seeing them, fairly or unfairly, as perpetrators of the mismanagement of funds rather than as unwilling partners.

In light of the changing expectations of society, it is worth while to consider a revision of the *Standards of Ethical Conduct for Management Accountants*. The current standards accomplish much of what the AICPA's Anderson Committee attempted to achieve, in that they are general in nature and principle-oriented. However, one means of reinforcing the professional image of accountants in private industry would be to provide more specific guidance to those accountants on how to apply the standards.

The proposed additions to the *Standards of Ethical Conduct for Management Accountants* include the following:

1. *A directive to management accountants to be open and candid in all their dealings with public practitioners.* This openness is fundamental to the public's

perception of accountants as professionals. The current standards require full disclosure of relevant information that could be expected to influence users of management accounting reports. However, when set against the strict confidentiality requirements of the current NAA ethical standards, management accountants may hesitate, in certain situations, to be totally straightforward with auditors. Full co-operation between management accountants and auditors is the only way to ensure the fair presentation of financial statements. This does not imply that the management accountant should do the auditor's job, nor does it fail to recognize the potential for honest mistakes or oversights. It does, however, require recognition on the part of both public accountants and management accountants that providing the public users with both relevant and reliable information is extremely critical to the public's perception of an accounting profession which can be labelled as 'ethical'.

2. *A requirement to document fully the accountant's thought processes in arriving at significant management decisions and accounting decisions affecting financial statement amounts and disclosures.* This requirement would help management accountants to strive for higher standards rather than meeting minimum requirements with respect to subordination of judgement, due professional care, planning and supervision, and the gathering of sufficient relevant data. Disagreements between professional accountants over such issues as accounting disclosures should be documented and, if necessary, discussed with the auditors. Documenting thought processes would show that the accountant has both technical competence and a thorough approach to problem solving in fulfilling his or her professional duties. Planning memos would evidence that accountants had taken responsibility for adequately planning projects for which they had significant responsibility, and that they had a strategy for supervising those to whom they had delegated responsibilities. Finally, thorough documentation of the evidence gathered to support management decisions would indicate that the accountant had taken responsibility for assembling enough evidence of sufficient quality to support the decision. The documentation process would help to underscore the professionalism of the accountant, as well as facilitating interaction with government agencies, internal auditors, and external auditors.

3. *A directive to be on the alert for ethical issues that may affect the accountant's ability to perform his or her services objectively and with integrity.* This goes beyond the current approach that only requires the accountant to deal with ethical issues that they happen to encounter in the conduct of their duties. Accountants should take a proactive approach to addressing ethical issues in the corporation and the profession, rather than just meeting a minimum level of acceptable behaviour. A positive search by accountants in their job for potentially significant ethical problems will bolster the public's confidence in the accounting profession's ability to regulate itself.

Management accountants have the professional and technical competence to recognize weaknesses in their companies' internal control structures, and they are in a much better position than the auditor to identify those weaknesses.

The Appendix proposes revisions to the current *Standards of Ethical Conduct for Management Accountants* necessitated by the changes proposed above. The revisions are shown in italics and could serve as an appropriate basis for commenting on the proposals made in this chapter.

BENEFITS OF THE PROPOSED CHANGES

The proposed changes to the *Standards of Ethical Conduct for Management Accountants* will help to accomplish the following goals:

1. *Serve the public interest.* The public interest encompasses all those individuals and entities that rely on the accounting profession for information. Few would deny that the ethical controversies of recent years have been harmful to the accounting profession and to the companies involved. However, greater ethical sensitivity and openness will benefit the public as a whole, including shareholders who lose hundreds of millions of dollars in scams like the ESM Securities and ZZZZ Best cases.
2. *Broaden public confidence in the accounting profession as a whole.* This is no small task in the current environment. In order to enlist the public's support for the profession, accountants must be seen as going beyond the minimum cosmetic changes necessary to get by. The recommended changes set a new tone of co-operation among professional accountants and emphasize the need of management accountants to take an active role in detecting and solving ethical problems.
3. *Demonstrate management accountants' continuing commitment to professional excellence.* Management accountants have long been a valued resource in organizations, and they have extended the accounting profession's reputation for technical and professional excellence into a wide variety of environments. The current environment provides an excellent situation for these accountants to exercise leadership in the attainment of the ethical goals of society and the profession. Corporate expectations will also be fulfilled as the management accountant demonstrates the ability to work with auditors, exhibits skilled approaches to planning, supervising, and documenting projects undertaken, and recognizes weaknesses in the company's internal control structure.
4. *Allow the accounting profession to maintain self-governance and professional certification.* If the federal government determines that intervention in the accounting profession is necessary in order to properly control ethical excesses, all accountants will be harmed. The usefulness of professional certifications will be questioned at the very least, and the potential exists for the federal government to conduct or supervise all audits. A proactive approach by all accountants on all fronts to go beyond minimum ethical standards will help forstall these types of results.

CO-OPERATION AS AN ALTERNATIVE TO WHISTLEBLOWING

Management accountants face a unique dilemma as described in this chapter. They are expected to be loyal to 'the management team' and yet to put the public interest above all else. The pre-eminence of the public interest has been recognized not only in the AICPA code of conduct, but in the courts as well. For example, the *Petermann* v. *International Brotherhood of Teamsters* case created an exception to the employment-at-will doctrine (the employment contract can be terminated by either party at any time and for any reason) for considerations of public policy. The importance of the public interest creates practical problems for the management accountant.

One suggested solution has been to 'blow the whistle' when there is a problem the individual feels should be revealed to the public. Elliston *et al.*[4] indicate that the act of whistleblowing occurs when four conditions are met. First, an individual must perform an action or series of actions intended to make information concerning organizational wrongdoing public. Second, the information must subsequently be made a matter of public record. Third, the information must involve non-trivial wrongdoing by an organization. Lastly, the individual who performs the action must be a member or former member of the organization.

Despite their expressed concern for the public interest, accountants have long opposed whistleblowing. Generally accepted auditing standards have historically required a sequential process of reporting problems such as discovered fraud: first at a higher level of management than the level at which the fraud occurred, then to highest management if co-operation is not forthcoming, then to the audit committee. The recent enactment of Statements on Auditing Standards 60 and 61, however, now require the auditor to communicate 'reportable conditions' in the internal control structure, disagreements with management, and difficulties in performing the audit (e.g. lack of client co-operation) directly to the audit committee. Audit committees are often (and ideally) made up of outside directors who represent the interests of the public. Though auditors are not whistleblowing, their responsibility to the public interest is being recognized in the standards. Members of Congress are urging even more disclosure in light of the recent savings and loan failures.

Whistleblowing has been held by management accountants as indicating disloyalty to the company. Yet the objectivity requirement of the NAA code requires that they 'disclose fully all relevant information that could reasonably be expected to influence an intended user's understanding of the reports, comments, and recommendations presented'. Management accountants may be torn by the conflict between their organizational responsibilities and their professional responsibilities. Whistleblowing may result in censure by both the organization and their professional colleagues.

An atmosphere of co-operation among professionals will not eliminate this tension, but offers the professional accountant a creative alternative to whistleblowing. Many have suggested that if the accountant is not able to solve an ethical dilemma internally, he or she should resign from the company rather than go public. While recognizing that professionals may often have to pay a price to stand for what they believe is right, this approach punishes the person acting with integrity. It also represents a failure on the resigning accountant's part to serve the public interest, though this is overshadowed in most people's minds because the individual seems to suffer the most.

What the public reasonably expects of the accounting profession is co-operation and honesty in working together towards the goal of providing users with fairly presented financial statements. If every segment of the accounting profession wants to be recognized as being 'professionals' all must assume an equal burden in meeting the expectations of the public. A revision of the NAA code similar to the one suggested here offers an approach to communicating to management accountants the importance of co-operation and openness with auditors, which will allow them to meet the professional's responsibility to the public while still effectively serving their employers.

SUMMARY

In short, the current ethical environment in the accounting profession and in society as a whole calls for management accountants to reflect on ways that current ethical standards may be improved. Admittedly, other steps could be taken to increase the co-operation among accountants in their various professional roles. However, this chapter was intended to explain the effects on management accountants of recent changes to AICPA ethical standards, and to suggest changes warranted in NAA standards. It is hoped that this will create a dialogue among management accountants, internal auditors, and external auditors regarding these important issues.

NOTES

1. AICPA (1986) *Restructuring Professional Standards to Achieve Professional Excellence in a Changing Environment*, AICPA, New York.
2. AICPA (1988) *Code of Professional Conduct*, AICPA, New York, p. 6.
3. National Association of Accountants (1983) *Statement on Management Accounting No. 1C, Standards of Ethical Conduct for Management Accountants*, NAA, New York.
4. Elliston, F., Keenan, J., Lockhart, P. and van Schaick, J. (1985) *Whistleblowing Research: Methodological and Moral Issues*, Praeger New York, p. 15.

APPENDIX: SUGGESTED CHANGES IN THE NATIONAL ASSOCIATION OF ACCOUNTANTS' STANDARDS OF ETHICAL CONDUCT FOR MANAGEMENT ACCOUNTANTS (RECOMMENDED CHANGES ARE ITALICIZED)

Management accountants have an obligation to the organizations they serve, their profession, the public, and themselves to maintain the highest standards of ethical conduct. In recognition of this obligation, the National Association of Accountants has promulgated the following standards of ethical conduct for management accountants. Adherence to these standards is integral to achieving the *Objectives of Management Accounting*. Management accountants shall not commit acts contrary to these standards nor shall they condone the commission of such acts by others within their organizations.

Competence
Management accountants have a responsibility to:

- Maintain an appropriate level of professional competence by ongoing development of their knowledge and skills.
- Perform their professional duties in accordance with relevant laws, regulations, and technical standards. *This should include an active, ongoing search for potential internal control weaknesses.*
- Prepare complete and clear reports and recommendations after appropriate analyses of relevant and reliable information.
- *Fully document the accountant's thought processes in arriving at significant management decisions and accounting decisions affecting financial statement amounts and disclosures.*

Confidentiality
Management accountants have a responsibility to:

- Refrain from disclosing confidential information acquired in the course of their work except when authorized *or when dealing with public practitioners engaged by the organization*, unless legally obligated to do so.
- Inform subordinates as appropriate regarding the confidentiality of information acquired in the course of their work and monitor their activities to assure the maintenance of that confidentiality.
- Refrain from using or appearing to use confidential information acquired in the course of their work for unethical or illegal advantage either personally or through third parties.

Integrity
Management accountants have a responsibility to:

- Avoid actual or apparent conflicts of interest and advise all appropriate parties of any potential conflict.
- Refrain from engaging in any activity that would prejudice their ability to carry out their duties ethically.
- Refuse any gift, favour, or hospitality that would influence or would appear to influence their actions.
- Refrain from either actively or passively subverting the attainment of the organization's legitimate and ethical objectives.
- Communicate unfavourable as well as favourable information and professional judgements or opinions.
- Refrain from engaging in or supporting any activity that would discredit the profession.

Objectivity
Management accountants have a responsibility to:

- Communicate information fairly and objectively.
- Disclose fully all relevant information that could reasonably be expected to influence an intended user's understanding of the reports, comments, and recommendations presented.

9

Enough is enough:
an employer's view – the Pink affair

Gerald Vinten

This chapter presents an unprecedented employer's view of 'whistle-blowing', and it therefore fills a significant gap. Whistleblowers sometimes become folk heroes, and this has certainly been the case with Graham Pink. The press has tended to portray the employer in satanic robes, and neglected to tell the employer's story. As there is both valid and invalid, ethical and unethical whistleblowing (and much that is in between), caution is necessary in relating these events.

Mr Pink's sincerity has not been questioned, but his conduct has, which raises some interesting ethical questions. For example, what was the opportunity cost of Mr Pink's lengthy campaign, especially in terms of diverting attention and resources from patient care? It is unusual for an employer in such a situation to offer redeployment, but that is what happened here. Mr Pink had complained that he wanted to be able to give more concentrated patient care, and this is what he was offered – care on a one-to-one basis. He refused the offer, being prepared to accept nothing less than reinstatement in his old job, even though not all the staff were happy to work with him again.

Was the rejection tempered by pride, or should it be called a sense of dignity? Was Mr Pink's unwillingness to compromise or negotiate unreasonable, or understandable in the circumstances? How far should an employer be expected to go to deal with an employee who disagrees with management policy? At what point should an employee consider that the concern has received sufficient airing? Was Mr Pink unwilling to take on the managerial necessity of operating within resource constraints? Was it legitimate to use Stockport as an occasion to mount a campaign that some perceived as being a direct attack on the government? Is it part of a mature democracy to be able so to do? The following account, put together from documentary sources, press, television and personal interviews, tries to answer such questions.

In view of the numerous occasions that Mr Pink has now violated the most precious rights still left to the elderly (namely dignity, privacy and above all confidentiality) by his articles in the press, I would be grateful if you would consider removing him from this ward, therefore ensuring that the 'most vulnerable members of our society' [Mr Pink's own phrase] are indeed afforded the respect they deserve instead of being pawns in his campaign.

It was with these words, in 1990, that a ward sister summed up her feelings – and those of other nurses – at Stepping Hill Hospital's Care of the Elderly Unit, about the publicity generated by Mr Pink. Three years later, as Mr Pink attempted to open up yet another chapter of accusations (this time targeting medical staff at the hospital), it was decided that no further discussion would be entered into with Mr Pink on the matter of general standards of care for the elderly. Enough was enough.

This was the end of a long saga which took place between 1989 and 1993. One version of what happened may be traced through the headlines generated by Mr Pink. What it was like to be on the receiving end of such a sustained campaign is the subject of this chapter.

BACKGROUND

In 1989 Graham Pink, a nurse at Stockport Health Authority's Stepping Hill Hospital, embarked on a massive campaign involving hundreds of letters, articles, radio interviews and television appearances, about night-nurse staffing levels on the hospital's three-ward acute Care of the Elderly Unit. As evidence of inadequate staffing levels, Mr Pink employed harrowing descriptions of neglect suffered by elderly patients which, he claimed, was even putting their lives at risk. Managers on the unit did not accept Mr Pink's descriptions of the care given to patients, nursing colleagues protested to their managers and unions about them and independent National Health Service (NHS) patient watchdogs who visited the wards found no evidence to support them.

Until joining Stepping Hill Hospital, Mr Pink had not nursed acutely ill elderly patients. He trained as a nurse in the mid-fifties and, after two-and-a-half years' nursing, had left the profession for a career in teaching. After 30 years as a schoolteacher he returned to nursing. He held a variety of posts in Manchester where his experience was mainly in plastic surgery. While Mr Pink was to become 'Britain's best-known NHS whistleblower' (*The Daily Telegraph*, 16 March 1993), the long experience of the authority, the unit's managers and nursing staff, and their persistent attempts to air their views, went largely unheeded by the media. Only one journalist actually visited the wards.

Despite his four-year campaign – which was time consuming and costly for the authority and its staff, damaging to the morale of an excellent acute elderly unit and distressing to elderly people – staffing levels in 1993 on the wards about which he complained were substantially the same as in 1989, despite rigorous appraisal of the allegations levelled by Mr Pink.

The impression given in the media was that Mr Pink was disciplined for 'blowing the whistle' about conditions on the wards at night at Stepping Hill

Hospital. This was not the case. He was disciplined for breach of patient confidentiality: it is crucial that every healthworker respects a patient's privacy at all times.

SEQUENCE OF EVENTS

Graham Pink was employed on nights as a block charge nurse on 3 August 1987 in the three-ward Care of the Elderly Unit. A block charge nurse has a 'floating' role between set wards to provide supervision and expertise, to assist with particular procedures, to support junior staff in organizing their work, and to help out on the wards when necessary. Although not permanently ward based until 1990, Pink spent a number of successive nights working a full shift on Ward A14 in August 1989.

Mr Pink's many complaints to his managers during his time as a night block charge nurse related specifically to the inadequacies of his day-shift colleagues in failing to achieve his own perceived standards in such areas as filling in drug and nursing kardexes and name bands, giving handover reports, washing medicine glasses and removing teacups from lockers at the end of the shift. His first letter of complaint about staff shortages was to Stockport Health Authority's chairman on 24 August 1989, shortly after working continuously on one ward for a few nights instead of 'floating' between three.

The chairman was on annual leave when Pink's letter arrived, but the chief executive visited the ward that night. Despite the lack of visual evidence – but with no reason not to believe the word of this mature and dignified nurse (a magistrate and retired teacher) – the chief executive pledged: 'Something will have to be done.' He then requested from the hospital's general manager an assessment of the adequacy of night-staff cover on the unit.

On his return from leave, the chairman spent four hours visiting the wards on the night of 16 September, and he discussed the subject of staffing levels with Pink. Like the chief executive, he had been deeply disturbed by Pink's description of patient care, but did not find corroborating evidence on the wards. His reservations were reflected in his response to MP Tom Arnold's inquiry to the authority following a letter of complaint he had received from Pink. In his reply to Arnold on 20 October, the chairman wrote:

> I spoke to every member of staff on duty and, whilst all said they were under considerable pressure at times, there was very little support for the views expressed by Mr Pink. I am not dismissing Mr Pink's complaint and I have asked for a thorough investigation of the position but, at the moment, I am treating it with some caution.

There are always two sides to a story. The problem for Stockport Health Authority was that here was an individual with a personal view of a situation which others did not share; yet the reporting of his stories in the national and local press evoked such an intensity of response that it utterly overwhelmed any attempt by the authority to say 'not so'.

Despite Pink's repeated claims that nothing was done to address his allegations, and that was why he was forced to go to the press, his allegations were
thoroughly investigated: night staffing levels were reviewed; a number of
meetings took place; inquiries about acute elderly wards outside Stockport
confirmed similar night staffing levels; and on 28 September a special panel
(made up of non-executive authority members) visited night staff. On 23
October the assistant general manager and senior nurse manager met with
Pink to discuss his points, and the following day the assistant general manager met with night sisters and charge nurses for further discussion on night
staffing. Meanwhile, letters passed between Pink and his managers, and on 14
November Stepping Hill Hospital's assistant general manager wrote to Pink:

> I am writing to you to summarise the meeting [of 23 October], and the correspon-
> dence we have had with each other, regarding the levels of nursing care in the
> geriatric area at Stepping Hill Hospital on night duty. In my opinion, the points at
> issue could be summarised by the following question: 'Are patients being put at
> risk by the staffing levels on night duty in the geriatric area?'
>   It is obvious that we both have different answers to this question. You will recall
> at our meeting, when I clearly stated that whilst staffing levels were not in my
> opinion ideal, I felt they compared favourably with the staffing levels available in
> other geriatric wards throughout the district. It would be nice to be able to im-
> prove staffing levels in all specialties if this were possible. However, I am con-
> fident that the best possible use is being made of existing resources.
>   I would confirm my statement to you, that it is not possible to increase the
> staffing levels in the geriatric area at night, without depleting levels of staff in
> other areas.

The letter concluded with a reminder on how to acquire assistance on the
ward during particularly busy periods and the request that he keep in close
contact with his night-nurse manager.

It is standard practice at Stepping Hill that, if a ward becomes especially
busy at night (e.g. when one of the other nurses is on a meal break, during
emergency admissions, bereavement counselling for relatives, etc.), nurses
are expected to telephone the night-nurse manager or night sister, who will
go to assess the ward and either

1. assist
2. send a nurse from another area of the hospital; or
3. send a bank (relief) nurse.

The key element of this system is that the night-nurse manager or night sister
assesses levels of care and demands placed on nurses by patients throughout
the hospital every night. Pink was again requested to take this course of action
in the following months, but there is no evidence that he did so.

The question therefore arises for an employer: What do you do when you
have listened to a complaint, have investigated it, found little or no evidence
to support it, explained your findings to the complainant, advised him what
action to take if he finds himself unable to cope with the situation on the
ward, and he still goes on writing letters of complaint to everyone from
hospital managers to union officials, MPs, the Secretary of State for Health
and the Prime Minister? The volume of correspondence was monumentally

time consuming for authority staff, as the people who received letters from Pink wrote in their turn to the authority for an explanation. Each received a reply, often with an invitation to visit the wards.

Early in April 1990 an MP (who had neither contacted the authority nor visited the wards) took, with Pink's approval, a quantity of Pink's extensive correspondence to the *Guardian*. The newspaper published an edited selection on 11 April. Out of 14 leters quoted, 11 were from Pink, and the three items from the authority gave little indication of the efforts made to address Pink's complaints.

If, as has been claimed, Stockport Health Authority had been vindictive, and had tried to punish him 'for going to the media,' they could have done something then. Instead, staff spent a great deal of time reassuring newly admitted patients and relatives that there was no cause for anxiety, and replying at length to incensed members of the public around the country that conditions at Stepping Hill's acute elderly wards were not as portrayed in the *Guardian* and inviting them to visit to see for themselves. The general manager and assistant general manager also met with Pink and asked him not to seek any more publicity because of the unnecessary distress it was causing prospective patients and their relatives.

Three months after the article in the *Guardian*, an incident occurred on Ward A14 involving Pink and a patient. It was Pink's publicizing of this event which was to be the turning point. Pink has always insisted that he has only ever told the truth. On this occasion there were a number of versions:

1. What he wrote in the official nursing record (kardex) shortly after the incident.
2. What Pink told fellow ward staff shortly after the patient complained to them.
3. What he told the night-nurse manager the following day, after the patient's relative had complained.
4. What he wrote on the accident form.
5. The account he published in a local newspaper, which led to suspension and the charge of breach of patient confidentiality.

The sequence of events leading up to this seems to be the following.

In the early hours of 15 July 1990, while on duty with Pink, an enrolled nurse and an auxiliary nurse had gone to attend to a patient. The patient said to them, 'Please don't let me fall again'. Both were surprised as they knew nothing of a fall, and asked what had happened. The patient indicated Pink and said, 'That man let me fall'. When they asked charge nurse Pink about it, he led them to understand that the patient had 'not fallen but had slipped and Mr Pink had lowered him to the floor'. He was asked if he had filled out an accident form, and replied, 'Not yet'. Later that day a relative complained to a member of the day staff that her father had just told her he had had a fall during the night. The night-nurse manager was advised of the relative's complaint when she came on duty, and she went to see Pink at 1 a.m. on 16 July. Pink told her that, as he went towards the patient, 'he was at the side of his bed and was sliding to the floor'.

All falls, accidents or incidents of any kind must be noted on the patient's kardex (nursing record) and a 'Report of accidents or other untoward occurrences to patients, staff, or any other persons on the premises' form (known simply as 'an accident form') should be filled in. The night-nurse manager instructed him to fill in an accident form.

On the patient's kardex, which Pink had filled in at 5 a.m. on 15 July, he had written, 'Mr— had a quiet, restful night'. On the accident form, which he completed on 16 July after his interview with the night-nurse manager, he wrote, 'Mr— stood out of bed to use a bottle and slid to the floor'. On 25 July, however, the *Stockport Express Advertiser* carried yet another version, when it published a front-page article and inside double-spread on Pink's lonely crusade, claiming: 'Since August 24 1989 he has written close on one hundred letters. He suffered condescension, vilification, smears, bullying, disdain and what amounts to demotion. He has never cracked, this is why. . . .'

What followed was Pink's version of events on Ward A14 from 4.30 a.m. on 15 July. There were two other nurses on duty that night with Pink, an enrolled nurse and an auxiliary nurse (both with longer experience nursing the elderly than Pink) – but at 4.30 one nurse was on her break in the dayroom, only seconds away. However, Pink claimed: 'Forty yards away, at the other end of the corridor and out of earshot, the only other person on duty is looking after the other 13 beds.' In fact, the area between the two sides of the ward is the nurses' station not a 'corridor', and the distance is 20 feet, not 40 yards (the entire ward measuring only 30 yards).

In the article he describes the patients by age, sex and medical condition (all immediately identifiable to other staff) and among them was Mr—, only here his fall, or 'slide' or 'slip to the floor', takes on a new and distressing dimension. According to Pink the staffing levels were so low, and he was so busy with another patient, that he was unable to get to Mr— when he called out. Having settled the other patient, Pink can now go to his aid:

> Little time has elapsed [since he called out] but the dying man is not in bed. He is lying on the ward floor in a pool of urine, crying. . . . His humiliation and pain are among the last things he is to experience. He dies three days later. . . . Why should a man have to be left lying, crying, on the ground in a flood of urine? Why will the authorities still not accept that, if staffing levels on the geriatric wards at Stepping Hill are not legally inadequate, they are morally inadequate? It offends everything I know to be right as a nurse and as a human being.

This incident was, Pink later claimed, the catalyst which drove him to his sustained publicity campaign over the next three years and he repeated it endlessly. Yet in the official nursing record Pink wrote, 'Mr— had a quiet, restful night'. Then there was the patient's own statement to a relative that, when he had repeated his call for assistance, Pink had gone over to him and said, 'I heard you once, don't call again'.

The newspaper article was devastating for immediate members of the patient's close-knit family. It was published the day after his funeral and they did not see it. But friends of the family did, so identifiable were the details Pink had given of the patient's age, sex, medical condition, ward and date of death, and they brought it to the family's attention. A relative made a formal complaint on 31 July. Pink was suspended on full pay on 9 August.

His disciplinary hearing, conducted by the general manager in accordance with NHS agreed procedures, was held on 12 and 29 October and 20 November 1990. The reason for the delay between suspension and disciplinary hearing was to allow more time for Pink to brief the Royal College of Nursing (RCN – the main nursing union) which took up his case at national level after he approached them. Until then he had not been a member of a trade union or any staff association. The support of the RCN's national and regional officers, who ignored the protests and views of its Stockport branch, angered local union members to the extent that they issued a joint press statement with the National Union of Public Employees (NUPE) distancing themselves from Pink's accusations.

The hearing upheld allegations on four charges, including breach of patient confidentiality. Although the hearing was formally and properly constituted, Pink, despite being given every opportunity to put his case through an experienced RCN representative, claimed in the media that it was a 'kangaroo court' and appealed. His appeal was originally planned for January 1991. However, he abandoned his RCN representative after the hearing and switched to the Confederation of Health Service Employees (COHSE). They requested extra time to prepare for the appeal and the authority made every attempt to accommodate them, even offering to convene during evenings and weekends, which was refused.

His appeal finally took place on 22, 23, 29 and 30 April and 8 July 1991. The appeal panel – chaired by the Health Authority's vice-chairman (a practising solicitor and experienced tribunal chairman) and assisted by authority members and an external assessor – upheld allegations on three of the four charges, including breach of confidentiality. The general manager took the view that, while he did not agree with Pink's claims about staffing levels, nor with his method of drawing attention to them, he was nevertheless genuine in his claim to have patients' well-being – especially the dying – uppermost in his mind. As an alternative to dismissal, Pink was offered a post in the community, giving respite care to patients in their own homes at night to allow stressed relatives a much-needed break.

THE PRESS RESPONSE

The press and national professional associations made little attempt to check Pink's version of events. Pink provided a ready-made platform from which to air individual opinions: about the government (politically the NHS is considered fair game, especially as a general election was approaching); about 'the crisis in nursing' (the RCN was launching its Whistleblow Scheme and ignored the views of its Stockport branch); about the erosion of trade-union rights (Pink wasn't a member of any until he was suspended); and about freedom of information and violation of rights (some rights organizations seem to feel no obligation to consider both sides of an allegation).

Despite the thousands of words published on the iniquities of Stepping Hill Hospital's Care of the Elderly Unit, only one newspaper made the effort to see for itself. A *Daily Mirror* journalist visited A14 at night shortly after the *Guardian* article appeared, reported Pink's allegations, offered no evidence to support them and wrote: 'A14 was bright and cheerful. Cards with messages of appreciation covered a notice board. Mr Pink had a qualified nurse with him, and they did their jobs with concentration and a kind word for everyone. It was a quiet night' (18 June 1990).

The *Guardian* did not visit the wards and their staff. As David Brindle, the journalist who edited Pink's file of correspondence in the article on 11 April, explained: 'I found a very special combination of factors which made me realize straightaway that here was something that would make a very, very, very good package for us. . . . The response was enormous . . . it was the most enormous response I have experienced in fifteen years of journalism' (BBC 2 *40 Minutes* television programme, 'Dear Mr Pink', broadcast 28 April 1992). *The Nursing Times* did not visit, despite giving the most protracted coverage to virtually every angle of the Pink case. The *Stockport Express Advertiser*, which had published the article on 25 July 1990 which led to the formal complaint and disciplinary action, also saw no reason to visit the wards.

After protests by the chief executive to the RCN about its public statements on the authority's handling of the case, the union's general secretary, Christine Hancock, described 'the Graham Pink case' in a letter to him in February 1992, as a *'cause célèbre'* and of 'national, almost symbolic importance.' She concluded:

> I am afraid that in a climate where employers have introduced confidentiality clauses forbidding staff to talk to the press; where nurses who raise legitimate concerns about staffing levels are met with inaction; and where there is widespread perception that quality of patient care is not the number one priority in the Health Service; that Graham Pink's case will continue to serve to illustrate underlying tensions.

The chief executive pointed out to Christine Hancock that Stockport did not have a confidentiality clause forbidding staff to talk to the press; it had met Pink's concerns with full investigation; and Stockport had numerous quality-of-patient-care initiatives. There seemed to be a lack of interest in publishing anything Stockport had to say, if it contradicted Pink.

When the authority's chief nursing officer undertook a review of staffing levels and published a report confirming that existing staffing levels provided adequate care and safety for patients, *The Nursing Times* published its own report, commissioned from 'one of the leading authorities on skill mix' and based on Pink's analysis of the ward, 'proving' Stockport's staff levels were inadequate. Invited to visit Stockport and discuss its report, the then editor, Linda Davidson, wrote: 'I must say that I have serious reservations about the usefulness of such a meeting to discuss the expert's analysis. What could we really achieve?' (11 September 1990). Stepping Hill Hospital nurses complained in a press statement in May 1992: 'We don't understand why the media prefers the views of one former nurse to those of the large number of nurses actually working in the unit.'

Two organizations did visit, the Stockport Community Health Council and the Health Advisory Service. The former is an independent NHS patient watchdog. Its members made three night visits during 1990 – one on 6 June, and two (unannounced) on 16 August and 2 September – and found no evidence to support Pink's claims. The Health Advisory Service is an independent body which periodically visits hospitals to assess services for the mentally ill and the elderly, and reports directly to the Secretary of State for Health. Its team visited Stockport for three weeks in August 1991 (by which time a fourth ward had been added to the unit) and the following extract from its report, *Services for Mentally Ill People and for Elderly People in the Stockport Health District*, published in December 1991, relates to the Care of the Elderly Unit: 'The quality of care provided on the acute elderly admission wards at Stepping Hill Hospital is particularly impressive. These are four extremely busy acute admissions wards, satisfactorily staffed by day and night and delivering a level of service which meets the high standards expected.' Pink had been maintaining in the press as late as 25 September 1991 (*Nursing Standard*) that 'It is sad that having spent two years trying to improve the care of these elderly and frail patients, I have achieved nothing.' When the 'particularly impressive' quote was published in December, Pink responded by questioning the rigour of the team's inspection (*Manchester Evening News*, 10 March 1992).

On 20 January 1992, Pink was presented with the 1991 Freedom of Information Award 'for drawing attention to poor standards within the National Health Service' (*The Nursing Times*). In February the chief executive inquired how Pink was nominated, and what efforts were made to verify his information, given that no one had taken the trouble to contact the health authority. On 11 August the Campaign for Freedom of Information advised by telephone that the campaign itself had decided to nominate Pink on the basis of the information and correspondence they had seen, and confirmed it had not contacted the authority for comment on whether or not the position was as presented by Pink. Pressed further, the director of the campaign confirmed on 7 September: 'We studied a dossier of approximately 1,000 pages of correspondence and documentation supplied to us by Mr Pink.'

On 7 November 1992 the *Guardian* published a two-page launch of a series of five Charter 88 pamphlets under the banner *Violations of Rights in Britain*. Pamphlet 3 was by Pink, and was reproduced almost in full, including his by-now standard allegations about Stockport's neglect of elderly patients and his account of his disciplinary procedure. The only reason the authority knew this was being published was that the previous afternoon a radio station rang to ask what the authority thought about it. The chief executive immediately rang the *Guardian*'s editor, Peter Preston, and expressed the view that it was inappropriate to publish an article about Stockport Health Authority without offering a right of reply. Preston told him he didn't have a right of reply.

On 11 November the chief executive wrote to the co-ordinator of Charter 88 asking what steps were taken to verify the claims made by Pink. After a telephone call and a further letter requesting an answer, Pam Giddy, editor, *Violations of Rights in Britain*, Charter 88, replied on 11 January: 'We do not believe that there was anything in the Violation paper written by Graham Pink which had not already been published in one form or another.' For an organization dedicated to violations of rights in Britain, it is a quaint assumption that prior publication renders verification unnecessary.

Indifference to anything Stockport might have to say was not limited to its management. On 29 April 1992 the RCN Congress at Blackpool had Pink as the speaker at its crowded lunchtime fringe meeting. He repeated his well-known allegations about Stockport to rapturous applause and then began to answer questions. Bravely, given the almost unanimous support there for Pink, a nurse from Stockport's Care of the Elderly Unit (and also the RCN steward for the union's Stockport branch) stood up to ask him why the first time she was aware of his allegations was by opening the *Guardian*, and why he had not approached her at the time, or joined the union then.

Pink answered, but when the nurse attempted another question, the chair, Norah Casey (also editor of the RCN's journal *Nursing Standard*) silenced her with an ultimate irony:

> We're not here to discuss the semantics of joining an organization. The purpose of this seminar was to talk about gagging clauses and whistleblowing as an issue. If we sit here and talk about my ward appearing in newspapers before anywhere else, or whether Stepping Hill Hospital has a bad reputation as a result, we are going to get nowhere. *It isn't about Stepping Hill.*

Thus was a senior nurse and long-time union member – who had just listened to Pink comparing the ward she worked on with prisons and death camps – effectively gagged by a member of her own union, in favour of someone who only joined after suspension for breaching one of nursing's fundamental principles, and who abandoned its representation halfway through the disciplinary process in favour of another union. To the staff at Stepping Hill Hospital it was very much 'about Stepping Hill'.

Pink made an interesting admission at the meeting when he commented:

> I, of course, overstepped the mark, I admit it . . . Er . . . I have said things in my letters, I've written to people and I had no right to do so and some of the things, I have said I could possibly have been had for libel, I'm sure that's true. But I was so incensed at what was happening and I was so disturbed that nobody seemed interested.

The chief executive had visited Pink on duty and it had been a quiet night. The chairman had visited Pink on duty and it had been a quiet night. A *Daily Mirror* reporter had visited and it was a quiet night. The general manager of the hospital spent a night on the ward with Pink and it was a quiet night. A BBC television camera team spent two nights filming on the unit, and they were quiet nights. The Stockport Community Health Council made three night inspections, two of them unannounced, and they were quiet nights.

This is not for a moment to deny that there are periods when a number of circumstances combine to produce a situation where the ward staff cannot respond to all of the demands being made on them. It is on just such occasions that the responsible nurse on duty is expected to telephone the night-nurse manager for assistance.

There appears to be a popular assumption that nursing the elderly is unrewarding, depressing and even futile. Yet nurses actively choose to nurse elderly people, have special training and take a progressive approach to care with the emphasis on rehabilitation and returning patients home. Patients do die – many are in their eighties and nineties and acutely ill – but the noticeboards on the wards are testimony to relatives' gratitude for the care they have received. As the noticeboards also bear witness, from equally grateful relatives, many also recover and return home with an improved quality of life.

Forty-two ward staff were moved to write to the media in their own defence in May 1992:

> Most of us nursed patients on these wards long before Mr Pink arrived, and we continue this work, of which we are very proud, day and night, despite the denigration of the Unit in the media. Conditions at the Unit have never been as Mr Pink describes them. Our patients have always been well cared for and every effort made to support and help their carers and families. It is an insult to our professionalism to suggest that we would do otherwise. . . . His repeated assertions that we support him, and would 'speak out' about staffing levels and poor care but are afraid to do so, are totally untrue. He does not, and has never had, our support. We disassociated ourselves from his opinions from the outset.

Pink has always claimed that he has never had anything but praise for his fellow night staff. There is, however, implicit in his descriptions of their wards a condemnation of the nurses who staff them. As Pink put it in the *40 Minutes* television programme, 'Dear Mr Pink', broadcast on BBC2 on 28 April 1992, 'They work because they need to. I'm sure they enjoy what they're doing and they're very good nurses, but they're there because they need the money.'

In January 1993 he was the profession's 'best-known whistleblower' and was voted on to the UK Central Council for Nursing, Midwifery and Health Visiting (UKCC), the governing body of the nursing profession. Among his first statements after election was, 'I plan to pursue those who decided no action is to be taken over the nurse managers I reported for misconduct' (*The Nursing Times*, 3 February 1993).

INDUSTRIAL TRIBUNAL

On 24 January 1992, the *Metro News* reported that Pink would be taking Stockport Health Authority to an industrial tribunal and that he would be represented by an eminent QC, 'the George Carman of industrial tribunals'. Henceforth, almost every article published by or about Pink included a plea for donations to be sent to his compaign fund in London to pay his legal costs. For Stockport Health Authority the industrial tribunal had represented a simple case of breach of patient confidentiality. Normally an industrial tribunal takes one-and-a-half days with the applicant represented by a full-time officer from the union. Ten days were booked and the documentation presented to the tribunal numbered over 2,000 pages. For months beforehand, and right up to the evening before the tribunal began on 15 March 1993, attempts were made by Stockport to reach a settlement. At the heart of the case were two basic principles – one about protecting patient confidentiality, the other about the need to speak out when patients' safety is put at risk – which Pink claimed were irreconcilable, but which the authority claimed were not.

The first principle, patient confidentiality, is enshrined in the UKCC's *Code of Professional Conduct* (2nd edn), which requires (Clause 9) nurses to

Respect confidential information obtained in the course of professional practice and refrain from disclosing such information without the consent of the patient, or a person entitled to act on his/her behalf, except where disclosure is required by law or by the order of a court or is necessary in the public interest.

In the authority's standard employment form, Clause 14 states: 'If in the course of duty an employee comes into the possession of information regarding patients and their illness such information should be regarded as in confidence and as such not divulged to anyone who does not have the right to this information. Contravention will result in dismissal.'

The second principle, safety of patients, also covered by the UKCC's *Code of Professional Conduct* (2nd edn), requires that a nurse 'Act always in such a way as to promote and safeguard the well being and interests of patients' (Clause 1) and '. . . make known to appropriate persons or authorities any circumstances which could place patients in jeopardy or which militate against safe standards of practice' (Clause 10). Stockport Health Authority's view was that it is possible to satisfy the latter principle without breaching the former. The two possible mechanisms for this – adequate anonymization or informed consent – are well recognized in professional codes.

Despite the authority's best endeavours to speed up the process, most of the first five days of the tribunal were lost in delays and adjournments. The second five days saw the general manager on the stand being questioned repetitively, line by line, about four-year-old correspondence as Pink's QC attempted to establish a defence. The issue of breach of patient confidentiality had become irrelevant. The authority had 14 more witnesses. It was predicted that at this rate the tribunal would go on for a further eight to ten weeks and cost an additional £250,000 – raising total expenditure to £340,000. The authority, with great reluctance, conceded a technicality in the disciplinary process and withdrew. And so it was back to the media for Pink. If his versions of the incident involving the patient seem contradictory, his versions as to whether or not he had committed a breach of patient confidentiality seem no less so.

In his Charter 88 pamphlet he had claimed: 'There was no breach of confidentiality. I did not give the patient's name nor any information by which he could be identified.'

On BBC Radio 4's *The World Tonight* on 6 June 1993, Pink said:

Yes, my terms of engagement make it perfectly clear that I must not go outside the hospital to speak to anyone about anything. It's quite clear, it says if you do this you will be dismissed. Not that you *might* be dismissed. So Stockport, certainly, was acting quite correctly by its own rules.

On local radio station GMR, *At Five*, on 21 June 1993, Pink appeared to have lost track of the concept of breach of patient confidentiality altogether:

> *Allan Beswick*: They say that the information you gave allowed that patient to be identified, indeed the relatives of that patient complained exactly thus.
> *Graham Pink*: But the relatives already knew about the situation.
> *Allan Beswick*: Notwithstanding that, you went public, that's what was wrong, according to them.
> *Graham Pink*: Yes, but you can't break confidentiality if you are revealing something to a person who already knows it and that if that person who already knows it is a direct relative. Now what it says in my terms of employment is you must not reveal information to people who do not have a right to it, but surely the relatives of a dead patient have every right to know what happened, so if they were to look at that closely they would see that in no way would it be said that I had broken confidentiality.

There was no way the authority could match the intensity of Pink's campaign. Suspended on full pay from August 1990 until September 1991 he appeared to spend all his time generating publicity. For instance, on 21 November 1990, the day after his disciplinary hearing ended, a local paper carried banner headlines, 'PINK RAPS "HOSPITAL SEX" SLUR' (*Stockport Express Advertiser*, 21 November 1990), an irrelevance with no bearing on the Hearing but which was guaranteed to attract a headline or two. The story was picked up nationally the next day. Five days before his appeal was due to start, 'HEALTH CHIEF IN NEW PINK SLUR' (*Stockport Express Advertiser*, 17 April 1991) and 'JOB "SLUR" FURY OF A BATTLING NURSE' (*Manchester Evening News*, 17 April 1991) appeared.

He exhibited a similar flair after his appeal failed. As the authority awaited his decision whether to accept or decline the alternative post, newspapers, nursing journals and local radio carried the dramatic news, 'Whistleblower Graham Pink collapsed last week and blames his illness on stress caused by his appeal hearing' (*The Nursing Times*, 24 July 1991). He also claimed for the first time that he had collapsed during the disciplinary hearing the previous year.

During his illness, which prevented him conveying his decision to the authority all through July, August and into September, he threatened the authority's chairman with legal proceedings for libel, began an appeal with the North West Regional Health Authority, participated in radio programmes (including attending the BBC's Manchester studios) and gave interviews to at least seven newspapers telling them that he would not be accepting the alternative post.

ISSUES RAISED

There seems to be an automatic assumption among some media, and thus among the public, that a whistleblower is the one individual in an organization brave enough to tell, at whatever personal cost, a truth known to other, but less courageous souls. Pink's former colleagues, angered by the likening of their wards to prisons and death camps, were moved to write to the media, 'We have not experienced the difficulties in caring for patients on these wards that Mr Pink claims to have had.'

Surely there is a requirement, before the automatic acceptance of a whistleblower's 'facts', not only to check the circumstances claimed but also the whistleblower's credentials. Before accepting him or her as an expert is it not necessary to look at the whistleblower's own experience, work history, how many posts held, for how long and reasons for leaving? Why were the press and other publicists so ready to accept Pink's version and so unwilling to go to look for themselves?

Pink is regularly quoted putting a monetary figure on what it has cost Stockport Health Authority to fight him, and that it should have capitulated immediately and devoted these sums to patient care. Much of the cost of Pink, however, is not quantifiable in financial terms. The massive correspondence, the lengthy investigations, dealings with the media and preparation for the industrial tribunal, were simply an added burden to the managers concerned.

Nor is it possible to speak in money terms of the effect on morale among the nursing staff who saw their wards, and their professional standards, denigrated week by week in respected nursing journals, and even day by day in the local and national press, on radio and on television. Nurses from Stockport's Care of the Elderly Unit attending external courses and seminars would have delegates from around the country peering at their identity badges and saying, 'Stockport? Isn't that where they've got those terrible geriatric wards?' That public unease existed is undeniable for the unit's staff. Too often acutely ill patients, accompanied by acutely anxious relatives, have balked at admission to these 'infamous' wards. Too often staff have faced hostility, and even aggression, from relatives of newly admitted patients whose only knowledge of the wards has come from the pages of a newspaper.

For over three years Pink's assertions about Stepping Hill have been used as a basis for raising questions on the issues of NHS patient care and freedom of speech. His actual campaign, however, raises many others. For instance:

- What is the responsibility of the press to investigate allegations before reporting them?
- Are public service managers 'fair game'?
- If so, should they be expected to respond forthrightly and combatively to unfair allegations? Would this politicize them?
- Are ordinary public service staff 'fair game'?
- How far can you attack a public service without this carrying personal implications for those who work in it?
- Why have industrial tribunals, which were meant to be places for practical men and women to address their conflicts practically, become so expensive and legalistic?
- Why are the public and press so cynical about statements which are made by public service managers? What kind of accountability can there be if any information given is assumed to be distorted and untrue?

- Why is there so little understanding of patient confidentiality?
- Why did the dignity and privacy of patients, and their right not to be used as political pawns, never surface in the debate?
- If an organization, which accepts free speech and which recognizes the legitimacy of dissent, can be characterized as oppressive on the unsupported testimony of one individual, what is the incentive to adopt policies of constructive debate?

POSTSCRIPT

As a postscript, it is interesting to see a similar pattern emerging after Pink was elected on to the UK Central Council for Nursing, Midwifery and Health Visiting. A letter in *The Nursing Times* on 26 January 1994 from Mary Uprichard, president of the council, criticized Pink's article 'In strict confidence' two weeks before, for its lack of understanding of the council's business. He was castigated for discourtesy in writing in the press before raising his concerns at a council meeting, and for being offensive to members in suggesting that they are not able to participate in debate and decision-making. Indeed, Mary Uprichard suggests that Pink was present when decisions were made that he subsequently criticized, yet he said nothing at the time. Under these circumstances, and it has to be regarded as public censure, Mary Uprichard decided to send her reply to every member of the council and to the editor of *The Nursing Times*.

Three months later Pink resigned, claiming the council did not stand up for standards. In an open letter to his fellow council members, he said: 'In all honesty, I am unable to continue to be a part of your secretive, indifferent, undemocratic and disingenuous body'. He added that he would be 'betraying' the nurses who voted for him by staying on.

Part III

PERSONAL PERSPECTIVES

10

Official secrecy: civil servants, secrecy and the defence of the realm

Robin Robison

> See the Lord is going to lay waste the earth and devastate it; he will ruin its face and scatter its inhabitants – it will be same for Priests as for people, for master as for servant, for mistress as for maid, for seller as for buyer . . . the earth reels like a drunkard, it sways like hut in the wind.[1]

In August 1985 I joined the Cabinet Office as a junior member of staff. I was nearly 22 and possessed of a superficial and somewhat naive view of government and the civil service. I was also politically immature: the views I held were what might be expected of a middle-class Scotsman with public-school education – they were not carefully thought-out views gleaned from personal experience. The Cabinet Office position was a job – it paid the rent, and also provided reasonably interesting employment for someone with an inclination towards history, politics and current affairs. I started off in the Central Statistical Office (CSO), which at that time was part of the Cabinet Office, under the Prime Minister. (It is now an agency under the Chancellor of the Exchequer.) My first job was in a section that compiled *Financial Statistics*, an esoteric publication known mainly to economists, academics and a few journalists.

The PSBR (Public Sector Borrowing Requirement) was a hot political potato at the time, and I was the most junior person in a line of civil servants whose job it was to provide Nigel Lawson (then Chancellor) with an advance notice and analysis of each month's PSBR. (This was done in conjunction with the Treasury who inhabited the other end of the Great George Street offices.) Through this work I became accustomed to the debate about presentation of figures, seasonal adjustments and the other points that make the staple diet of statistics. There was quite frequent and intense debate between the CSO and the Treasury about the classification of the financial instruments within the national accounts (e.g. ECGD promissory notes). These disputes sometimes reached the top, with a series of letters being exchanged between Jack Hibbert, Director of the CSO, and Sir Peter Middleton, then Permanent Under Secretary of State at the Treasury.

This may well sound academic and obscure, but how and where items were placed within the national accounts had serious effects on economic indicators and at times statements in the House when the figures were used as briefing material. Perhaps more importantly was the way that *Financial Statistics* and other figures were used in policy-making and economic-forecasting. Clearly, classification within the accounts had an important role with regard to this area. During the 1980s, two directors of the CSO threat-ened to resign over issues connected to presentation of statistics, showing that seemingly obscure figures can have political implications.

After two years at the CSO, I was transferred to the support staff of the Cabinet Office Secretariat at 70 Whitehall. I was positively vetted – a process through which all members of staff at 70 Whitehall have to go through. Positive vetting involves a scrutiny of a person's background. Therefore my friends were approached, and I was interviewed by a security officer. In September 1987 I started life in 70 Whitehall as a general-purpose clerk. This position in the Cabinet Office provided a useful insight into the whole system, as we were privy to many of the Cabinet committee papers, diplo-matic telegrams, letters and all manner of communications.

I had been attending Quaker meetings for five years, and by 1987 I was on the verge of membership – thus my faith was having a profound effect on my worldview. The positive-vetting system looks very carefully at political views to see if they are of an extreme kind, e.g. membership of organizations that resort to violence and certain kinds of personal failings. Religion is thought of as a private matter, of no concern to the authorities, unless for some reason it may lead to violent activities.

Many Quakers, including myself, take the view that spirituality is by no means confined to the specific religions represented by the organizational structures of the churches. The institutions have often been in partnership with the state, but there has always been a spirituality in the organized churches that has challenged, and still challenges, the often cosy relationship between the institutions and the state. I would argue that it is this spirit found in and outside the churches that gradually moves human beings in the direction of a more loving (and therefore more democratic society) ex-pression of organized society.

What is whistleblowing? The obvious definition is of someone making public an activity or action which they believe should be in the public domain, and without their action the issue would be likely to remain private. This is often thought of as making a stand for good ethical princi-ples in public and private organizations. However, it is salutary to ask what we mean by 'good ethical principles'. Within the context of the secu-lar society of the 1990s' Britain, this is generally taken to mean human-itarian principles, those developed over the centuries, and now generally accepted by the majority of the population as the standards to which we should aspire as the citizens of a 'civilized country'. For the majority of the population, until the middle of the last century, the arbiter between good and bad ethical behaviour was the Church. We may not recognize it, but we are the inheritors of a religious tradition that goes back to the beginnings of the Christian church, and indeed is mirrored in different societies in their own cultures.

Although I was on my own within the Cabinet Office (there was no one with whom I could share the doubts I was having about the system, and the Staff Counsellor is there for members of the intelligence and security services), being a member of a Friends Meeting meant that there was a group of people to whom I could turn in the knowledge that I would be listened to carefully and sympathetically.

Over a period of many months I came to realize that I was becoming increasingly uncomfortable with the tension between the world that I was seeing in my work and the spirituality that I was experiencing at Meeting, both on Sunday and during the week at Westminster Friends Meeting House. I decided to share my discomfort with my local meeting.

The basis of the concern that I took to my local meeting were doubts about the morality of spying and other covert activity. In other words, I doubted that the means justified the end; and more than this, I was convinced that covert activities of various kinds could undermine peace in the long run. This, I felt, was especially dangerous in a country that had become quite obsessive about secrecy, and whose security and intelligence services operated almost entirely in secret, in an unaccountable world divorced from Parliament and people.

While I worked in general clerical support I had come to have doubts about the use of the classification system. Not surprisingly, most documents in the Cabinet Office were classified. However, it was by no means always clear why some documents were classified at a particular level. (It is fair to say that the classification of a document cannot be fully understood unless one is in full knowledge of all the relevant facts; the permanent undersecretaries undertook a review of the classification system while I was in Whitehall, but decided to leave things as they were.) Nevertheless, the general practice tended towards being secretive rather than open. I often wondered at the classification of Cabinet committee minutes. For example, I remember an economic committee's minutes were classified secret. Technically 'secret' meant that the information could be of damage to the well-being of the nation or the security apparatus. In this case it seemed to me that these minutes were classified secret in order that as few people as possible should see them, as a leak could well have been embarrassing to the government.

This raises the question of whether confidentiality or secrecy is ever justified. Clearly both are justified in all walks of life at some time or other. In the context of policy-making by a government, it is legitimate for ministers to be able to conduct their discussions in private. The difficulty is in drawing the line between this acceptable and proper confidentiality and unnecessary and dangerous secrecy. Governments of all complexions are guilty of using the system to their own advantage, and perhaps this is to be expected. The real problem lies in the fact that the British system does not allow the legislature a real or biting role in scrutinizing the executive. Select committees sometimes manage to be thorns in the side of government, but there is far too much toadying to the government, both in the House and in committee.

More all pervasive is the secret culture in Britain, a mixture of misplaced deference to authority, apathy and lack of appreciation of the importance of real participation in government by the people for the people. This culture was very evident within Whitehall, in the posters found around the walls with words like 'careless talk costs secrets, keep our secrets secret', and advice about how to talk about the office. There was also a booklet entitled *Their Trade is Treachery*, very much out of date now, with the demise of the Soviet Union and its empire. Its tone is quite paranoid and anti-Russian. I am not defending spying, which I think is immoral, but in order to define a 'traitor' it is necessary to define enemies; as a pacifist I find difficulty with this attitude.

Although not in a position to take part in the writing of answers to parliamentary questions, I witnessed much of the discussion within White-hall about the presentation of information. It always struck me that our elected representatives are at a huge disadvantage, and often know far less about many subjects than a junior civil servant. The doctrine within which all civil servants in Britain operate is ministerial accountability to Parlia-ment. The civil servant is in theory accountable to the minister, and the minister is in turn accountable to Parliament. Thus the civil servant has no role to play beyond the confines of his or her department. According to the established doctrine, the civil servant has no role to play in taking their concerns belong the civil service, no matter what is troubling them. This includes appearances before House of Commons select committees, when civil servants are there to speak on behalf of their ministers, and are not entitled to go beyond their brief, which they will have agreed with their minister beforehand.

Officially the Joint Intelligence Committee does not exist, and ministers would refuse to answer questions about it in the Parliament. I was a clerk in the support staff. It was the quantity and also the kind of intelligence mater-ial that troubled me, and the fact that no parliamentary committee has any access to this kind of information. The fact that no parliamentary body has access to intelligence information means that not only is there no monitoring of the specific uses of intelligence but there is also no check on the way the intelligence services encroach on many areas of life, quite unsuspected by most people. For example, GCHQ has many contracts with academic institu-tions throughout the UK. These contracts are for research into electronic and radio technology associated with interception of communications. While electronic research itself is clearly desirable, it is also a matter of concern that in some instances academic institutions are involved in assisting espionage. The whole question of classified research is raised by these contracts. A growing area of interest to intelligence agencies, and we know this from the comments by people like Robert Gates, Director of the CIA in the USA, is the economic field. Much evidence from other sources confirms the need for real scrutiny of the use of intelligence information (see reports in *The Financial Times* 'TINKER TAYLOR, SOLDIER, BANKER', 15 July 1991, *The Daily Telegraph*, 'TO KILL OR WATCH AND WAIT?' 28 January 1992, and DTI select committee proceedings over many months, 1991–2). It is fairly obvious that there is a cosy relationship between some sections of the intelligence world and the commercial sector. When the establishment is confronted with these kind of arguments there are several stock responses. The first is that all government departments and agencies are accountable to the people through ministers of the Crown in Parliament. This view has been given the full weight of an official Statement by the Cabinet Secretary in 1985 and 1987, then Sir Robert Armstrong. His memorandum made it clear that, as far as the official view is concerned, civil servants are responsible to the Crown – meaning the gov-ernmment of the day. The memorandum laid down certain procedures for civil servants who feel they are being asked to do something which is un-ethical or unconstitutional, or against their consciences. They have a right of appeal to the head of the home civil service, via their permanent undersecre-tary. Sir Robert (now Lord Armstrong of Ilminster) has stated on other occasions that he considers going public wrong, no matter what might be troubling someone's conscience. Indeed he has said that one can transfer one's conscience to one's minister. In paragraph 14 of the 1987 memoran-dum, Armstrong made it clear that if, after having appealed to the head of the home civil service, the individual felt obliged to resign they would still be under a duty of confidentiality – no matter what the reasons for disquiet were. The point was made in several places that the ultimate responsibility lies not with civil servants but with ministers. This rests on the assumption that ministers of the Crown are truly accountable to Parliament.

It is impossible to escape the view that there is a fictive element in the theory of ministerial accountability. First, Cabinet ministers are vastly over-loaded and cannot possibly keep a firm hand on the departmental tiller. Furthermore, government is an increasingly complex business, and minis-ters rely heavily on their civil servants for information and advice on most matters. Evidence from Cabinet ministers has indicated that intelligence and security matters are even less under their control than other matters. There is nothing wrong with ministers relying on civil servants – that is what the civil servant is there for – but this should be recognized constitutionally in order that these powerful bureaucrats are accountable. One way that Parlia-ment can exercise control is over spending levels, but in relation to intel-ligence and security, Parliament is kept in the dark. In this respect the Security Service Act 1989 is deficient:

> Most importantly, the Act does not provide for any real form of Parliamentary oversight if we disregard the censored reports which it receives. . . . The comp-troller and Auditor General does not audit the service in spite of the fact that a former Auditor General Sir Gordon Downey, believed that he should. Equally important is the fact that the Public Accounts Committee has no role in relation to its expenditure.[2]

With the banning of union membership at GCHQ in 1984, the final vestiges of accountability were removed from a very powerful intelligence organiza-tion. Such a move made is clear that the establishment did not value a tradition of dissent within an organization like GCHQ.[3] Given that there is no parliamentary scrutiny and that GCHQ is not even mentioned in the Security Service Act 1989, this was an alarming change for the worse.

While at the Cabinet Office I came across correspondence relating to De-nnis Mitchell, who worked at GCHQ for over thirty years. Mitchell had become troubled over many years in service at what he saw as an in-creasingly inward-looking and unaccountable system. As his experience and access to information grew wider he experienced doubts which he ex-pressed to his line management. In the end Mitchell wrote to the Cabinet Secretary, who gave no assurance about the matters raised by Mitchell. Mitchell then tried to raise the matters with parliamentarians (members of the Privy Council), and after he had done this he was injuncted in 1986; he is therefore not able to speak at all about his specific concerns arising from his long experience at GCHQ. There are five areas of ethical concern to Mitchell: (1) who is targeted; (2) the methods used and whether they were properly authorized; (3) who the beneficiaries of the product are; (4) for what purpose the information was required; and (5) what use was made of it. Mitchell's concerns coincide to a large extent with my own, and it is helpful to have someone of such long experience at a fairly senior level within an entirely different part of the intelligence machine. Even without knowing the details of Mitchell's concerns, it is apparent that he too has had considerable doubts about the use of intelligence information, and this is inextricably linked with the question of accountability. Were there to be real and effective supervi-sion of the intelligence services then there could be much more confidence in their activities. However, in order to achieve this accountability it is necess-ary to question the need for the apparatus as it stands. If Parliament decides that we do in fact need the large machine that exists today then we must be clear why we need it.

Mitchell's experience shows that the establishment does not seem to be genuinely interested in listening to the concerns of those with troubled consciences. Mitchell has had meetings with the intelligence staff counsellor, Sir Philip Woodfield, and it seems from those meetings that Woodfield's role is mainly to attempt to avert embarrassing and unwelcome disclosures. The new Official Secrets Act 1989 in principle makes it much more difficult for those from within the machine to air their concerns beyond the confines of the department. I did not have access to Woodfield, not being an employee of one of the agencies, but I did seek permission to attend conferences about government secrecy, and told my security officer once I had been ap-proached by a member of the press. In the light of Mitchell's experience I found it hard to see any point in attempting to address the problems that I saw from within the system. I was also coming to the realization that I was temperamentally unsuited to the civil-service life, at least in the Cabinet Office. It is possible that had I been employed in a different department I would have felt able to stay in the civil service. There is a need for people to work for change within organizations, and for those who work for change outside the institution that they found they were unable to stay within.

The recently retired Permanent Undersecretary of State at the Ministry of Defence, Sir Michael Quinlan, has provided an interesting unofficial re-sponse to concerns expressed by people like Mitchell, Massiter, Ponting and myself. Quinlan is someone who has clearly developed a well-thought-out defence of the current ethical practices within the civil service. He set out his views very lucidly in a talk given to the Christian Responsibility in Public Affairs Group, the text of which was subsequently published by the First Division Association, and the Civil Service magazine *Port Cullis* in January 1991. His main point is on the ethics of role. He argues that in a complex, modern, industrialized society like 1990s' Britain, there has to be a division of role, and each job has its own code of ethics. But over every one are the moral absolutes or Christian ethics. Quinlan's point is that in his experience those absolutes are very rarely threatened. He says:

> An admirable colleague recently retired is on record as commending the with-holding of 'the last ounce of commitment'. I recognise what he says, but I am a shade uneasy about its vulnerability to misrepresentation. One may think a par-ticular policy a square circle, and indeed within the confines of Whitehall one may argue fervently to that effect; but once the decision is taken it is a matter both of duty and professional pride to help make the very best square circle that effort and imagination can contrive . . . the duty of confidence is similarly not condi-tional on good actions by others.

Quinlan sets his views of civil-service ethics squarely within the param-eters of the Armstrong memorandum, saying that civil-service account-ability operates wholly through ministers, and that this principle must always remain the case – even in front of select committees. There are a number of civil servants of a variety of ranks whom I have spoken to who also maintain that their personal morality has never been challenged. We all draw lines in different places, so that the point of departure will be different for each of us. The orthodox views expressed by Quinlan remain valid only in proportion to the success of the system as a whole. For many reasons it is becoming increasingly clear that the system is not working. Even with a wholly pragmatic approach the time for reform is long overdue. Sir John Hoskyns advocated that 'there should be more open government, so that past failures would not be concealed, helping instead to push ministers up a learning curve'.[4]

In the last twelve years there have been several pieces of legislation passed that have a direct bearing on this subject. This is not the place to enter into a detailed examination of all the nuances and implications of that legis-lation, but I will look at the most relevant aspects of that legislation. The three most pertinent Acts are Interception of Communications Act 1985, Security Service Act 1989 and Official Secrets Act 1989. These three Acts of Parliament all have much in common.

The Interception of Communications Act was implemented largely be-cause of the criticisms of the British government over the Malone case, where the European Court were unhappy at the lack of legal controls over interception. The European Court of Human Rights then put pressure on the British government to bring tapping within the law, and not just by the prerogative. Principally a warrant must be sought from the Secretary of State by a security service before a tap may be placed. However, the safe-guards are minimal. Only one of the categories under which a warrant may be issued is clear cut: that of 'preventing or detecting serious crime'. The other two are: 'In the interests of national security, and for the purpose of safeguarding the economic well-being of the United Kingdom.' National security is never defined, and the consistent approach over many years has been that it is for the government of the day to judge what is or is not in the interests of the nation. This is without any real or open debate in Parliament to guide the executive in making this judgement. Much of the activities of the intelligence and security services come under the royal prerogative, and thus there is no part for the legislature to play in making judgements. There is no attempt made to define 'economic well-being'. It is so open ended as to allow enormous scope for the various agencies to act on their own initiative.

The tribunal set up by the 1985 Act has very few powers. They may only investigate whether there has been a relevant warrant sought for and issued under the due procedure. They may not question the judgement of the executive with regard to what constitutes national security. The commissioner in theory has access to all information, but may withhold (with the consent of the Prime Minister) any information that is deemed to be prejudicial to the operation of the security and intelligence services, or the detection of serious crime, or the economic well-being of the UK. The technology of GCHQ makes it very simple for them to listen to any conversation they like without having to obtain a warrant from anyone and, as they are not covered by any legislation, their activities are entirely under the prerogative. There is some evidence that GCHQ is used in this way, and the quantity and type of SIGINT I saw made me wonder who was being targeted, and who was taking the decisions. This is strenuously denied in the most recent report of the commissioner appointed under the Interception of Communications Act 1985 (Chap. 56).[5] The commissioner makes a point of saying that economic intelligence is not industrial espionage; it is good to hear this but it still does not answer the question as to what is really meant by the economic well-being of the UK. It is possible to imagine a situation in which the economic interests of one nation were directly contrary to those of the UK, and that with economic intelligence we may attempt, covertly, to gain an advantage. It is possible that this type of activity could contribute more tension to an already difficult international scene. We could, of course, trust that the probity of individuals like the commissioners under the 1985 Act, and the Security Service Act 1989, would mean that major illegal acts will not happen. However, it is difficult to see how two individuals can do what is done in Canada and the USA by several paid staff with the benefit (all be it restricted in this field) of freedom-of-information legislation.)

The Security Service Act 1989 is notable for its brevity. Again there are appointed a commissioner and a tribunal whose terms of reference and scope for action are exceedingly narrow. The Act makes it clear that it is for the security service to determine, not the tribunal or commissioner, what category of person may legitimately come under investigation by the security service. Neither national security nor what constitutes undermining of parliamentary democracy are defined. The evidence of Cathy Massiter and others is that dissenting groups who are totally within the law are, or certainly have been, likely to come under scrutiny. The Official Secrets Act

1989 removed the totally ridiculous element from official secrecy, but it is in fact a much sharper instrument, without the vestiges of a public-interest clause for the protection of civil servants and others with troubled consciences. When the Act was debated in both Houses of Parliament there were many calls for the insertion of such a clause. The establishment line was well put by Lord Hunt of Tanworth, who said that such a clause was not required, and that juries would not convict those of honest and honourable intent. Once again this leaves considerable scope for the executive. The instinct is always to keep such matters within the 'club'. I got this message very strongly in a conversation I had with a recently retired senior civil servant who had had some responsibility for tapping warrants. He was quite adamant that the public just had to trust particular individuals, and that once the system was opened out a bit it would be very difficult to stop the process. This is obviously an argument in favour of continued use of the prerogative at the sole discretion of the executive branch of government, and is a continuation of the Armstrong line that whistleblowing is always wrong. This is government by 'them' for 'us'; very much Whitehall saying that they know best. Who is to make the judgement about what is best for the nation? The establishment has always put their faith in a small group of politicians and administrators who take all the really big decisions. The way that decisions were taken about a British nuclear bomb is a very good example of this belief in practice.[6] This spans the period 1945–85, and without exception prime ministers of both Labour and Conservative administrations kept discussions and decisions within a very small group of ministers and officials. The Cabinet was only ever informed of the decisions, and had virtually no say in the process. A trenchantly held view of all the prime ministers involved was that the circle of people should be kept to a minimum, and the strong implication was that others were not to be trusted to come to the right conclusions. An argument in favour of this secrecy would be the need-to-know principle. It is very strange in a democracy that such fundamental decisions should be kept within such a small and secretive circle. The official line is always that disagreement with nuclear policy is fine in a democracy like Britain, but the very strong impression from government and the establishment is that anti-nuclear views are beyond the pale. There is evidence of a smudging of roles between politicians and intelligence and other officials over the anti-nuclear issues and, with a lack of scrutiny this, one may be tempted to think this was in some ways inevitable.

It would be wrong to give the impression that Quakers are totally against government as a concept and in practice. It was William Penn who wrote: 'The glory of Almighty God and the good of mankind is the reason and end of government, and therefore government in itself is a venerable ordinance of God.'[7] Just as there has always been a tension among Friends over the dichotomy between the individual leading and the group wisdom, so there has also been a tension between those whose faith will not let them take part in government of any kind, and those who express their faith by diligent service in the community and government. Both kinds of witness are

healthy and good. In this context it is apposite to mention the Quaker involvement in the industrial revolution when they took a leading role in
some areas. Despite this full involvement in the capitalist world there were
considerable tensions within Friends, especially around slavery, which resulted in Quakers first of all giving up slaves, and then ending up leading the
campaign to end slavery. This tension has been most recently evident in the
troubled consciences of Friends who cannot accept the part they are made to
play in defence spending by paying through direct and indirect taxation.
There is an argument that we live in a democracy, and that we vote for
governments that believe in nuclear weapons, but the knowledge of how
decisions were made undermines this position.

To a large extent the civil service in the UK, and Parliament and the
governmental system, is a product of the settlement at the Restoration, and
the 'Glorious Revolution' in 1688. While I was working in Whitehall there
were all kinds of celebrations of the 1688 settlement. I found this ironic, as it
is clear that the system that was established in 1688, and which was the root
of the way that the UK has governed itself ever since, is showing clear signs
of strain. Reforms in the nineteenth and twentieth centuries have resulted in
a universal adult franchise, but still an anachronistic and overcentralized
central government whose power lies too much in the hands of the executive. The USA, with its different system (thus making direct comparisons
pointless), and a more powerful legislature, is worth considering. The
Founding Fathers had the power of George III in mind when they balanced
the power of the executive with congressional powers. However it is important to note the way in which the presidency and US executive has been
encroaching upon congressional powers, and indeed circumventing Congress altogether. Perhaps more importantly the USA shows that in order for
the people to handle power with responsibility, it is necessary that they are
well informed and willing and able to fulfil their role as citizens rather than
subjects. There is a fundamental way that one of the reasons that I decided to
speak out publicly was a rejection of the kind of world that that political
arrangement created. Quakers grew out of a spiritual and political revolutionary ferment, and would not exist if they had accepted the prevailing
authority. This has meant that they have always, and still do, look to a better
order of society that more reflects the kingdom of God. Without being fully
conscious of it I was caught up with this vision and, in the end, I had no
choice but to obey. It could be said that I was arrogant in taking upon myself
the judgement of what is or is not morally acceptable, but I submitted my
leadings to Friends who, in the way that they have always done, tested what
I said. I then waited to see if this was in accord with the leadings of Friends
corporately. This tension between accepting the need for an ordered society
and the vision of something different will always exist, but it is the very
existence of this creative tension that results in change for the better:

> Not as partisans of a certain type of government, nor as those who despair
> altogether of the state as something inherently evil and necessarily immoral shall
> we make our contribution, but as those who while recognising as realists the
> tensions of life, give priority to the spiritual values. We shall acknowledge the

legitimacy of social organisation and control. We may even agree with William Penn that government is 'a part of religion itself, a thing sacred in its institution and end', and engage more earnestly in its labours and responsibilities. We shall believe that . . . peace on earth is possible to men of good will, and that the individual and the group may mutually assist each other to their highest self-realisation. We shall apply to the nation as to the individual the searching question, What shall it profit a man if he gain the whole world and lose his soul?[8]

NOTES

1. *Isaiah* 24: 1–2, 21–1.
2. Birkinshaw, P. (1990) *Reforming the Secret State*, Open University Press, Milton Keynes.
3. See Norton-Taylor, R. (1989) *In Defence of the Realm?*, Civil Liberties Trust,
4. Hennessy, P. (1986) *Cabinet*, Basil Blackwell, Oxford, p. 193.
5. Lloyd, LJ (1992) *Report of the Commissioner for 1991*,
6. See Chapter 4.
7. Preamble to the Great Law enacted at Chester, Pa., 1682.
8. H. J. Cadbury (1937).

POSTSCRIPT

Since this chapter was written, there has been unprecedented Government initiative in this field. Most recently, this has included the Intelligence Services Bill, which includes a provision for a Committee of both Houses of Parliament to have some oversight of the intelligence and security agencies. This Committee will meet *in camera* and will report to the Prime Minister rather than directly to Parliament. In order for these initiatives to have some real and lasting benefit, it is essential that members of our legislature are increasingly vigilant and probing in their scrutiny of the executive.

11

Charles Robertson: in the eye of the storm

Alan Lovell and Charles Robertson

The sensitivity and potential significance of financial information goes beyond the obvious shareholder and management boundaries giving the accountancy profession and its members an intriguing public-interest dimension to their activities, a dimension which the profession itself is keen to trumpet on occasions. Professional codes of ethics tend to place heavy demands upon their members and the higher a professional association aspires in terms of social and political status, the more exacting the code of ethics is likely to become. Members of professional bodies are required to act in ways which uphold the expected behaviour of 'respected professionals' and any deviations from those norms are usually dealt with expeditiously, with the deviant member likely to face a variety of penalties, the ultimate being withdrawal of membership. It might seem reasonable to assume that those members who not only strive to uphold their profession's required code of conduct but also resist pressure from their employing organization to act in ways which are both contrary to acceptable professional practice, but illegal as well, would receive support from a wide constituency including their professional association, fellow members of the profession, fellow employees and the wider public. If the principled employee ultimately finds him or herself faced with no option but to 'blow the whistle', that support could be crucial in protecting the employee concerned from the wrath of the employing organization. However, the available evidence does not support this assumption. The outcome for those considering 'blowing the whistle' is invariably one of considerable emotional and material loss (see Soeken and Soeken, 1987; Winfield, 1990).

Those employees who ultimately find themselves faced with no option but to 'blow the whistle' on the organization malpractice which they have sought to change, rarely have their cases examined in detail and, as a consequence, the emotion, pressure and torment which often characterize the context of a specific case are lost. The following is itself a précis of a particular case and, while it cannot hope to capture all of the drama, pressure, emotional turmoil and isolation experienced by the subject of the case, it is hoped that the presentation will cause the reader to reflect upon the factors which often cast the whistleblower as the 'deviant' – the one performing abnormal/unacceptable behaviour – the outsider.* Possibly a more positive description than whistleblower would be 'principled dissenter at work'. This may seem little more than a semantical point, but the term 'whistleblower' carries with it negative connotations and may present vested interest with a convenient shield behind which to stand.

The subject of the case is an accountant, Mr Charles Robertson, who held a very senior position with an international insurance organization. As a member of a profession which holds itself out as one of the leading professions and espouses an allegiance and commitment to that elusive concept, 'the public interest', it was considered appropriate to present the case in the form of a 'public inquiry', with the author adopting the role of 'inquirer', seeking clarification and asking questions when it is appropriate.

Inquirer: Good day, Mr Robertson and welcome to the inquiry. I believe your case involves the alleged manipulation of internal accounting information. While this in itself would not have been an illegal offence, you claim that it was converted into one by a conspiracy on the part of certain employees of your former employer.

Robertson: Yes, that is so, although my 'claim', as you describe it, has been accepted by an industrial tribunal on a unanimous verdict.

Inquirer: The inquiry is interested in the specifics of your case inasmuch as they allow the actual behaviour of one of the country's leading business organizations and the support systems of the professional accounting bodies to be studied.

Would you like to explain your case, providing contextual information where this is appropriate? I will only interject when I believe a point of clarification might be helpful, or where a particular aspect requires more detailed examination.

Mr Robertson, the floor is yours.

Robertson: Thank you. I am a member of the Institute of Chartered Accountants of Scotland and I had always been proud to be a member of that institute. As you would expect, I began my initial working life in a chartered accountant's practice, but shortly after qualifying I moved out of private practice.

Inquirer: Was there any particular reason for this?

Robertson: No, not really. I simply did not see myself remaining in a practising environment and so moved, when an attractive opportunity became available, to a commercial organization. My interests and expertise have always been in the finance and financial accounting fields and in particular in the area of taxation. I joined Guardian Royal Exchange (GRE) in 1973 as Assistant Taxation Manager and by 1980 I had been promoted to Chief Accountant (Taxation).

---

* The term deviant is defined as one who displays behaviour which differs from acceptable/normal behaviour (*The Collins English Dictionary*, 1986). However, synonyms include crank, blackleg, outsider and scab.

Although my line responsibility was to a person who had the job title of Assistant General Manager (Finance), my regular dealings were with the General Manager of Investment and Finance. While this last job title may not sound too senior, this is not the case. The person holding this position in GRE is very senior and the person in question also held a position on the main board of directors. This information is relevant because my line manager does not figure in my case until I received my notice of suspension. Prior to this he plays no real part.

The problem which eventually led to my dismissal erupted in early 1987, but the history to the saga goes back a good deal further. I believe it would be helpful to the inquiry if I explained the circumstances which preceded the final crisis.

Inquirer: Yes, please go ahead.

Robertson: As I have said, I began my employment with GRE in 1973, but in 1982, during an investigation with my taxation manager into reinsurance transactions undertaken between GRE (UK) and some of its overseas subsidiaries, we discovered certain irregularities. A number of retrospective adjustments had been made to the accounts of particular overseas subsidiaries, most notably the Australian subsidiary. The adjustments in themselves were not fraudulent if they had stayed within the company's own internal reporting system. It is entirely up to individual companies how they choose to report the performance of their constituent parts within their own management accounting systems. It only becomes a problem for a person such as myself, who has to deal with the company's wider constituencies, if these 'adjustments' are retained in the final accounts which are published to the outside world, or are used without adjustment to support the tax returns to the Inland Revenue.

Inquirer: I apologize for interrupting you, Mr Robertson, but what was the reason for your investigations in the first place? Was this the result of your own doubts about the probity of the accounts, or was there some other reason?

Robertson: We were undertaking the investigation in order to respond to a number of very specific questions which the Inland Revenue had raised in correspondence. The Inland Revenue had been trying to resolve some long-standing queries with the company, but a variety of factors had contributed to the queries remaining outstanding in 1982. During the course of our investigations my taxation manager and I discovered accounting adjustments which had the effect of deflating the 1974 UK profits by £3 million. The adjustments related to some retrospective reinsurance payments to an Australian subsidiary. I brought this to the attention of the company stating that I was duty bound to bring the matter to the notice of the Inland Revenue.

Inquirer: Could you explain what you mean by 'duty bound'?

Robertson: Certainly. I can answer the question in a number of ways. At one level it is a question of personal choice. It is not in my nature to defraud other people. I am not a zealot. I simply believe that society deserves honesty and integrity from all its citizens, particularly those who have been granted positions of trust and I regarded myself to be in such a position.

This brings me on to the second reason. My professional accounting body *requires* me to act in an ethical and honest manner. Even if my personal values allowed me to condone the behaviour I had uncovered, my professional accounting institute gave me no such leeway. My institute's code of conduct is very clear about the position of its members, irrespective of whether they are employed in public practice or as a salaried employee in industry or commerce.

The third reason for my behaviour can be explained by the nature of my position within the company. I was responsible for dealing with the Inland Revenue over the company's tax affairs. I had total authority for this aspect of the company's business. If I had acted in any way less than scrupulously with the Revenue, I could have undermined the reputation of the company. I had a duty to the company to be honest with the Revenue.

Inquirer: I understand that your claim of 'total authority' over the company's tax affairs was disputed by the company at your industrial tribunal.

Robertson: That is correct, but I was able to refer the tribunal to the company's own job description of my position which reads: 'The job holder has delegated to him unlimited authority to settle the Group's liability with the Inland Revenue.' So you see I can justify my actions on three counts. While the first is a very personal statement, I include it because, notwithstanding the second and third requirements, I would still have acted in the way that I did, because that reflects my personal values. However, even if my personal judgement would have allowed me to ignore the irregularities, the requirements of my professional accounting body and the specification of my job required me to act in a way which displayed integrity and trustworthiness.

Inquirer: Thank you for that explanation. Please carry on.

Robertson: We (my taxation manager and I) had lengthy discussions with the very senior management of the company to ensure that all other dealings with overseas subsidiaries had been 'at arms' length'. This term describes business dealings which reflect market prices. Without this assurance the company might stand accused of illegally arranging its dealings with overseas subsidiaries to reduce its UK tax liability. I required the assurance in writing and finally received it in early 1984.

Inquirer: That is a long while to wait to obtain the assurance you required.

Robertson: It took many requests.

Inquirer: How did the Revenue react to this disclosure?

Robertson: Well, at their instigation, I asked the most senior executives responsible for underwriting in each division of the company, as well as the Reinsurance Manager, to ensure that I would be informed in future of any unusual underwriting transactions involving significant sums. If there was any doubt concerning the way a transaction had been handled in the accounts, then I requested that I be informed so that I could assess the taxation implications of the transaction. I was also interested in any transactions which might not be considered 'at arms' length'.

The Revenue assessed the company for the back tax due of £1.56 million. The Inspector of Taxes did not assess the company for penalty payments or interest because at that stage I was not aware of any purposeful irregularities. The omission of the £3 million was treated as an innocent mistake, because that is what I understood it to be. In the circumstances it was a successful outcome for the company.

Inquirer: Nevertheless, £1.56 million is a considerable sum of money, even for a large company. Were there any repercussions arising out of this affair? For example, were relations between yourself and colleagues in any way affected? I ask this because reactions, assuming any were detectable, could be either positive or negative.

Robertson: I am glad you have asked the question in terms of individuals rather than, for example, 'how did the company react?' I had always had a great deal of respect for Guardian Royal Exchange as an organization. However, the behaviour of certain individuals within the company has filled me with dismay.

After 1982, when I advised my General Manager that I was duty bound to disclose the £3 million to the Inland Revenue, his attitude towards me cooled noticeably. Looking back, I am now convinced that ever since I advised the Revenue about the £3 million adjustment I became a *persona non grata* as far as he was concerned. Indeed you will find that the role of my General Manager is crucial to my case.

Inquirer: But having obtained the written assurances from top management you required and with the £1.56 million repaid to the Revenue, did that not end the matter?

Robertson: No, unfortunately. During a subsequent examination of old papers I came across a note which related to a meeting held in 1975. This note was to change completely my understanding of the £3 million adjustment. It proved that my predecessor as manager of the taxation department had been involved in planning and setting up the £3 million retrospective payment. I now knew that its non-disclosure was not a simple and innocent omission. It had been a calculated deceit.

I was faced with a dilemma of what to do with the evidence. It now seemed clear to me that over the years several senior people must have been aware of the questionability of the £3 million adjustment and had deliberately kept me in the dark. The £3 million adjustment would need to have been approved by the very senior management. I was in a quandary. I did not want to be the cause of any severe unpleasantness for two former colleagues who had retired. A court appearance and any subsequent penalty would have been very difficult at their time of life. I had obtained written assurances that there were no more tax skeletons in the past and that I would be informed of any future unusual underwriting transactions. However, I was aware that a fraudulent deceit had been carried out. I was genuinely stressed by this situation, especially as the issue at stake was not an abstract ethical concept, but about real people – people I knew at first hand. Given that the Inland Revenue had received the back taxes it was due, and out of loyalty to the company and sympathy to certain individuals I felt unable to notify the Revenue. In effect my decision was not to make a decision.

Inquirer: Does this not contradict your earlier statements about commitment to a professional code of ethics, your own personal code of conduct and the requirements of your position within GRE?

Robertson: I agree that there appears to be some inconsistency at this point, but I have not said that I had decided to conceal the information. I was merely in a quandary about what to do, particularly with respect to the two retired colleagues and what any legal proceedings might do to them. I was genuinely unsure about the possible outcomes and the justification of these outcomes.

I appreciate that there is an argument that says I should have left that to the courts to decide, but it would be my decision to bring the apparent fraud to the courts' attention. It was a very heavy responsibility. I was not playing God, I simply was not sure that the purity of my conscience and the integrity of the law justified what a court action might do to the individuals concerned, and to the reputation of the company, which was also a consideration. The fact that I had been central to the Revenue being paid their outstanding tax did make me feel that a kind of equity already prevailed.

In a sense I sat on my hands. I did not make a decision as such, but kept the evidence in my private files and continued to ponder what to do. I do not claim this was a 'correct' action, whatever that might mean. These decisions are far more complex when there are real people involved. While I do not claim my behaviour, with respect to the two retired gentlemen, is without criticism, I hope it does prove that I am not an insensitive or vindictive person.

Inquirer: How did things develop after this affair?

Robertson: With great difficulty. A series of incidents showed clearly that my general manager was seeking to make my life difficult. My taxation manager resigned and I had to wait five months before my general manager would even discuss the matter of his replacement. An incorrect and critical comment about my performance was placed upon my staff appraisal form. It took ten months of repeated requests for an explanation for the comment and for the comment to be removed. In addition a letter which had been sent to the company by my former wife contained malicious and untruthful statements. From statements the general manager made to me it was clear he had either spoken to or received a communication from her. The company (or at least the senior officials) denied this and after repeated attempts to resolve the issue I was left with no alternative but to serve court notices on both the company and my former wife. As a result I was able to see the letter my former wife had written and the company finally agreed to remove the letter from my file. However, these and other incidents took place over an extended period of time and were extremely wearing. I felt compelled to write to the Managing Director about the behaviour of my general manager. As a result of this letter the attitude of my general manager did mollify. I did not kid myself that I and the general manager would ever be bosom friends, but it was good to have his scheming and conniving laid to rest, or so I thought.

Inquirer: So, the general state of relations between yourself and other senior managers within the company had improved as a result of your internal correspondence with the Managing Director and remained so until the question over reinsurance dealings with overseas subsidiaries surfaced again?

Robertson: Yes, that is so. With the written assurance from the senior management that all dealings with overseas subsidiaries were 'at arms' length' I felt confident that I could settle all the company's outstanding tax matters with the Inland Revenue and when I received a very detailed letter from the Inspector of Taxes itemizing 30 questions which required responses, I had no qualms in approaching various managers within the company for their responses to some of the questions.

Inquirer: Which issues did the most significant questions address?

Robertson: The major queries still revolved around the extent to which dealings with overseas subsidiaries could be considered to be at arms' length. However, by now, albeit belatedly, I had a written assurance from the company that all such dealings were at arms' length, and so I circulated my requests to senior managers for information with no feelings of apprehension.

Inquirer: But in fact the second phase of your case begins at this time, does it not Mr Robertson?

Robertson: Yes, indeed. It will be necessary to mention a number of dates to the inquiry which relate to a series of meetings and correspondence. I trust that this detail will not appear daunting because it is crucial to record and recognize the timing of events. They provide important pieces of information in the overall jigsaw of the case.

In most respects I made good progress in obtaining the information necessary to answer the inspector's 30 questions. However, the Reinsurance Manager then told me that he had not kept the papers containing the calculations which were done in agreeing the rating for the Australian fire catastrophe treaty. I received a series of memos in which he endeavoured to show that the rating was at arms' length market term. When I replied to the last of these memos saying that I did not think the Revenue would be satisfied with the explanations he had offered, I received a request for a meeting from two other managers. The current Reinsurance Manager was about to retire and the request for the meeting came from the man who was due to become the new Reinsurance Manager and his boss. Both men requested a meeting with me at the earliest opportunity.

As soon as they arrived in my office the two managers told me that there was nothing more the company could do to justify to the Inland Revenue that the rating was at arms' length terms. The reason for this then became crystal clear. To my astonishment I was informed that the reinsurance department had been instructed by a senior GRE official to give the Australian subsidiary 'special particular' terms, which were very favourable compared with arms' length market terms. The reason the company could not supply the calculations to prove the integrity of the calculations was simply that the rates did not reflect arms' length market rates. In addition, other subsidiaries in South Africa, Holland and New Zealand were mentioned as having received similar treatment. The two managers asserted that in each case the senior official argued that the subsidiaries could not, at the time, afford arms' length market rates. Neither of the managers were prepared to say who the senior official might be, but they did say that they were reasonably confident that all transactions since 1985 had been at arms' length.

I took notes during the meeting and shortly after the meeting telephoned one of the managers to confirm a number of the points. There was no misunderstanding between the three of us present at the meeting as to what had been said during the meeting.

As I mentioned, I was dismayed because statements made by the two managers were contrary to assurances made to me by senior company officials. I informed both of the managers that this information disturbed me greatly and that I would have to raise the issues at the highest level. I remember saying that I would need to bring the matter to the attention of the Chairman.

The information, if true, meant that a whole series of profit computations which I had used in my negotiations over recent years with the Revenue to determine the company's annual tax liabilities, contained intentional irregularities, the very deceit the company had committed before and assured me would never happen again. Not only was the Revenue being cheated, and thus ultimately the general public, but I also felt betrayed.

Shortly after the two managers left my office I received a telephone call from my general manager and I informed him of the information I had just received.

On the 28th January (the day after the meeting) I sent a memorandum to my general manager which focused upon the claims of the two reinsurance managers. I also addressed copies of the memorandum to the Chairman, the Deputy Chairman, the Managing Director and the two other general managers. However, because I was unsure how or where to contact the Chairman and Deputy Chairman, I said in the memorandum that I relied on my general manager personally to ensure that the Chairman and Deputy Chairman receive their copies. My memorandum highlighted the claims of the two reinsurance managers and I stated that: 'I was no longer prepared to accept the word of any full-time operations executive, including the Managing Director.'

Inquirer: That is strong language. You even singled out the Managing Director as being possibly untrustworthy. Why did you involve the Chairman and Deputy Chairman at this stage?

Robertson: I was not suggesting that the Managing Director was guilty of any deceitful or underhand act, nor, for that matter, any other specific manager. *However I had been told by the two reinsurance managers that a senior manager had authorized the 'adjustments'. Thus, on their evidence, one of the senior managers appeared to be guilty.*

In my memorandum I was merely highlighting that the information I had received placed me in a position in which I did not know whom to believe. Two managers, with no apparent axe to grind, and with detailed operational knowledge, had volunteered information to me which contradicted assurances I had received from top management regarding the reliability and integrity of the official accounting information I had been using in my negotiations with the Inland Revenue. The reference to the Managing Director was merely to illustrate the depth of my concern and uncertainty. I considered this a very serious matter.

I did feel personally betrayed, but if the allegations were true, and please remember that the statements were made by two managers under no duress, then the ramifications for the company would be very damaging. Highly respected city institutions are not expected to act in deceitful ways, particularly with a government agency.

Inquirer: So what was the response to your memorandum?

Robertson: The memorandum was sent on the 28th January and the following day I received another telephone call from the general manager. This time his tone seemed apologetic, but his message puzzled me. He informed me that he had been asked by the Managing Director to instruct me 'never again attempt to communicate with a non-executive director, other than through proper line management channels'. Effectively this would mean me notifying the Assistant General Manager (Finance), who in turn would notify the general manager, who would then notify the Managing Director and so on. In addition the general manager asked if I would be able to attend a meeting at the company's head office in London, on the next day, the 30th January, to consider what should be done in relation to the issues raised in my memorandum. The people who would be attending the meeting were mentioned and these were the Managing Director, my general manager and two further senior managers, but neither the Chairman or Deputy Chairman.

I was prepared to travel to London the following day for the meeting, but I was disturbed by the statement that I was never to communicate directly with the Chairman or Deputy Chairman again. I do not consider that it is normal for a person in my position to communicate directly with the Chairman or Deputy Chairman, but this was not a normal situation. To have those avenues denied to me filled me with even greater consternation. I was clearly being denied access to these people, and given the seriousness of the situation and the uncertainty surrounding those involved, I considered this to be an unreasonable constraint.

Inquirer: Did you raise your concerns at the meeting, or did you respond more quickly than this?

Robertson: Although I was pleased the Managing Director had responded speedily to my memorandum by convening the meeting, I was apprehensive that, given the gravity of the situation, neither the Chairman nor the Deputy Chairman would be present. I needed to express my concern about their absence and so I sent a fax to the Managing Director.

Inquirer: Would you explain what you said in the fax.

Robertson: Certainly. I stated that I regarded the statements by the two reinsurance managers to be extremely serious and that I felt that the Chairman and Deputy Chairman should be notified at once. Just to reiterate, I did not suspect the Managing Director personally, but given the situation, I could not afford to exclude anyone from possible association with the deceit. I assumed he would understand this and would not take my concerns personally.

Given the delicacy of the situation I considered it important that both the Chairman and the Deputy Chairman should be present at the meeting on

30th January and said so in my fax. If either of them was unavailable I asked for another non-executive director to attend in his place.

The Managing Director did not reply to me directly, but instructed my general manager to pass on a message which the Managing Director had written on his copy of the fax. The message said simply, 'Please advise Robertson I shall do no such thing'. Thus, I was effectively being barred from communicating with the Chairman and Deputy Chairman, and any non-executive director. Given that 'the senior manager' who had authorized the favourable terms with the overseas subsidiaries might be one of the managers attending the meeting in London, I felt very apprehensive. But at least I had the statements of the two reinsurance managers and thus those at the meeting would have to wrestle with the principle which these two managers had raised.

Inquirer: So you travelled to London on the 30th January, ready to discuss the issue of the particular reinsurance contracts with the senior managers you have mentioned?

Robertson: Yes, the senior managers were there. However, just before the meeting was due to start the two reinsurance managers walked into the room.

Inquirer: Their presence surprised you?

Robertson: Yes it did. I had been told that only the senior managers would be there. The two reinsurance managers sat next to me and the three of us looked across a very large table at the senior mangers. One of the two reinsurance managers (my allies, or so I thought) made a point of looking at me with a very fixed, serious expression on his face.

Inquirer: So what was the purpose of the two reinsurance managers presence at the meeting? Was it for the other managers present at the meeting to hear at first hand the statements and claims of these two managers?

Robertson: I presumed that was the purpose and I certainly hoped it was.

Inquirer: And were your expectations fulfilled?

Robertson: No! One of the reinsurance managers made a statement that claimed I had misinterpreted what he and the other reinsurance manager had said at the meeting on the 27th January and he produced a memo which he purported was an accurate record of that meeting. I knew that neither of the two reinsurance managers had taken any notes during the meeting so I was interested to see what the memo contained. I quickly read the memo, handed it back and reiterated that my memo of the 28th January was factual in every respect. I had not misunderstood or misinterpreted the conversation, or any part of it. Indeed I reminded one of the reinsurance managers that I had telephoned him shortly after the meeting to confirm a number of points.

I was flabbergasted. I turned to the two managers in disbelief. An argument developed between one of the reinsurance managers and myself which was only terminated when my general manager intervened by saying that there was no point in the meeting continuing in that vein. And so we turned to the particulars of the case.

The meeting concluded with one of the senior managers present agreeing to work with the two reinsurance managers to provide, as soon as possible, the remaining information necessary for me to reply to the Inland Revenue. It was also agreed that there would be a thorough internal examination of all reinsurance transactions with overseas subsidiaries from 1979 to 1986 to certify that they were all at arms' length terms.

The two reinsurance managers were aware that I had taken notes during our meeting on the 27th and I subsequently notified them that I could provide them with a copy of the notes if they so wished. However, I had not been made the same offer of the notes which one of the reinsurance managers produced at the meeting, although when I raised the matter at the meeting in London, I was informed that I had been on the circulation list for the notes. Later events will suggest that they were never sent to me.

At no time did any of the senior managers challenge either the two reinsurance managers or myself to try to understand the nature of the disagreement. The allegations originally made by the two reinsurance managers were so important that I could not understand why the senior managers were so passive.

Either the two reinsurance managers were lying, or I was. There was no basis of a misunderstanding between us. They were denying that they had said that special favourable terms had been given to overseas subsidiaries upon the instructions of a senior GRE official. They either made that statement or they did not.

My original memorandum of the 28th was dismissed as merely an incorrect interpretation of statements made at the meeting of the 27th January. The version of the meeting of the 27th provided by one of the reinsurance managers was believed and not mine. I returned home shell shocked. I really did not know whom I could trust.

Inquirer: But the outcome of the London meeting was that you would receive certification that the company's dealing with overseas subsidiaries were all 'at arms' length'. Would this not have satisfied your needs?

Robertson: First of all it would depend upon the precise wording of the certification, but more importantly you must view this assurance in the context of the case.

I had just attended a meeting where two managers had denied statements which I knew they had made to me, and the most senior managers in the organization had made no attempt to explore what had to be a very serious accusation. The whole affair was a set-up.

Inquirer: What do you mean, Mr Robertson?

Robertson: Simply that. If I had attended the meeting in London as one of the senior managers called to hear this very serious accusation from a respected manager and colleague, then I would want to hear his version of the story and to understand why such an important and puzzling misunderstanding could have arisen. Yet none of this happened.

I immediately wrote to one of the reinsurance managers asking to see the notes he had claimed had been sent to me, but which still had not arrived. Two days later I had to send a further letter, because still no reply was forthcoming. The use of fax machines was, and is, very common within the company and there would have been no problem in sending a copy of the notes within minutes of receiving my request.

A further day later, on February 5th, I telephoned my general manager stating that I had still not received any response from the reinsurance manager. I established that my general manager had a copy of the 'missing' notes and so I asked if he would send a copy of the notes to me so that I could study them. Initially my general manager agreed to this request, stating that he would clear it first with the reinsurance manager in question. I pointed out that this was unnecessary because I had supposedly already been sent a copy of the notes, so I was not asking to see something I was not supposed to see.

He agreed to send a fax of the notes to me immediately, notifying the reinsurance manager that he was doing so. However, within half an hour of this telephone call I received another call from my general manager to say that he had been unable to contact the reinsurance manager and had consequently decided not to send the fax to me until he had discussed the matter with him.

I made some inquiries and established that the reinsurance manager was attending a meeting at the head office in London, where my general manager worked. I relayed this information to my general manager and informed him that it was now possible for him to notify the reinsurance manager and fax the note to me. My general manager refused, but said that he would 'leave a message for the reinsurance manager to contact him before he left the London head office'. I said that I could not understand why a main board director had to clear this matter with a manager, particularly as I was already on the mailing list.

At 5.15 p.m. on that same afternoon I received a fax of the 'notes' from the reinsurance manager's office.

Inquirer: Were the notes as contradictory as suggested?

Robertson: They omitted any mention of the reinsurance managers' statements made to me on 27 January 1987, i.e. that the reinsurance department had been instructed by a senior GRE official to give the subsidiary companies in Australia, South Africa, Holland and New Zealand 'special particular' terms which were very favourable to the subsidiaries and not reflective of arms' length market terms. Also they said I had stated that my duties were on behalf of HM government. I had not said this. As I stated earlier, I considered that I had a duty to deal honestly with the Revenue, but I would never say that I was working on behalf of the Inland Revenue. That statement was a misinterpretation. Whether it was an intentional misinterpretation is unclear, I will leave you to ponder.

Inquirer: What do *you* think, Mr Robertson?

Robertson: I know what I said. The statement which the reinsurance manager imputed to me in his 'notes' was quite specific. I said nothing of the sort. My only reference to obligations and the Revenue was the one I have mentioned. I have a duty *to* the Revenue, and that duty is on behalf of the company, not the Revenue – that is all.

Inquirer: Having finally received a copy of the reinsurance manager's notes, what did you do next?

Robertson: Having been rebuked for communicating, or at least trying to communicate, with the Chairman and the Deputy Chairman I had since then not directed any of my correspondence to them. But now my situation was far more complex. I had attended a meeting at which all the relevant members of the senior management team had been present, and not one of them had been interested in exploring the issue. The opportunity had been there to question the reinsurance managers and myself, particularly me, but no one was interested. Indeed, other than the argument between the reinsurance managers and myself, not a cross word was said at the meeting on the 30th January.

I felt totally isolated. What was I to do? It seemed to me that I had one of three courses of action open to me. Either I:

1. decided that I had taken the issue as far as I could and that now I should keep my head down and accept whatever the company offered by way of an explanation of the overseas reinsurance dealings;
2. decided that I could no longer work in an organization like this and tender my resignation; or
3. would stay within the company and try to resolve the issues from within. After all my employer was a highly respected organization and I could not conceive that the senior management would jeopardized the reputation of the organization for the sake of some, admittedly, serious errors of judgement.

It was possible that the actions of the senior manager who authorized the adjustments were a reflection of some misplaced loyalty. That is, the individual was trying to make as much money for the company as possible, and even defrauding the Inland Revenue could, in his opinion, be justified in this context.

If the original accusations made by the reinsurance managers were unfounded, then a written statement to that effect from the two managers would have been sufficient. I could accept that as long as the blame for the incident was not placed on my shoulders. In addition the company would have to give signed assurances about the reinsurance transactions together with documentary proof.

All of these things had to be possible. I wanted to resolve the matter from within. I enjoyed working for the company. I had friends there. My roots were and still are in the area. My job was interesting and very well paid. At my age and with my specialism it would be extremely difficult for me to find alternative and equivalent employment I had a great deal to lose, but it seemed inconceivable to me that I could ever suffer because of this affair, given that I was the totally innocent party. I never really considered the consequences of losing my job because the prospect of my position being at risk never entered my head. Thus, practical considerations did come into the decision to try to resolve the problem from within the company, but the principal driving force was my belief in principles – values borne out of my personal beliefs, those of my profession and the reputation of the company. *Inquirer*: Mr Robertson, you say that you had not communicated with the Chairman or the Deputy Chairman since your admonition, but that was on the 29th January. The following day you experienced the traumatic meeting in London. One of the comments you have just made suggests that, while you had been prepared to refrain from contacting either the Chairman or Deputy Chairman prior to the London meeting, you were less prepared to accept that constraint following the meeting?

Robertson: Yes I was, and I would ask you and the inquiry's audience to consider what you would have done in my position. All your normal lines of communication had effectively been closed off. It was highly likely that at least one of the senior managers present at the meeting in London was implicated in the deceit, either directly or indirectly. Clearly this assumes that the reinsurance managers were being truthful when they made their statements to me on 27th January, but their subsequent denial of the statements at the meeting in London on 30th January only served to support those original allegations, as far as I was concerned.

The London meeting was most disturbing for me. Not only was the behaviour of the reinsurance managers puzzling and reprehensible but so too was the behaviour of the senior managers present. I could not explain their passive, uninquisitive behaviour without returning to the thought that they had discussed the issue beforehand and come to a view on which they were not prepared to be challenged. But what had informed that view? Why did they not want to question me, or allow me to examine the issues with them, while I was there, in front of them?

At best I could only explain their behaviour as inept and negligent. At worst they could be implicated, embarrassed and conniving. Because of this I write to the Chairman on 2nd February informing him of my worries. He telephoned me upon receipt of the letter, saying that he would 'take up' the points I had raised with him regarding the meeting in London on 30th January. On the 12th February I received an internal memo from the Chairman acknowledging receipt of my letter. Distressingly for me he also made a statement, which in other circumstances would have been perfectly reasonable, but in my situation was a body blow.

Inquirer: Would you explain to the inquiry what this statement was?

Robertson: The Chairman stated that he and the Managing Director were always in close contact with one another on important issues, including the situation regarding the correspondence with the Inland Revenue over the reinsurance issues. He indicated that he was aware that further investigations had been instigated (I presumed he was referring to the exercise which had been promised at the meeting in London) and that he believed that these investigations would be concluded in a short while.

Given that he was in contact with the Managing Director he did not see the point in me corresponding with him as well and duplicating the correspondence he was receiving. He told me, in a courteous way, to stop corresponding with him.

As I said, in other circumstances this would be a perfectly reasonable position to adopt but given everything which had gone before, how could I trust anything which was said or promised to me by any of the gentlemen who were at the London meeting? I could not trust them and now the Chairman had told me that he wanted his knowledge of the situation to be dependent upon the information passed to him by the Managing Director. I had been effectively isolated. The only lines of communication left open to me were ones of which I was deeply suspicious.

Inquirer: You have described a very difficult situation and one which was becoming increasingly more fraught and tense. How did the situation develop?

Robertson: Basically I sat and waited for the findings of the investigation of the reinsurance contracts with overseas subsidiaries. On the 17th February I received a note outlining the results of the investigation. The inquiries had covered the period 1979–86 and it was concluded that the terms used with overseas subsidiaries reflected 'commercial rates'.

Inquirer: Would this have been adequate to satisfy the Inland Revenue and provide you with the assurances you required?

Robertson: At the very beginning of my evidence I referred to the phrase which the Inland Revenue had used in their correspondence. The phrase was 'at arms' length'. This phrase has a particular and well understood meaning, whereas 'commercial rates' can mean a variety of things. A definition of what is 'commercial' will be dependent upon the state of a market and the power relationships within that market. For example, a company might sell one of its products or services at a price which does not fully recover its attributable costs. This could still be justified as a commercial decision, on the grounds that it was acting as a loss leader, but the customer would need to be an independent party. If, however, the customer is a fellow division within a group of companies, and the 'loss leader' role of one of the division's products has the effect of reducing the group's tax liability within a particular tax authority, then the acceptability of the transfer price would deserve challenging, and that is exactly what the Revenue was concerned about.

Please remember also that whatever documentation was produced by a senior manager within the company regarding the reinsurance deals, it was I who would have to negotiate with the Revenue authorities. I had to have confidence in the information I was using, and that I most certainly did not. So you see, it is not simply a case of what would be satisfactory to me, but rather what would be acceptable to the Inland Revenue.

I had also asked for two additional aspects to be considered before any documentation regarding the contracts with overseas subsidiaries could be accepted. The first was that the document which was to include the phrase 'at arms' length' should be signed by the Chairman. Second, I wanted an explanation of why the two reinsurance managers had made statements to me containing extremely serious allegations, but which they subsequently denied at the meeting in London on the 30th January. The need for this information was to establish how much credibility I, or anyone else, could place in any statement made by officials of the company regarding the reinsurance dealings.

I responded to the report's findings by sending a note to the general manager responsible for the report, with copies to the Chairman, the Deputy Chairman, the Managing Director, my general manager and the other general managers. I wanted the debate to involve as many of the relevant people as possible.

On 20 February, I received a memo from the Chairman. In it he said that he had read the report, as well as my reply to the report. He went on to say that he was satisfied with the outcome of the investigations and asked me to proceed with resolving the reinsurance matter with the Revenue on the basis of the information I had received.

He then instructed me to 'desist from addressing senior management, who have shown you much patience and co-operation, in the tone of your latest memo, which I have advised the general manager in question not to answer.' He concluded by stipulating that he required me to involve a senior manager in all my further dealings with the Inland Revenue on the reinsurance matter. The manager was the boss of the two reinsurance managers who made the original accusations to me.

Inquirer: That is a devastating memorandum, Mr Robertson. If I may I would like to review that memorandum. You had been told to resolve the company's outstanding tax affairs with the Inland Revenue on the basis of the information provided, but which you considered inadequate in order to respond to the Revenue. You had also been severely rebuked by the Chairman of the company for the language you had used, and finally as an apparent sign of the company's mistrust of you, the Chairman had placed another manager alongside you presumably to monitor your actions and correspondence with the Revenue.

Robertson: Yes, that is precisely the effect of the Chairman's memo.

Inquirer: For the benefit of the inquiry could you provide evidence of the language you used which so offended the Chairman and presumably other senior management at the company?

Robertson: Certainly, I will read to you the memo I sent on the 17th February, the one which spurred the Chairman's comments:

> Thank you for your memo of 16th February confirming that between 1980 and 1985 no terms have been approved for reinsurance arrangements to subsidiaries other than on a commercial basis. However, I should prefer your memo to use the terminology suggested in my memo of 28.1.87 i.e. it should cover the period 1.1.79 to 31.12.86; instead of 'commercial' it should state 'arms' length market terms'; and it should also be certified by the Chairman of the company.
>
> Furthermore, before replying to the Inspector of Taxes letter of 11th September 1986, I shall require a full explanation of why I should accept your word that no reinsurance covers have been given to overseas subsidiaries in the period 1.1.79 to 31.12.86 at other than arms' length market terms in the light of the opposing statements of the reinsurance managers made to me on 27.1.87 as shown at (i) to (iv) of my memo of 28.1.87. To put it another way, why then did the reinsurance managers make their 'erroneous' statements? I again repeat what I said at the meeting on 30th January, that what I say at (i) to (iv) of my memo of 28.1.87 is absolutely correct.

That is the complete memo.

Inquirer: Well the passage 'I shall require a full explanation of why I should accept your word' is a little provocative, but presumably you were feeling a little provoked yourself?

Robertson: No so much provoked as beleaguered, threatened and isolated. I believe my choice of words conveyed my emotions precisely. I truly did not know what or whom to believe. How could I?

The general manager who had conducted the latest investigation of reinsurance contracts with the overseas subsidiaries had been one of the senior managers who had been present at the London meeting and had shown no willingness or interest in exploring the claims made to me by the two reinsurance managers. Why should I now trust him? I was simply being straightforward and honest in my choice of words.

Inquirer: It would appear that relationships between yourself and all of the relevant senior managers had reached a very tense and undesirable state. What did you do in response to the Chairman's instructions?

Robertson: I attempted to comply with the requirements of the Chairman, while not compromising my own principles.

A few days after I received the instructions from the Chairman I received a communication from the senior manager who had been detailed to oversee my discussions with the Inland Revenue. I must remind you that he was the boss of the two reinsurance managers. His memo set out a proposed response to the Revenue's inquiries, but I judged that it was not going to be acceptable to the Revenue. It did not contain the use of the term 'at arms' length rates' and it failed to address the points raised by the insurance managers on 27th January.

I replied in a most civil way, pointing out where the draft response required amending. I sent a suggested second draft, including the term 'at arms' length'. I also asked him to support me in refuting a claim that my approach was misguided, and my language offensive. I concluded the memo with the sentence 'I look forward to hearing from you'. I trust you will agree that this wording reflects a person who is not setting out purposely to antagonize people. Although I was now working through the senior manager, I did not allow my personal hurt to get in the way of my professional judgement, but neither was I going to be inhibited by his position.

On the same day that I sent this memo (23rd February), I also sent a note to the general manager who had conducted the latest investigation, saying that it had been brought to my intention that the tone of my earlier memo had caused him offence. I assured him that had not been my intention and apologized to him.

Inquirer: So you had taken steps to build as many bridges as possible?

Robertson: My position was a very difficult one. I did not consider that my various memos and correspondence had done anything other than express my heartfelt emotions on the subject of the reinsurance dealings. I had experienced a great deal of anguish and although I felt that it was I who should be the recipient of apologies, I also recognized that if words I had said or written had caused offence, then I should apologize.

I wrote a third item of correspondence on the 23rd February, this time it was a letter to the Chairman.

Inquirer: But had the Chairman not instructed you to desist from contacting him?

Robertson: Yes, but that was in relation to correspondence he might already receive from the Managing Director. My letter was addressed to him and only him and concerned some matters I had raised with him earlier in the month. I asked him how his investigation into the contradictory statements made to me by the two reinsurance managers was progressing. I also asked why we could not use, in our correspondence with the Inland Revenue, the required phrase, 'at arms' length'. I also notified the Chairman that I had sent an apology to the general manager who had apparently been offended by my memo.

On 27 February I received a memo from the Chairman which made the following points:

1. The Chairman was satisfied with the most recent investigation into reinsurance dealings with subsidiary companies and he had nothing more to add on the matter.
2. The general manager who had authored the report had informed him that as far as he (the general manager) was concerned he had no objections to me regarding his use of the term 'commercial' as if it were 'at arms' length'.
3. And, finally, he trusted that the correspondence could now stop.

Inquirer: Did that satisfy you?

Robertson: If I was prepared to ignore the statements which the two reinsurance managers had made to me on 27th January, under no duress; if I was prepared to ignore the way I had been treated so disrespectfully and how my requests for an explanation of the two managers contradictory statements had been continually dismissed; if I could forget the way I had been patronized and yet required to present the company's case to the Revenue with information I could not trust, nay had been told by two managers was doctored, then yes, I could have been satisfied. But I am not that type of person and although my actions were borne out of my own value system, if the code of ethics of my professional accounting body are studied, then my personal values are the type of values my professional body requires all its members to hold.

The Chairman's reply concerned me. There was a very clear attempt to close off the whole affair, and yet I was left in the worrying position that I was being required to use 'doctored' accounting information in my dealings with an agency of the government. I could be risking contravening the Taxes Acts by presenting information to the Revenue about which I had good grounds for believing was 'unsafe'. If I succumbed now, I might relieve myself of the very real pressure I was experiencing at work, but my own reputation and self-respect would be destroyed. This was no virility test, I just believe that ultimately we each have to be true to ourselves.

I replied to the Chairman's letter, asking how I was expected to deal with the Revenue when fundamental questions remained unanswered. I really had begun to feel, for the first time, that my position was in some jeopardy, whatever I did, and I sought his advice on how I could resolve the situation.

But I was not prepared to be mollified without the contradictory statements of the two reinsurance managers being resolved.

Inquirer: An *impasse* it would seem, Mr Robertson.

Robertson: I do not see why. Was I really being so unreasonable in wanting an explanation of the two managers' contradictory statements? Are accountants expected to be as flexible and malleable as their clients and employers require them to be? Are there not laws which have to be respected?

To prove that I still believed that the developing situation was resolvable I sent a copy of this latest letter to my general manager, so that he did not feel I was being underhand by corresponding directly with the Chairman. I also asked my general manager if he could assist in any way. This was on 2nd March. In response the general manager came from London to my office in Ipswich on 5 March to discuss the matter with me. At the end of the discussions we had that morning he gave the impression that he was sympathetic to my predicament and accepted my insistence that the response to the Inland Revenue should include:

1. what the two reinsurance managers had told me on 27 January 1987, that reinsurance transactions had been authorized by a senior GRE official at other than arms' length terms;
2. that they had subsequently retracted what they had said; and
3. details of the investigation which was subsequently carried out to confirm the integrity of reinsurance dealings from 1979 to 1986 between the UK parent company and its overseas subsidiaries.

As I say, the general manager agreed with these requirements, subject to his own idea that the wording be approved by a firm of solicitors. Two hours later, after lunch, the general manager returned and asked me whether there were any circumstances in which I would *not* insist in the response to the Inland Revenue including what we had agreed that morning. We discussed this for some time without reaching any agreement. When leaving my general manager said he would give more thought to what I had insisted upon, but would be in touch again as soon as possible after he had discussed the matter with the Chairman, whom he described as 'ruthless'. On 10th March my general manager telephoned to say that he had not forgotten and would be seeing the Chairman the next day. On 12th March he telephoned to give me the feedback on his meeting with the Chairman. He told me that a meeting would be arranged between myself and the reinsurance manager who had 'constructed' his own version of the fateful meeting in my office on the 27th January, when the reinsurance manager returned from a trip to America, a trip he would commence on 13th March, that is the next day, and would return from on 19th March. In the meantime my general manager instructed me to reply to the Inspector of Taxes along the lines I had been disputing since 27th January, otherwise he would go to see the inspector himself.

Inquirer: So you were given an ultimatum?

Robertson: Yes. I was required to comply with the command before I would have an opportunity of discussing the key issues with the reinsurance manager. If I complied with the instruction, in an uncritical way, I would be as implicated in any wrongdoing as the rest. I believed we had reached a point of no return. An ultimatum is exactly what it was, but it was not an ultimatum imposed by me. I had been placed in a totally untenable position and I was deeply troubled.

I reflected long and hard about everything which had gone before. The memos, the meetings, the denials, the rebukes, the accusations and the betrayals. I would not claim that it is possible to be totally objective in such a situation, but as far as it is possible to be, I believe I was thorough and honest in my assessment of the situation and had identified the only 'correct' course of action open to me.

On 16th March I wrote to my general manager. The company might argue that this letter marked a crossroad in the affair, but that is not so. The crossroad, if there is just one, was the telephone call of my general manager on 12th March.

In my letter of 16th March I stated that I required a written undertaking, signed by the Chairman, the Managing Director or my general manager, accepting that all my actions throughout the affair were approved by the company, and that my insistence for an explanation of the contradictory statements by the two reinsurance managers was totally reasonable. Without this undertaking I would make a full disclosure to the Inland Revenue. I appreciated that my challenge represented a last throw of the die.

As you will realize this ultimatum was itself a response to an ultimatum. Even at this late stage I wanted the affair resolved within the company and this letter represented the last option I had available to me. The company had refused all the previous requests I had made, and in a last desperate attempt to make them see reason, I made the statement which I did, although I must stress it was not an empty statement, I just hoped they would not force me to carry out the action.

My letter stressed, once again, that the penalty for fraudulently delivering, making or submitting an incorrect return or claim for allowance or relief is 200 per cent of the amount of the underpaid tax. This would amount to £3.1 million for the 1974 incident, plus whatever might be involved during the seven-year period between 1979 and 1985. I also made the point that it could not be in the interests of the company to have the Inspectors of the Inland Revenue's Special Transfer Pricing Office in its offices examining the reinsurance arrangements with the overseas subsidiaries in depth and interviewing the appropriate staff.

I must stress that had I been allowed to see the reinsurance manager before I was required to reply to the Inspector of Taxes, then I would not have been making these statements. If the prospect of resolving the contradictory statements of the two reinsurance managers had been available to me still, I would have wanted to have pursued that course of action. However, the company denied me that opportunity.

Inquirer: So, the company, in the form of your general manager's telephone message, had delivered an ultimatum to you, and you in return had refused to comply, stating that without total support from the company for the stand you had taken, you would have no option but to make your papers available to the Inspector of Taxes.

Robertson: That is correct.

Inquirer: How did the company respond?

Robertson: On 19th March I was called to the office of my immediate line manager. Also present was the Personnel Manager. A prepared statement was read to me. The statement went as follows:

> I have been asked to convey to you that it has been decided that you are to suspended from your duties forthwith, pending the Company making further investigations.
>
> It is felt that your letter of 16th March is defamatory to the Company, and the correspondence is defamatory to senior individuals of the Company. We are most concerned at the manner in which you have aired this matter, which we find ill befits the conduct that we expect of a senior manager, and I have to say that the issue appears to us to be one of gross misconduct.
>
> Therefore, pending a full review of all the circumstances, we are suspending you on full pay. As soon as possible we will be in touch with you to arrange to discuss the matter further.
>
> If there are any aspects to the matter you wish to raise with me now, or if there are any factors which you would wish us to bear in mind in conducting our further investigations which may help to explain you actions, please feel free to voice them. However, at this stage, we are not asking you to defend your actions. You will be given every opportunity to do so when you are called in for further discussions.

Inquirer: What was your response?

Robertson: I told them that I considered the whole thing was a load of codswallop, as any investigation would simply prove me to be right. How could any investigation function better with me away from the company rather than still working within it? It appeared to me to be an attempt to coerce me into withholding information from the Inland Revenue. The meeting was conducted in a calm manner, although I left with no dates as to when I could expect to hear from the company.

On April 10th I received a letter from my general manager enclosing the record of the company's investigation into my conduct. The statement was quite clear in highlighting that the investigations were not concerned with my concerns about the reinsurance dealings, but with *my* supposed 'gross misconduct'. A series of phrases, taken from much of the correspondence I have referred to today, were then itemized as examples of my gross misconduct.

My memo of 28th January which included the phrase 'I am no longer prepared to accept the word of any full-time Operations Control Executive including the Managing Director', and my assertion on 2nd March that the Chairman and others had been 'less than frank', were examples cited. Both these examples were considered by the company to be 'highly derogatory and insubordinate statements'.

However, both of these extracts appeared in correspondence dated well before 16th March and yet no offence had been taken at the time. Only towards the end of the company's report does my letter of 16th March receive attention.

The company now appeared to be saying that correspondence which at one time was not worthy of comment, now justified the description of 'grossly defamatory statements . . . the potential consequences of which could be as serious as summary termination of your employment'. Yet on 5th March 1987, only 14 days before my suspension, my general manager had expressed 'the high regard he had for me'. Having suspended me the company now seemed to be searching for 'evidence' to justify their actions, yet they cannot avoid the inconsistencies and contradictions in their statements and actions.

Inquirer: Would you expand upon that last statement.

Robertson: Well, in addition to the complimentary statement to which I have just referred, I had very recently received a discretionary salary increase, which presumably indicated that the company considered my performance justified the salary enhancement. In addition the company had agreed to finance my attendance at a tax conference in Amsterdam, to be held later in the year. This does not seem to me to be the actions of a company towards an employee who is considered to be acting in a grossly defamatory fashion and liable to be dismissed.

Inquirer: The communication from the company regarding their investigations into your conduct suggests support from within the company for the actions taken against you. What are the investigative or appeals procedures within the company to handle situations such as your own?

Robertson: My contract of employment stipulated that I had the right to appeal to the grievance committee and therefore to the Joint National Council. GRE refused to comply with its own procedures. Whereas both the aforesaid committees should have been evenly split between representatives of management and representatives of the union, all six members of the committee which was convened to hear my appeal on 22nd June 1987 were representatives of management – three directors and three managers!

My appeal was rejected and I was sacked with effect from May 31st.

Inquirer: You were thus out of work as a result of behaviour which you maintain was totally in the interests of the company. From your opening remark it is clear that you took your case to industrial tribunal and that you were successful. Would you please provide some insights into that experience.

Robertson: Yes, I took my case for unfair dismissal to an industrial tribunal, but without the assistance of a solicitor. I obtained the names of five local firms of solicitors, which I was informed were very strong in the areas in which I was seeking advice. The first four firms I approached felt they should not advise me because of a conflict of interest. They had a lot of business with GRE! However, the fifth firm seemed very sympathetic and agreed to advise me. Having given the firm the fullest particulars and documentation of the case, they advised me that my chances of success were slight. I was shattered. None the less, I recovered from that very discouraging blow, carefully examined the appropriate sections of the employment Acts, purchased some relevant books and started to prepare my own case.

Inquirer: I find it most surprising that you were unable to find one legal practice to handle your case out of five you approached.

Robertson: Surprising it may be, but true it certainly is.

At the industrial tribunal the company was represented by a barrister who specialized in employment law and a firm of employment law consultants. I represented myself. It felt a little like David and Goliath, but I was sure of my case. Despite the show of strength by my former employers their case collapsed.

Inquirer: Would you explain why and how.

Robertson: The evidence provided by the company, especially my general manager, was full of inconsistencies and contradictions. Their case placed heavy emphasis upon my 'gross misconduct' over a period of time. Yet I was able to show that by awarding me a discretionary pay rise, by agreeing to finance my attendance at a conference overseas and by compliments paid to me during the period of the dispute, my behaviour could not have been that provocative as to warrant dismissal. I was able to convince the industrial tribunal that the only reason for the company's action was my letter of 16th March.

Despite the company's assertiveness at the tribunal hearing that the last internal inquiry into the parent company's dealings with overseas subsidiaries had revealed no irregularities, my general manager finally and reluctantly agreed under questioning that *no* documentary evidence existed of that inquiry.

Following my suspension the company had also commissioned Coopers & Lybrand (the company's auditors) to carry out an investigation into the company's reinsurance dealings with overseas subsidiaries. This investigation had been announced by my general manager to the Inland Revenue at a meeting which took place on 26th March, a week after my suspension. Yet at the company's appeals committee hearing convened to hear my appeal, my general manager had implied that the investigation by Coopers & Lybrand had begun prior to 16th March, i.e. he implied that I had sent my letter of the 16th March despite knowing of the inquiry by Coopers & Lybrand. This was untrue. In fact the announcement of the investigation by Coopers & Lybrand was necessary to pre-empt any decisions by the Inland Revenue to set up their own inquiry into the company's tax affairs by their own fraud inspectors. The investigation by the firm of accountants was in several parts, the first being to study the evidence relating to the £3 million profit understatement of 1974. Despite the evidence which I knew existed, the accountants were able to produce an interim report which could find nothing amiss in the company's actions. The Inland Revenue found the report 'disappointing', to quote the official response, and the fraud inspectors of the Inland Revenue are investigating the company's tax affairs as we speak!

At the tribunal hearing my general manager claimed no recollection of the agreement he had made with me on the 5th March regarding the response I was to make on behalf of the company to the Inspector of Taxes. However, I was able to show that at the two meetings convened by the company to hear my case and then my appeal, meetings which had both been held prior to the industrial tribunal hearing, he had not challenged my references to that agreement.

I was also able to show that in addition to the appeals committee organized by the company being purposely incorrectly convened, the ACAS rules concerning the confidentiality of evidence and the need for the defendant to be informed of any new evidence submitted were ignored.

Inquirer: I understand that your principal witness was the Inspector of Taxes.

Robertson: Yes, Mr Hoye, who was the Inland Revenue Inspector of Taxes at the time of the case, gave expert witness at the tribunal hearing. His evidence supported my own and obviously helped corroborate the case I was constructing against the company.

Inquirer: And so as you mentioned earlier, the company's case collapsed and the unanimous ruling of the industrial tribunal was that you had been unfairly dismissed.

Robertson: Yes. The exact wording of the tribunal decision was:

> We have listened to the evidence: we have read the correspondence. We have arrived at the clear conclusion that the more probable reason for the applicant's dismissal was the reason which the applicant has suggested. We do not accept that the reason was the abusive tone of the memoranda and telephone conversations.

The statement continues:

> If we have found that the reason for dismissal was the abusive communications, we might have had to look at the question of contributory conduct. As, however, we have come to the conclusion that the reason for the dismissal was not the reason which the respondents have shown us, that does not arise.

In addition to the tribunal unanimously agreeing that I was unfairly dismissed, the tribunal ruled that I was also required to be reinstated in my job, an outcome which I understand is recommended in about only three cases in every 1,000 which go before industrial tribunal courts.

Inquirer: So your stand had been vindicated. You must have felt elated. A successful outcome to what must have been a very painful and disturbing period of your life.

Robertson: I was elated. The many months between my sacking and the industrial tribunal hearing had been full of periods of great anguish, wondering whether justice would prevail. There were times when I felt low – very low. However, this was not the end of the trauma, in some ways the worst was yet to come.

The company initially agreed to my reinstatment, but shortly before Christmas the company reneged on that agreement. I received a letter from the Managing Director stating that the company would be appealing against the industrial tribunal decision, but irrespective of the outcome of the appeal the company would refuse to re-employ me. I was devastated, but I decided to force the company to show its disrespect for the industrial tribunal decision. I arrived for work on the day stipulated in the ruling of the industrial tribunal and tried to enter my office. I was escorted from the building by two uniformed police officers who were waiting for me. This incident was captured on film by Anglia Television and some of the cameramen were manhandled and chased from the premises by GRE security officers.

The decision by the company to appeal against the ruling of the industrial tribunal court meant that I had to prepare my case afresh and I had the anguish of a further nine months wait before the appeal hearing. In the meantime I was dependent upon social security payments. Cynically, shortly before the appeal was due to be heard the company withdrew its objection to the industrial tribunal decision. I had been put through an emotional 'ringer' once again, but may be that had been the intention from the start. I had also spent £6,000 on legal costs in preparing my case for the appeal, but now I was told that I had wasted my money.

Inquirer: Although the company decided not to pursue the appeal, am I correct in understanding that they still refused to abide by the reinstatement order of the industrial tribunal?

Robertson: Yes.

Inquirer: So notwithstanding the ruling of an industrial tribunal court, an employing organization can choose to ignore a reinstatement order?

Robertson: That is correct.

Inquirer: But presumably the company had to pay a significant penalty for refusing to comply with the reinstatement order?

Robertson: The company received the maximum penalty under employment law legislation for refusing to recognize the reinstatement order – £4,264 – hardly a disincentive. In fact the total of the sums awarded to me for unfair dismissal and for being denied the right to take up my post as Chief Accountant (Taxation) was £15,452. My total income prior to dismissal had been around £50,000 p.a., so £15,452 was a relatively small cost to remove a principled employee.

Inquirer: Were the sums awarded to you reduced for any reasons? They seem remarkably low considering the case you have described.

Robertson: The very maximum the tribunal could have awarded was £17,684, but adjustments were then made for my age and length of service reducing it to £15,452. Employment law legislation does not appear designed to inhibit unscrupulous employers. The average award made to employees who won their cases for unfair dismissal in 1990–91 was £1,773. And at the end of the process who will employ you? Presumably employers do not want dishonest employees, but neither do they appear to want employees who might resist their own unscrupulous behaviour. Following the successful outcome of the industrial tribunal, I responded to 40 job advertisements, achieved one interview but was unsuccessful. I eventually obtained temporary employment with a leading charity, which contacted me after reading of my case in a Sunday newspaper, and then, finally, I was successful in securing the post of finance officer of a local theatre company at a quarter of my previous salary – but this process took nearly three years!

In the meantime, notwithstanding the industrial tribunal decision, GRE continued to treat me as if I had been dismissed for gross misconduct and refused to pay my immediate pension entitlement. This would have been a great help to me, but the company continued to do everything it could to frustrate me and make my life as difficult as possible.

Inquirer: Did you take out a civil action for unfair dismissal against you former employers?

Robertson: I considered it, but was advised by my solicitor that my legal expenses would be prohibitive, there was no legal precedent and the outcome was far from certain. He also warned that judges did not like finding against our big 'reputable' companies. He advised me to settle out of court. By this time I was very tired and emotionally drained. I had fought my campaign virtually singlehanded and although I had won the moral and legal arguments, I recognized that it had been at an enormous cost to myself. With great reluctance I agreed to an out-of-court settlement which amounted to a net £56,596 in addition to the £15,452 the industrial tribunal had awarded me. When you consider that my future earnings from the company would have amounted to approximately £1 million and my final pension would have been considerably enhanced, you can begin to appreciate the financial loss I have experienced.

Inquirer: Mr Robertson, you have mentioned your qualification as a member of the accountancy profession. Did you contact your professional body at any time to enlist their help in your struggle with GRE?

Robertson: I did, but not until after the industrial tribunal. Until then I had complete faith in the integrity of my case. While I was still the head of taxation at GRE I did not believe that the affair would end in my sacking, not until, that is, the events immediately leading up to the ultimatum I received on 12th March. During the months leading up to the industrial tribunal hearing I was fully occupied preparing my case. I was not aware that my professional body had any systems to handle the ethical dilemmas of its members, although I was subsequently informed that a committee did exist to consider such matters. In the 25 years I had been a member of the institute I had not been aware of this.

Following the industrial tribunal decision, however, and the company's refusal to reinstate me, I was in a difficult situation. I wrote to my institute asking for help on a number of matters. I asked if my membership fees could be waived until I was able to secure employment. I also asked if the institute had any mechanisms to allow members to make contact with organizations who were seeking to appoint an accountant. I also asked if the institute could provide me with the names of legal practices which specialized in employment law to act for me at the appeal hearing. The institute agreed to waive my fees, but they were unable to help on the other two counts. They felt unable to name firms of lawyers for fear of being seen to favour one firm over another. The chairman of the institute's Consultative Panel of Members not in Public Practice (the ethic's committee I mentioned earlier) also felt unable to help. After reading my case material he concluded that there was nothing the institute could do as the situation, in his view, was now a matter of law rather than ethics. I had hoped that my institute might take up my case with GRE and possibly investigate the role of Coopers & Lybrand in the affair. I wanted the institute to consider whether there was a conflict of interest between Coopers & Lybrand preparing an objective report on the reinsurance operations of the company and its other role as the company's auditors. I also wanted the institute to study the report submitted by Coopers & Lybrand to assess the quality of its findings, given that those findings had a direct bearing on my position. Even though Coopers & Lybrand had not carried out indepth interviews with either myself or Mr Hoye, Inspector of Taxes, the chief witnesses in the matter, the firm of accountants could produce a report giving the company a clean bill of health. On the other hand their report said that I had been untruthful. However, at the industrial tribunal I had no difficulty in proving that this was not so.

You will recall that the Inland Revenue has since instigated its own investigation into the reinsurance dealings of the company. What so disappointed me regarding my own institute was that four years after my dismissal, with all the evidence in front of them including the damning criticism of GRE's behaviour contained in the tribunal findings, they could find nothing wrong with the investigation undertaken by Coopers & Lybrand. I was informed that if I wished to take the issue further then I should approach the Institute of Chartered Accountants in England and Wales (ICAEW), because it was one of its members who had signed the report.

Inquirer: Did you want to take the issue further?

Robertson: Most certainly, but my case would have been greatly enhanced if I had received the support of my institute, not just in terms of approaching my former employer but also by supporting my call for an independent inquiry.

Inquirer: The institute might respond that it does not have the resources to investigate the authenticity of every case of ethical dilemmas faced by its members.

Robertson: But my industrial tribunal hearing had already been held. All the details I have presented to this inquiry today are available from the records of the industrial tribunal hearing. I had not only received a unanimous verdict of unfair dismissal, but very exceptionally I had also secured a reinstatement order. The industrial tribunal decision actually states that there was no conduct of mine which contributed to my dismissal. On the other hand the decision states that some of GRE's senior officials were endeavouring to obstruct my efforts to make a proper disclosure to the Inland Revenue. What more evidence is necessary?

Coopers & Lybrand are a large international firm of accountants. These large accountancy practices carry tremendous influence within the profession and while I hoped that the role of Coopers & Lybrand would be investigated by my institute, I was extremely doubtful that such an investigation would be undertaken.

The institute argued that had I contacted them before I was dismissed they might have been able to play a mediating role between myself and GRE. I find this very difficult to understand. It suggests that the institute would have tried to find some middle ground between myself and the company, but the situation was quite clear. There are times when an act or behaviour is wrong. Compromise is not always an option and this was one such case. Given this approach by the institute it is clear that they would not have been able to make any positive contribution to my situation, or for any other members faced with a situation similar to mine. The message is clear.

Inquirer: And what, in your opinion, Mr Robertson, is that message?

Robertson: That members cannot expect help, of any substance, from their institute if an ethical conflict arises between a member and his or her employing organization.

Inquirer: It could be argued that you are asking your professional body to act in the manner of a trade union, to which they might take exception.

Robertson: Whether I am asking for professional associations to act as trade unions is a moot point, *but if a professional body is not prepared to lend one of its members support in a case such as mine, where the evidence is as overwhelming as it is, what is their role? How does it expect its members to uphold the high ethical standards it espouses?*

Inquirer: Mr Robertson, during your long struggle with GRE over the reinsurance dealings; your dismissal; your fight for justice culminating in the industrial tribunal hearing and then the appeal; and your struggle to gain access to your pension entitlements, it would not be surprising if you had experienced periods of great isolation, depression and anxiety. Were you completely on your own?

Robertson: During my stand concerning the reinsurance dealings of the company and the subsequent struggles, my secretary at GRE was my confidante and my source of strength. During my low periods, she encouraged me to continue with the fight. It is a cliché, but I do not know how I would have coped without her.

After the industrial tribunal we were married.

Inquirer: Do you have any concluding comment you would wish to make to the inquiry?

Robertson: I believe that the final comment should be that of my legal adviser, who has more experience in this field than most. He said of me and my case: 'No one would fail to be moved by his predicament. . . . I have never come across a case where I felt that a man had been so unfairly served by his employers and indeed the law.'

Inquirer: Mr Robertson, that is a powerful and poignant statement with which to conclude. Thank you very much for your evidence.

REFERENCES

Soeken, K. and Soeken, D. (1987) *A Survey of Whistleblowers: Their Stressors and Coping Strategies*, Association of Mental Health Specialities, Laurel, Md.

Winfield, M. (1990) *Minding Your Own Business: Self-Regulation and Whistleblowing in British Companies*, Social Audit, London.

12

Academic whistleblowing on the beat:
the policeman's lot

Simon Holdaway

INTRODUCTION

My inclusion in this volume seems presumptuous. I don't regard myself as a whistleblower. During my nine years of police service, especially after returning to my constabulary from university in 1973, and to work as a sergeant, I found many features of policing distasteful. The most difficult was the attitude of police colleagues towards groups of people within the population of the inner-city area for which I and my colleagues had responsibility. Black and Asian people were derided; suspects were perceived to be guilty and unworthy of anything other than the most basic consideration; and the population was generally tainted with distrust. Rightly or wrongly, I didn't find it easy to cope in this atmosphere.

My experience of the police, however, does not launch me into a description of the doings of ogres dressed in blue serge, who routinely 'fit people up' with trumped-up charges, beat them unmercifully and vilify them at every opportunity. A shift in an inner-city police station brings officers into contact with diverse situations requiring, among other personal attributes, firmness, kindness, care and a measure of assertiveness. The complexity and diversity of skills required by officers is considerable; dangerous situations have to be faced, very occasionally.

These and other features of policing were to be found in the life of my station but, and this was the point that tugged at my conscience, the sensitive use of discretion, proper use of arrest powers and, at times, use of physical force were overlaid by not infrequent and extremely damaging incidents when people were mentally and physically abused. This often happened within the confines of the police station where they had no access to a solicitor, friend or confidant. A disregard for people up against life in the inner city and an embittering cynicism turned what was meant to be a police service into a soured force.

None of these circumstances led me to blow the whistle on my colleagues by exposing publicly a case in which someone had been personally abused.

I wasn't up to that and can't pretend to rank among the morally courageous who have broken rank to their personal cost. A significant reason for this, probably the main one, was that I had once been as immersed within the police world as any of my colleagues. A mixture of unease about my personal credentials and straightforward guilt did not provide the mettle required by a whistleblower proper.

Other former and serving officers have fulfilled this more dramatic and challenging role. PC Joy of Kent Constabulary, for example, who told the press that his colleagues were massaging arrest figures to improve clear-up rates; and PC Singh of Nottinghamshire Constabulary took his chief constable to an industrial tribunal with an allegation of racial discrimination. He won his case and demonstrated the widespread use of racist language within the police and his own chief constable's insensitivity to the experience of black and Asian officers serving in his force. Assistant Chief Constable Allison Halford of Merseyside Police, who has recently settled her case of sexual discrimination against her chief constable, has also certainly moved into a whistleblowing role.

A rather different, unintentional type of whistleblowing is by the officer who lets us peep behind the curtains of privacy that shield the policy world. The Chief Constable of Strathclyde, for example, recently made a racist remark during an address at a cricket dinner. He was reprimanded by his police authority.

Finally, there is the whistleblowing that challenges accepted wisdom in the interests of the police. Speaking within the context of the last general election, Commander David Stevens of the Metropolitan Police commented on the relationship between crime and social deprivation. Street crime had increased in areas of London 'where they are having a tough time'. The largest increases in crime occur in the areas of greatest social deprivation and 'the government must address the electorate in terms of solutions'. The implication of Steven's views are that the control of crime and, therefore, the police mandate does not lie solely with police officers. They cannot stem a flow of crime stimulated by inadequate social and other government policies.

My efforts make mundane reading in the annals of whistleblowing. When in 1975 I resigned from my constabulary to take up a university lectureship, a sense of personal relief was dominant. I could not only embark on a new career but also use my contractual obligation to publish as a platform from which to argue the case for police reform. The role of the academic social scientist includes making clear that what is often taken for granted as common sense is, from other perspectives, tentative and partial. My task was to demonstrate that the common sense of my erstwhile police colleagues was, in fact, a very partial perception and presentation of 'reality' (Holdaway, 1983)

Being an academic whistleblower is really pretty safe and I don't pretend to rank among my colleague authors. Part of my work over nearly twenty years as an academic, however, has been to try to be an agent of change by using with integrity the research I have undertaken about the police. This has, of course, not been my only concern because my experience of eleven years work as a police officer also led me to value the university and work of the academic as essentially one of the pursuit of knowledge for its own sake, free from the censorship that finally led me to resign from the police. A privilege like this carries with it a responsibility to use research findings to try to influence change. But I have not always understood policing, academe and the place of knowledge in the world in this way.

POLICE SERVICE

My police service as a constable began in 1966, after two years as a cadet. My police career was built on the experience of a 16-year-old grammar-school boy consistently performing at 'Beta level'' who achieved five O-level passes in two goes and who had cultivated an acute awareness of not being an academic achiever. I needed a job that would keep me out of trouble – so my mother must have reasoned as she pondered the future of her youngest son. Recruitment to the police cadet corps, in effect full-time secondary school with drill, judo and loads of sport thrown in, followed by a cadet posting in a station, seemed just right. My parents encouraged me to join. If accepted, I would be kept off the streets, dismounted from my Lambretta scooter, restrained by disciplined, controlled employment and, at a stroke, would avoid recruitment into the trade of travelling salesman for a groceries' company or a similar work open to a grammar-school failure.

The cadets corps was good, very good. I was made a house captain and earnt a reputation for possessing an abundance of what was then regarded as the quasi-biological attribute of 'leadership'. I was a leader and, so the word was put about, a future senior officer. This 16-year-old 'Essex lad' was no less impressionable than any other and he quickly cultivated a militaristic style, at that time fitting of a future chief.

Being impressionable is conducive to the acquisition of impression management, a key skill required by senior police rank (and academics for that matter). The need for senior officers to demonstrate their possession of real abilities rather than present an appearance of them is a recent innovation in policing. In my day, and this is still the case to an extent, the key to promotion was to admit to having an abundance of the vital, unquestionable commodity called 'common sense'. This meant affirming allegiance to the view that the police are *the* bulwark against increasing crime and disorder within the nation; that policing is about the eradication of crime mostly through police control; and that the force, or more accurately, *our* force, should be defended against criticism at all costs. In time I came to perceive the world rather differently and decided I no longer wanted to be a police officer. There was no great drama about my awakening, neither was there any drama about my departure. I didn't have the stomach for that.

Police training school followed the cadets and a posting to an inner-city division. At that time all the attributes of policing I later came to question were in my possession. In sociological language, I was fully socialized into the occupational culture! At 19, PC 257 'H' Division Holdaway was author-itative, (authoritarian more like), and ready to 'do the business'. For me the police was a wonderful job that I more than enjoyed. I nicked 'em, pushed 'em around and shared the primary mission of my colleagues to hold down the riffraff who threatened the apparent stability of life in our area. People who took a contrary view were either 'do-gooders', corrupt or stupid.

The complex world of policing was simplified by a wonderfully effective turn of mind that worked in the interests of what we, the rank and file, defined as 'common sense'. Then as now, the pay was excellent, the work varied, important and offered great opportunities to engage in many dif-ferent tasks. An appreciation of the use of discretion when using the law, the key role of peace-keeping in routine police work, and the opportunity to find a way of balancing the many, complex demands made of officers were there for the taking. But we 'bobbies' didn't understand policing in these terms. Our self-sustained culture prompted us to interpret police work as the uncomplicated exercise of arrest powers; the essential pursuit of excite-ment; the retention of absolute control through the use of authoritative force; and as a self-justified activity in self-justification.

LEARNING TO DRAW BREATH

My problems really began when I met the undergraduate studying social administration who was to become my wife. Her values and understanding of police work were rather different from my own but she had the stamina and patience to suffer my views, waiting, as it were, for her opportunity to blow the whistle on me. Once again, there was no drama as she introduced me to the world of reasoned argument that was rather different from the argy-bargy with drunks after closing time and to the knowledge that people who associate with social workers and the like were not the precious do-gooders my police world would have me believe. Gradually I began to realize that it was possible to understand something of why people get into personal difficulties, that personal responsibility is in some way constrained by social factors. The fail-safe explanations of crime and criminality offered by the police world were questionable, in my head at that stage if not in my practice of policing the streets.

Meanwhile the performance and appearance of PC Holdaway seemed to appeal to his senior officers. A telephone call from headquarters summoned an interview about the career path to senior rank I might be groomed to follow. 'I'm going to be a senior officer', I told myself as I practised my signature followed by 'Chief Superintendent'. Promotion exams led to my qualification for sergeant rank with just over two years in the job and an interview for the accelerated promotion course at the National Police Col-lege, Bramshill, as it was then called.

Failure then struck – I was not selected for accelerated promotion and had to wait longer to be promoted to sergeant than I had already served in the force. This was more than unsettling and it was my wife, as she had become, who suggested I might take a couple of A-levels by correspondence course and think about university study. A year of nights, lates, earlies, court appearances and A-level essays followed. Keeping the promise of a university education within reach, a provisional place at a number of universities, among them an offer to read religious studies (with sociology and politics in the first year) at Lancaster, were secured. Lancaster university was where I wanted to go and, after the A-level results were published, where I was able to go.

My intention was to ask for three years' extended leave, conditional on the retention of pension and other contributions. Then I discovered that a constable at my station had secured police funding of full pay to study geography at Durham University. I had little to loose and pitted my case against his, initially without success. The final court of appeal was an interview with my chief officer and when this was granted a pretty abrasive encounter occurred. He delegated the interview to one of his assistants who told me that the two cases were not comparable and I was therefore free to remain in my force or take unpaid leave, supported by a student grant. I decided to take leave when, just four days later, I was recalled to headquarters and told that I would be granted leave on pay. A semblance of honesty led me to point out that a U-turn like this did not foster confidence. After the initial interview I could not guarantee that I would return to my force after graduation but, surprisingly, this was fully accepted. I was able to go to Lancaster University on pay, which is what I did in October 1970, putting the police behind me for three years.

LANCASTER UNIVERSITY

Lancaster University proved to be a superb context to develop my undergraduate studies in sociology, the subject I chose for finals. My gratitude to the staff in the departments of sociology and religious studies cannot be adequately expressed. At Lancaster I was encouraged to articulate theoretical arguments, to read books in plenty and, I hope, to learn to write. It was wonderful. The one subject I did not choose to read about on any of my courses was the police – that could wait because I was too interested in the theoretical and methodological dilemmas posed by sociological and theological subjects. Questioning what other people regarded as common sense was now the starting-point of inquiry. I was taught how to take breath and, if a whistle was to be blown, to argue rationally.

Having been awarded a first-class honours degree it was natural to think about postgraduate study. After graduation I returned to my force and was promoted to sergeant, managing to secure a posting to a multiracial area of one of Britain's major cities. The thought of returning to policing invoked mixed feelings. On the one hand my force had financed my studies and there was an obligation to repay a debt. I also thought it was necessary for a sociology graduate to demonstrate that it was possible to work for the repressive arm of state control, so frequently dismissed by many of sociology's armchair experts.

If I was going to pursue postgraduate research from the theoretical and methodological perspectives that interested me, I needed to be a participant and an observer in a 'natural setting', documenting what the subjects of my research took for granted about one or more aspects of the world. There was an incredible opportunity to slip back into my force virtually unnoticed and to 'get the seat of my pants dirty with real research', as one of my sociological gurus put it. I had a unique opportunity to keep a diary secretly while working as a police sergeant and to use the data gathered to write a sociological analysis of policing based on how the rank and file actually think about and perform their work. The opportunity was not to be missed.

On the other hand, I really could not conceive of how to cope with the scenarios that engaged my mental speculation. What would I do if a police officer hit someone in my presence? What would I do it I thought someone had been fitted up with evidence? How would I cope with police racism? We mentally speculate about the worse that might happen to us, at least I do. Thankfully, it is not possible to be precise about how one will react when a previously imagined situation becomes 'real'. Perhaps the most realistic stance is to know what you hope you stand for, and to hope. But, when push comes to shove, don't be surprised if you find yourself a good deal weaker than you reckon might be the case. I was aware that if academic curiosity was a driving force for my research, that curiosity was tempered by moral concern to weigh police practice and, in the longer term, to change it. The issue was really whether ethics were to be the tail that wagged the researching dog? With the end of my undergraduate days drawing nigh, I returned to my force. How would I fare?

POLICING

Back in blue serge and flushed with first-class honours, I arrived at the headquarters to meet my divisional commander. He welcomed me and encouraged his graduate sergeant with 'Where have you been then, university? What subject did you take?' The frustration surged. If I was glowing with academic pride he seemed intent on minimizing my achievements and to find little or no relationship between university and police worlds.

Next stop was the Chief Superintendent of the subdivision in which I was to work. He was also suitably sensitive, greeting me with: 'The last thing I want is men with beards. I spend half my time telling men to get their hair cut.' He continued, 'You will have no time for research. We have to get on with policing the ground and haven't time for experiments. What I want is people who can lead men.' Despite having read numerous articles about the research method of participant observation that requires a bland adaptation to whatever faces a researcher, I immediately found myself torn between opportunities for research and commitment to the police service, my university sponsor. This *entrée* was parabolic; ethical decision-making is not a dispassionate pursuit. It is not an objective enterprise and I should not have been surprised if I was caught between what I thought ought to be the case and what was the case.

The irony was that if I had followed the cannons of sociological research these senior officers' comments would have tasted as meat and drink. Their recommendation I should 'get into policing again' was unwitting advice to rediscover the 'common sense' of police work – the very theme of my research and, indeed, of important sociological developments at that time. What little research had been completed on the police indicated that the legal framework within which they were said to work shielded a rather different practice when law was used by the rank and file; the lower ranks possessed the power within their organization to ensure that they retained a considerable measure of control over the performance of their work (Banton, 1964; Skolnick, 1966; Cain, 1973). I found myself in a unique position to document the world of the police rank and file, adding to a very small body of knowledge about their occupational culture and, perhaps in the long run bring about some change to policing.

After weighing the options – requesting permission for research access from headquarters and/or from my lower-ranked colleagues, resignation, and so on – I decided to begin covert fieldwork. This seemed the only realistic option; alternatives were either unrealistic or involved an element of the unethical only marginally more commendable than covert observation (Holdaway, 1982). Further, as a legally empowered police officer, I was a member of a powerful institution of our society who would mostly deal with the less powerful. The argument that all individuals have a right to privacy (that is to say, freedom from observation, investigation and subsequent publication based on the investigation), is strong but should be qualified when applied to the police. Published research and my previous experience of police work demonstrated the power of the lower ranks, not least their resistance to external control of their work. An effective research strategy had to pierce their protective shield.

This problem is encountered during research of many organizations. However, the case for covert research is strengthened by the central and powerful position of the police within our society. They are constrained by the rule of law, a constitutional restriction on their right to privacy but one they often try to neutralize by maintaining a protective occupational culture. When such an institution is overprotective its members restrict their right to privacy. It is important they are researched.

One answer to this argument could be that I dismiss any effect senior officers might have on the behaviour and views of their subordinates. At my station there was minimal management of constables but, that apart, it would have been very restricting simply to place one's evidence in the hands of senior officers, believing that they would or could straight-forwardly alter the practice of policing by the lower ranks.

During the last twenty years a number of chief officers who are far more open than those I worked with have been appointed and they would indeed have been approachable. But they were not in post at the time I undertook my research and there is a wider constituency of interest in the police that

needs to be taken into account. Loyalty to one's occupation is not an absolute duty for the whistleblower. The covert researcher of the police works
within an extremely powerful organization that begs revelation of its public
and private face by first-hand observation – risky as that observation might
be. In part, therefore, I justified my covert research by an assessment of the
power of the police within British society and the secretive character of the
force. This does not mean that covert research into powerful groups is
ethical while that into less powerful ones is not; neither is it to advocate a
sensational type of sociology in which rigorous analysis of evidence gives
way to moral crusading. Although I came to this uncomfortable conclusion
when my research began in 1973, I would still argue in similar terms, despite
widespread changes in police policy and a marked movement in the abilities
of many – but not all – chief officers.

RESEARCHING THE POLICE

This description of my decision-making tends to convey an impression of
careful calculation. In fact, it was as much informed by a desire to complete
doctoral research and a sense that the drift of others' valued opinions
seemed in my favour. However, having made the decision in principle to
conduct covert research, I had to face its practical implications. This was
none the easier for my being a police sergeant, holding all the legal powers
of that office, as well as responsibility for the supervision of a large number
of officers who would be working to their 'street-wise' rules. I was not like
previous researchers, masquerading as a schizophrenic, an alcoholic, a mil-
lennarian, a Pentecostalist or a factory worker; I was a police sergeant for
real and had no idea when or if I would leave the field for the comfort of my
study. I had no idea if and how I would survive. My primary concerns were
a mixture of acute attention to fieldwork and a handling of dis-ease about
the way in which a good number of my colleagues went about their work.

Other research methods do not present these risks of participant observation. Unlike experimental, questionnaire and other more controlled
research methods, covert research is equivocal; those who are being researched control the situation as much as, if not more than, the researcher.
When the subject of the research is the police, whose work is highly unpre-
dictable and varied, a definition of limits of ethical tolerance is significant.
Codes of ethics like those adopted by the professional associations for social
scientists deal with predictable and planned research, conditions that are not
present in fieldwork. Indeed, their absence encourages the use of naturalistic
research methods.

During my first days of police duty and the beginnings of my covert
note-taking, I asked myself what I would do if an officer hit a suspect in my
presence or some other indiscretion took place. I was, I kept reminding
myself, not simply a sociologist but a sergeant with legal and other supervisory responsibilities. Contemplating ethical problems which *might* arise
hampered my capacity to document in detail. However, the police

unknowingly provided me with a pilot study. My Chief Divisional Officer posted me to a small station where, with two other sergeants, I was responsible for about 12 constables. The rough and tumble of police work soon began.

One night, when I was in charge of the station, a man who had threatened his wife with a pistol was arrested and brought to the station. He pleaded his innocence and a police officer kicked him on the backside as a reminder that his pathetic explanation was not acceptable. Excessive force was not used but what happened was not exactly conducive to behaviour at a tea party. Similar situations arose and I wrote in my research diary:

> It is still a problem working with another police officer who has very different ideas about civil liberties – patrolling with Sergeant X – in this case. Every time we stopped someone I had to manage a situation in which the possibilities of corners being cut were real. This causes a strain for the sociological observer.

The pretentious, high-sounding sociological observer was me, protecting myself from a police world with which I was not comfortable.

Other incidents presented different demands. During another night shift a young mother called the police after the sudden death of her young baby. In her grief-stricken state she made some remarks about the state of her marriage which I did not record. I recall wrapping the baby in a blanket and holding it in my arms as two silent colleagues drove with us to the mortuary. The mortuary attendant took the child and routinely placed it in refrigeration. One of my colleagues said that he felt like 'putting one on' the attendant for the way he treated the child. Incidents like this reminded me that the world in which I worked required the police to act with great sensitivity and with humanity – I needed to be reminded about that.

The name of the game during these days was survival. Did I want to be a police officer or employed elsewhere; I hadn't struck a balance between policing and research. A likely escape route appeared – an advertisement for a lectureship at a Midlands Polytechnic. Thankfully, my application was not successful but one of my referees wrote to commiserate, advising I should get on with my research and fix a time when I would leave the police. Then I would precisely know the end date of my sentence and the beginning of parole.

I was not the only one to wonder about my suitability for a police career. The PCs I worked with noticed that my ideas about policing were rather different from their own. When tea mugs belonging to the shift were changed we were presented with colours to suit our personality: My mug was yellow. 'Why yellow?' I asked naively. 'Because you're scared.' Senior officers found me tetchy and my Chief Superintendent doubted my suitability for the police service. I later complained of his insensitivity to another senior officer, who responded: 'You might disagree with Mr— but do you disagree with 99 per cent of the officers at the station?' He explained, 'There are two important things about police work. First, policemen must be willing to cut corners or else they will never get their job done. Secondly, it's because policemen have been happy to gild the lily that the law has been administered in this country.' He was right. We disagreed about these issues. It seemed my police career was gently but efficiently nearing its end, until a new officer took command of my division, heard about a minor problem called Holdaway and transferred him to another station. My pilot project had been brought to an end and an opportunity for the research proper opened up.

Now I knew that I wanted to complete my sentence and to be more secure as a covert researcher. Sociological research rather than the potential to blow a police whistle now underpinned my police service. I was a researcher with a unique opportunity to gather data in an unusual setting. It was wise to sit out the discomfort, wait to publish an analysis of policing and then try to influence police reform.

My academic supervisors were crucial at this time. I had enrolled as an external, part-time PhD student at one of the major centres of social-science research in the UK. Not so fresh from night-duty sleep I would arrive for a research supervision and try to explain my observations. These sessions must have been pretty intriguing for my supervisors. They sat dispassionately and referred me to relevant academic literature, a million miles from the study of the police but wonderfully relevant. When, for example, I described the ways in which officers seemed to be controlling the use of physical space within the station, it was suggested that I think about the ways in which an anthropologist had found that light falling into an Algerian house had implications for the ordering of behaviour. A link was then charted to Emile Durkheim's notions of the sacred and profane. Reworked like this my fieldnotes had the potential to analyse the police from sociological perspectives (Holdaway, 1980).

Another crucial source of refreshment was my supervisor's encouragement. During one supervision I heard, 'Yes, I can see the book now, chapters on this, this and this.' Transcending the immediate context of one's understanding of the world and offering strong encouragement to persist with the task of trying to analyse and theorize the apparently mundane features of social life are key aspects of a social scientist's work. Like my undergraduate tutors at Lancaster, I owe my postgraduate supervisors, Professor's Terence Morris and Paul Rock, an enormous gratitude.

A FRESH START

The new station to which I was posted was much larger than that for the pilot project. I now worked on a shift with an inspector, three sergeants and about 25 constables. It seemed important from the outset to tell my colleagues about my limits of tolerance to their behaviour. This was often done by engaging them in conversation about a particular issue or job in which they were involved. For example, one of my fellow sergeants was known to use 'unorthodox techniques' when questioning suspects. When we chatted about this issue he gave me a full description of what he was and was not willing to do during questioning, with illustrations of each point. His explanations were of great use in the research because it became possible to compare the illustrations with his subsequent behaviour and that of other colleagues. Fortunately, he enjoyed our discussions and became an important informant who was always content to provide details of the ways in which officers had dealt with an incident.

Any participant observer, overt or covert, intervenes in the research situation. The point is to know how and its consequences. It was noticeable that when PCs brought a 'dodgy job' into the charge room they would, if they had a choice, ask a colleague sergeant to deal with it. Other sergeants also intervened indirectly if they thought that I might spoil or misunderstand a procedure they wished to control. Eliciting accounts of what was going on in these situations was never difficult. The senior officers now began to air rather different views about me, and I found that I had settled into my police and research work as a covert, participant observer.

All this work took its toll. As the American sociologist, William Whyte, put it in his classic study of gangs in a Chicago slum, 'I also had to learn that the fieldworker cannot afford to think only of learning to live with others in the field. He has to continue living with himself' (Whyte, 1943) Covert research and the ethical questions it raises create conditions of stress within which a sociologist has to live 'with himself'. For me, there was a tension derived from working with officers who did not always share my values and assumptions about policing. So what, you might say, the world is nasty place? Yes, but I had to take responsibility for the manner in which these officers worked. I occasionally retreated from nasty situations – conversations and incidents over which I had no control. There were times when I had to sanction an officer whose conduct exceeded the bounds of acceptability. When I kept my distance or intervened like this there was a danger of seriously compromising my research. If I stayed and observed very difficult situations I would record the data and, in the longer term, make public what was essentially private information. What is to take priority – one's own comfort or the longer-term gains of research? When the chips are down, an argument about the priority of personal comfort can win convincingly.

Then there was the routine of actually doing the research. I had to concentrate on what was happening around me, commit precise details of incidents to memory and follow leads through a shift, sometimes for days and weeks. This added to the already-demanding work of being a police sergeant at an inner-city station. There were times when my research suffered because I was engrossed in police work. I took the view that defending counsel at Crown Court would not excuse me from following legal procedure because my mind was distracted by a doctoral thesis! Neither did I reckon that my PhD examiners would be particularly impressed if I argued that my data lacked detail because police policy and practice required me to ensure that I listed defendants' (more usually called prisoners) property with greater accuracy than my fieldnotes of canteen conversations. Research of the type I was undertaking and policing were not always in harmony. The upshot was a fascinating but demanding and very wearing situation.

Then there were times when I 'went native'. At the start of each tour of duty I reminded myself that I was researching and of its major themes. There were days when I was less attentive than usual; and days when I stood back from distasteful events. On one occasion, after hearing a conversation about race relations, I wrote in my diary:

> I reacted badly to the conversation yesterday and want nothing to do with such sentiments. I remember saying to myself, 'Underneath, these policemen are ruthless and racist.' I seem to have slipped into the mould easily during the last couple of weeks and wonder if I should have been so easy with my feelings. The balance of participant observation is one which can so easily be submerged and forgotten. Now it has been brought before me in glaring lights, and all the old issues of ethics loom large.

The final dilemma to be faced was that as a covert researcher I was documenting the work of people who regarded me as a colleague. The risk of being found out was always present and I had to be sensitive to any indication that others – sometimes friends – might know what I was doing. I kept shorthand notes on a scrap of paper in the back pocket of my uniform trousers and if I had to leave the station or charge office to make notes I listened for approaching footsteps. Some unexpected comments made me pretty wary:

> While at the station I telephoned my supervisor to arrange a tutorial. After returning to the communications room a constable said to me, 'Switch that tape recorder off sarge.'
> I asked, 'What are you on about?'
> 'Oh nothing.'
> I do not know what was meant and never found out, but the remark caused me considerable anxiety that my cover was blown.

There was another occasion, on 5 November, when I was on plain-clothes duty and decided that I should patrol a postgraduate seminar in the sociology of deviance at the university where I was a part-time student. I had charge of four constables, also in plain clothes, who were to patrol, looking for firework throwers. Just why we were in plain clothes was not obvious to me or anyone else but that is what happened every 5 November, so don't question my chief superintendent's wisdom! During the bus journey back from the seminar to my area I checked some research notes. As I stood up to alight, the night-duty telephonist, who had been sitting across the aisle, greeted me. Had she seen the notes and would she blow the whistle on me? I don't know. The question mark against my identity as a researcher was sufficient to be bothersome.

When these considerations are added to the sheer physical effort of policing – shift work, overtime, discordant leave days – the stress of covert research cannot be avoided: it has to be managed to the researcher's advantage. Imperfectly, I tried to use my situation to heighten my consciousness of what was going on around me, not least when potentially stressful incidents were likely to happen. For example, I was able to make a particular study of the police use of physical force, finding that I could tolerate its use more satisfactorily if I took detailed notes. This enabled me to check officers' attitudes against their actions, while clarifying the limits of my own tolerance.

Another help was the knowledge that I would not be a serving police officer for ever and ever. When Sheffield University appointed me to a lectureship they allowed me to remain in the field of policing for 12 months. A cost-cutting exercise for them but a research spur for me. Research became the central task and purpose of my work.

CHECKING THE EVIDENCE

Many whistleblowers become incensed by one event that illuminates a wider concern they eventually feel a duty to reveal. Not so for me, partly because I did not think of my research as a drawing of breath to expel a headline exposé of policing. I had to sustain as systematic and controlled an approach to the collection of data as I could manage. My interest was not in the implications of one or two incidents that affected me in a very personal way but on the routines of police work that were rather mundane. Spectacular cases that would have made good newspaper copy arose but my preference is not for 'smash-and-grab' research where the apparently radical sociologist is blooded by brief engagement with an institution of state control like the police. Fieldnotes can be written into a Filofax during a brief moment but they are the better recorded systematically over a long period of time after a round of nights (10 p.m. to 6 a.m.), earlies (6 a.m. to 2 p.m.) and lates (2 p.m. to 10 p.m.). Put in more sociological language I had to ensure that the data I collected were valid and reliable. My thesis was not to be an exercise in the articulation of prejudice.

I worked from the basic premiss that I should observe and record as much as possible, even of the seemingly routine and insignificant. Further, data would be gathered about as many officers and in as many contexts as possible. Published research helped to direct my attention to specific issues and my own documentation over a considerable period of time, two years in fact, prevented a 'smash-and-grab' approach.

To check out particular themes I would sometimes use rhetorical questions:

> One Sunday night I was patrolling with a colleague when a call to a fight came over the radio. The location of the call was too far away and the incident too trivial for a sergeant to attend, but we drove towards the scene at high speed. I asked my colleague: 'The only reason you drove like that was because you wanted to have a fast drive?' He replied, 'Yes, well, it's a bit of fun, isn't it? It all makes a bit of excitement and gets rid of a headache.'

This pearl of wisdom offered some verification of a theme that I had been considering and was able to continue developing.

Knowing what colleagues think of you is not always pleasant, yet the participant observer who elicits the views of other people can use their opinions to discriminate between more and less reliable details of evidence. Academic supervisors required me to reflect on my data, away from the bustle of the station but, just as important, police colleagues tended to make their opinions known, usually by way of a joke: 'In response to exceedingly conscientious British Transport police officers, a colleague remarked, "Right couple of lawyers we've got out there. They're trying to decide who cautioned him before he was arrested. Must have a sociology degree from Lancaster." ' Remarks like this appeared to confirm my impression of other officers' attitudes and likely actions in situations I witnessed and heard about.

There have also been times when other police officers have ventured to comment on the accuracy of my findings; officers on extra-mural courses, for example. And to a lesser extent I consider my membership of the police was and remains relevant to my analysis. The following incident will illustrate the point. On one occasion, after chasing a number of suspects who had committed a burglary, I returned home to my wife (I had been off-duty, unloading shopping at the time the suspects appeared), raging about what I would do to them if they were caught. At that moment I was completely 'native', displaying the characteristics of normal police craft. In short, the experience of having been a police officer is valuable in sustaining the empathy necessary to research founded on participant observation.

LEAVING: SOME RISKS

When the time came to leave the police service I found myself without any qualms about academe or regrets about leaving the work that I began when I left school at 16. At that time it seemed I had some unique data about the police. I had collected a great deal of evidence about the ways in which the lower ranks understood their work, contrasting this with the ideas written into the law and police policy. The most contentious areas of the police world I had documented were the use of physical force and 'verballing'. Less spectacular but no less interesting to me were the ways in which officers used physical space and time to sustain the experience of a world that was in accord with their understanding of policing. This understanding, sustained so powerfully, is the occupational culture of policing, what one student of the police recently called the 'Berlin Wall' of police work. We know from research evidence that most police work is not concerned with crime. The officers I observed nevertheless placed crime at the forefront of their work to the virtual exclusion of the many, other, important tasks they were required to perform by the public. Police work is a rather slow type of employment. Long periods of inaction are interspersed with some requests for police assistance that are incredibly diverse in character. The officers I observed created a world within which speed and excitement were retained at a premium, using cars and radio communications to sustain it. And so I could go on, contrasting the world of the lower ranks with an alternative social terrain documented by social-science research. The occupational culture is therefore a construction, a kind of apparition, sustained by the chosen routines and experience of policing.

One upshot of this view is that senior officers involved in policy-making and management are unlikely to change the powerful traditions and ways of working found in the occupational culture. Law and policy are moulded in the university of the streets; the police are less than fully accountable.

So this research, carried out from the inside, pierced the surface appearance of the police world to reveal a rather different reality. By describing and analysing what my colleagues regarded as common sense I was able to demonstrate they accepted a very partial view of police work, a contestable version of 'reality' shot through with the potential for illegality and error. This was not argued from the evidence of one or two dramatic incidents – my interest was the routine and commonplace. Social science, so conceived, blows a whistle on the safety of the taken-for-granted structures and contours of the police world. The appearance of police work is not its reality and portrayals of this world by senior officers, for example, who defended their rank and file, could be shown to be error. Simon Holdaway could now well and truly blow the whistle.

But this is perhaps a somewhat fanciful, inflated view of my research. Chief police officers would hardly have to defend themselves against the writings of a lone academic. A much more important concern for me when I left the police service was to protect the officers about whom I would write. My aim was to guard against undeserved harm being caused to them and some practical steps were taken to this end. Whenever I refer to my police research all names and places are changed in the cause of anonymity, and steps have been taken to ensure the security of the data. The officers with whom I worked cannot escape moral responsibility for their actions; neither can I. Writing about the police, however, making my data available to pressure groups, giving evidence to official inquiries and other means of engaging in attempts to change police policy provide a continuing context for working through the difficult moral issues posed by my research and my personal responsibility for its covert stance.

A rather different risk to the sociological community also had to be considered: it could be said that sociologists cannot be trusted! This is not a criticism that I have been made aware of. Rather more worrying was the possibility that I would be consigned to the dustbin of radicals who bang on about powerful institutions of the political state for the sake of it. There could be no better, no more available target than the British bobby. It would have been pretty easy to dismiss my work by charging me with engaging in a polemic about a readily accessible 'whipping boy'; by arguing that it is impossible to verify any of my data; and that I engaged in deception for the hell of it, hoping to pull off a nice little earner from the proceeds of my writing. In fact, although my book about the research drew academic attention it did not draw much police venom.

PUBLISH AND BE DAMNED

One of the first papers I published on my appointment to a lectureship at Sheffield University was in the *British Journal of Sociology* (Holdaway, 1977). In the paper I outlined my basic thesis that the occupational culture of the lower police ranks constructed a version of reality out of tune with the prevailing managerial reform of the service. The paper was peppered with illustrative quotes from fieldnotes and I hope it made a contribution to the sociological study of the police which, at that time, in 1979, was sorely neglected. Just before publication I recall the editorial office of the journal telephoning me to say that it wanted to issue a press release about the paper because it should capture a wider public interest. I hid for the next couple of days because I did not want to parry the questions of news reporters. One or two of the tabloids picked up some of the more exciting themes of the paper, and that marked the first public exposure of the work. An edited collection of sociological papers followed and I continued to write for an academic readership (Holdaway, 1979). The publisher of the edited collection snapped up the proposal I tentatively circulated to a number of houses and, as part of it, I wrote a paper about a 'mugging squad' (James, 1978). The essential theme of the article was the now familiar charting of how the squad re-formed its brief, to police to the tenets of the occupational culture rather than managerial preferences. This was the first published collection about polic-ing and, in a cautionary spirit, the text was sent to a libel lawyer, who honed in on my article and underlined virtually all of it in red. If the paper was to be published a risk of legal action had to be accepted. An added problem was that when I joined the police service and, again, when I resigned, I had to sign the Official Secrets Act, which forbade me from retaining any note or other information of any sort about my employment. Publication was a breach of the Act and I didn't fancy being a test case of any kind, despite the ridiculous wording of the Act at that time. We published nevertheless.

There was no response from the police but I did not court publicity for the article or book. As I said at the beginning of this chapter, I do not consider myself a whistleblower *par excellence*. Invitations to appear on television and radio were accepted, however, and the edited collection was followed in 1983 by *Inside the British Police* (Holdaway, 1983). This was also read by a libel lawyer before publication and cautious comments were made, but the opinion was that the book had been enjoyed and so it should be published! The ideas presented were gradually percolating into various organizations, a process that continued for a number of years. Opportunities to speak at conferences, to make more television appearances, to work with pressure groups, and so on, continued. Importantly, public debate about the police was opened up by the 1981 riots in a number of British cities and the publication of Lord Scarman's report, which was a watershed for police reform.

ACHIEVING CHANGE

One of the regular police criticisms of my work used to be that 'everything has changed, you are talking about what used to happen'. There is of course no final way of answering this challenge. So be it. The occupational culture is necessarily secretive, shielded from senior officers' gaze and, anyway, it is rather unlikely that a chief officer would admit to finding it the most stub-born of their problems. However, over the years there have been many signs that the occupational culture is alive and well. It has periodically seeped to the surface and to public view through newspaper reports of discipline cases and, more importantly, the recognition by chief constables that this is one of their major problems.

When I first began writing and talking about the occupational culture it was said by many police officers that I was arguing about a chip on my shoulder, about personal prejudice, about a grudge. Over a period of fifteen to twenty years, however, there has been a growing awareness among chief constables and others that the occupational culture, canteen culture as they have preferred to call and sanitize it, is indeed a stumbling-block of massive proportions for reform. For example, the last Commissioner of the London Metropolitan Police, Sir Peter Imbert, is reported to have set himself the goal soon after his appointment in 1988 to 'change police culture'. The term 'police force' was abandoned and the title of Metropolitan Police Service was adopted. With an acceptance that 'we must respond to well founded criticism', Sir Peter set in train the 'Plus Programme', which is a force-wide development of policy to flesh out his notion of police 'service' rather than 'force' and turn the inward-directed, self-interested focus of the lower ranks' occupational culture outwards to the public and their defined needs. From this perspective, crime control, through the making of arrests by officers, takes on a wider programme of policy and practice involving consultation and co-operation with locally based police, public liaison groups, dealing with people's fear of crime as much as 'actual levels' of crime, and adopting a positive approach to issues like racial attacks, domestic violence and crime prevention through close co-operation with other agencies, social services, local authorities, probation services, and so on.

Paul Condon, Sir Peter's successor, one of the youngest officers to hold this rank in recent years, was previously Chief Constable of Kent. There he adopted a *Policing Charter for Kent* in an attempt to change a police culture of deliberately under-reporting crime figures and inflating clear-up rates. This was a situation exposed by a real whistleblower, PC Joy, who went public with information that Kent's published crime figures and clear-up rates were continually massaged to the apparent advantage of the force. Placing more emphasis on documented public needs, Condon placed a rapid re-sponse to calls from the public, care for victims of crime and high-visibility street patrol at the centre of his charter, hoping that excellence becomes its own reward. How far an approach like this receives approval from col-leagues in the Association of Chief Police Officers is not known. A small number of other chiefs have their own programmes or, more likely, discreet initiatives for changing their force.

The point here is that among a growing number of chief officers and lower-ranked police managers there is a realization that the occupational culture is a reality posing the most profound threat to police reform. This awareness has grown over fifteen to twenty years, fostered and sustained by a mixture of nationally publicized, dramatic incidents, concerted press crit-icism and sustained prodding by academics. Whistleblowing does not need to be a revelation brought to public attention by a sudden exposé. The mundane, unspectacular work of academic research can over a period of time have a similar, desired effect.

REFERENCES

Banton, M. (1964) *The Policeman in the Community*, Tavistock, London.

Cain, M. (1973) *Society and the Policeman's Role*, Routledge & Kegan Paul, London.

Holdaway, S. (1977) 'Changes in urban policing', *British Journal of Sociology*, Vol. 28, no. 2, pp. 119–37.

Holdaway, S. (ed.) (1979) *The British Police*, Edward Arnold, London.

Holdaway, S. (1980) 'The police station', *Urban Life and Culture*, Vol. 9, no. 1, pp. 79–100.

Holdaway, S. (1982) 'An inside job: a case study of covert research on the police', in M. Bulmer (ed.) *Social Research Ethics*, Macmillan, London.

Holdaway, S. (1983) *Inside the British Police: A Force at Work*, Basil Blackwell, Oxford.

James, D. (1978) 'Police black relations: the professional solution', in S. Holdaway (ed.) *The British Police*, Edward Arnold, London.

Rt. Hon. Lord Scarman OBE (1981) *The Brixton Disorders, 10–12 April 1981*, HMSO, London.

Skolnick, J. (1966) *Justice Without Trial: Law Enforcement in a Democratic Society*, Wiley, New York and London.

Whyte, W. F. (1943) *Street Corner Society*, University of Chicago Press, Chicago, Ill.

General Index

Index of Whistleblowers